The Tasaday Controversy

Special Publications of the
American Anthropological Association

The Tasaday Controversy:
Assessing the Evidence

Edited by
Thomas N. Headland

a special publication of the
American Anthropological Association

scholarly series

special publications of the
American Anthropological Association

Scholarly Series Editor
Terence E. Hays

Published by the
American Anthropological Association
1703 New Hampshire Avenue, N.W.
Washington, D.C. 20009
202/232-8800

Library of Congress Cataloging-in-Publication Data
The Tasaday controversy : assessing the evidence / edited by Thomas N. Headland.
     p.   cm.   — (A Special publication of the American Anthropological Association : no. 28. Scholarly series)
    Papers from a special session held during the 88th annual meeting of the American Anthropological Association, Washington, D.C., Nov. 16, 1989.
    Includes bibliographical references and index.
    ISBN 0-913167-51-7
    1. Tasaday (Philippine people)—Congresses. 2. Impostors and imposture—Philippines—Congresses. I. Headland, Thomas N. II. American Anthropological Association. Meeting (88th : 1989 : Washington, D.C.) III. Series: Special publication of the American Anthropological Association : no. 28. IV. Series: Special publication of the American Anthropological Association. Scholarly series.
DS666.T32T37   1992   92-25352
959.9'01—dc20   CIP

cover photograph: Tasaday man Gintuy with one of his wives. Photo by Oswald Iten, March 1986.

CONTENTS

Notes on the Contributors

GERALD BERREMAN (Ph.D., Cornell) is Professor of Anthropology, University of California, Berkeley. His primary research has been on social inequality and environmental issues in the Indian Himalayas. Other interests include urban India, tribal peoples, culture change in the Aleutian Islands, and research ethics. He has been continuously involved in the Tasaday controversy since 1986 when, at the international Tasaday conference in Manila, he was appointed to the anthropological commission to assess the evidence. Among his publications are *Hindus of the Himalayas: Ethnography and Change* (1972), *Caste and Other Inequities* (1972), and *Social Inequality: Comparative and Developmental Approaches* (1981).

JOHN BODLEY (Ph.D., Oregon) is Professor of Anthropology at Washington State University. He conducted fieldwork in the Peruvian Amazon with the Ashaninka and Shipibo Indians, investigating the impact of expanding national society on traditional society and resource use. His publications include *Victims of Progress* (1975), *Anthropology and Contemporary Human Problems* (1976), and *Tribal Peoples and Development Issues* (1988).

ROBERT CARNEIRO (Ph.D., Michigan) is Curator of South American Ethnology at the American Museum of Natural History in New York. Besides an interest in the use of the stone axe in Amazonia, he has written about a number of problems in the cultural ecology of that region, especially matters relating to slash-and-burn cultivation and settlement patterns. More broadly, he is interested in all aspects of cultural evolution, particularly the rise of chiefdoms and states, and has written "A Theory of the Origin of the State" (1970) and "The Chiefdom: Precursor of the State" (1981).

LEVITA DUHAYLUNGSOD (Ph.D., Queensland, Australia) is currently Assistant Professor in the Department of Agricultural Education and Rural Studies, University of the Philippines at Los Baños. Her dissertation, *Confrontation with Commoditization in a Philippine Upland Village,* is a postmodernist research on her ancestral village about which she is presently preparing a document for return presentation to the community. Her interest in the Tasaday controversy arose from her husband's family's two decades of missionary work among the Tboli. This led to her paper, "The Development Saga of the Tadaday: Gentle Yesterday, Hoax Today, Exploited Forever?" (1990, forthcoming, with David Hyndman), which she presented to the Fifth Hunting and Gathering Society Conference in 1988. Together with Hyndman, she continues her research on the Tboli.

RICHARD ELKINS (Ph.D., Hawaii) is an International Translation Consultant with the Summer Institute of Linguistics. His research interests are the ethnography and descriptive and comparative linguistics of the Manobo subfamily of Philippine languages. He has lived in the Philippines since 1953 where he has spent more than 30 years doing fieldwork in several Manobo communities. His publications include *Manobo English Dictionary* (University of Hawaii, 1968), "Three Models of Western Bukidnon Manobo Kinship" (1968), "A Proto-Manobo Word List" (1974), "The Proto-Manobo Kinship System" (1982), and 25 other articles or monographs on Manobo linguistics, ethnography, and translation. One of the original dozen scientists to the Tasaday, he spent four days with them in 1972.

BARRY FANKHAUSER (Ph.D., Otago, New Zealand) is currently a Research Fellow in the Prehistory Department, Research School of Pacific Studies, The Australian National University, Canberra. His present research is on the chemical analysis of residues in earth ovens and on pottery. Other research interests involve the application of chemical and physical methods of analysis to archaeological problems, including thermoluminescence dating, nutrition and cooking of Pacific root crops, and sourcing of archaeological stone and obsidian. His publications include several articles on the cooking and nutrition of *ti* (genus *Cordyline*), an important plant in Polynesia.

THOMAS HEADLAND (Ph.D., Hawaii), the editor of this volume, is an International Anthropology Consultant with the Summer Institute of Linguistics and Adjunct Associate Professor of Linguistics at the University of Texas at Arlington. His primary research interests are hunter-gatherer societies and human ecology in tropical forest ecosystems. Between 1962 and 1986 he spent 18 years doing fieldwork among Negritos in the Philippines. Among his publications are *A Dumagat-English Dictionary* (Australian National University, 1974, with Janet Headland), *Emics and Etics: The Insider/Outsider Debate* (Sage, 1990, with Kenneth Pike and Marvin Harris), and 30 articles on Philippine society.

DAVID HYNDMAN (Ph.D., Queensland, Australia) works in the area of Fourth World studies in the Asia-Pacific region, especially in Melanesia and the Philippines. He has over 50 articles and book chapters and two books on his work in New Guinea, including (in press) *Ancestral Rainforests and the Mountain of Gold: The Political Ecology of the Wopkaimin of New Guinea*. His current research in the Philippines concerns the political ecology of autonomy in the Cordillera and, in collaboration with Levita Duhaylungsod, a political ecology analysis of the Tboli and the Tasaday hoax in Mindanao.

OSWALD ITEN (Ph.D., University of Zürich) is a Swiss citizen who currently works as a freelance reporter. His doctoral thesis was related to economic anthropology (*Economic Pressures on Traditional Society, A Case Study of Southeastern Nuba Economy in Modern Sudan,* European University Papers, Peter Lang Publishers, 1979). Iten opened the hoax controversy with his startling news article (1986a) after his visit to the Tasaday in March 1986. (His address is Waldhof, CH-6314 Unter geri, Switzerland.)

CLAY JOHNSTON is a computer software trainer for linguistic, translation, and literacy applications at the Summer Institute of Linguistics (SIL) in Dallas, Texas. He served for ten years with SIL in the Philippines as a field worker among the Cotabato Manobo people of Mindanao. He has published several articles on linguistic features of the Cotabato Manobo language.

RICHARD B. LEE (Ph.D., California, Berkeley) is Professor of Anthropology at the University of Toronto and a Fellow of the Royal Society of Canada. His research interests in ecology, history, and Marxist theory center on the study of hunting and gathering societies, particularly the !Kung San of Botswana. His books include *Man the Hunter* (1968), *Kalahari Hunter-Gatherers* (1976), *The !Kung San* (1979), *Politics and History in Band Societies* (1982), and *The Dobe !Kung* (1984), in addition to over 60 articles on related subjects. His long-standing interest in the historical status, current predicaments, and public perceptions of peoples known as "hunters and gatherers" led to his involvement in evaluating the Tasaday evidence. He was recently awarded an honorary doctorate by the University of Alaska for his research and advocacy of foraging peoples.

WILLIAM LONGACRE (Ph.D., Chicago) is Professor of Anthropology and Head of the Department of Anthropology at the University of Arizona, where he has served on the faculty for more than 25 years. He has had visiting professorial appointments at Yale University, the University of Hawaii, and the University of the Philippines. He was a Fellow at the Center for Advanced Study in the Behavioral Sciences in Palo Alto. He has conducted extensive archaeological research in Arizona and ethnoarchaeological fieldwork in the Philippines, and has numerous publications reporting the results.

CAROL MOLONY (Ph.D., Stanford) is Associate Researcher, University of California, Irvine, and Visiting Professor, San Jose State University. She specializes in linguistic anthropology of Philippine and Indonesian languages and their speakers. Her current research is with immigrants to California from the Moluccan (or Spice) Islands of eastern Indonesia. Since 1970 she worked with Moluccan immigrants to the Philippines and the Netherlands. Her four volumes and two dozen articles focus on language change when the speakers come into contact with other groups. One of the original dozen scientists to the Tasaday, she spent fourteen days with them in 1972.

EMMANUEL NABAYRA studies anthropology at the Ateneo de Manila University and once headed a missionary organization providing literacy and other basic services to cultural minorities in Davao del Norte and Davao Oriental, also in Mindanao, Philippines. He did extensive research (1965–76) on belief systems and folklore among the Dibabawon, Ata Manobo, Manggwangan Manobo, Mandaya, and Mansaka tribes. He has published a book on literacy and articles on the Mandaya tribe of Davao.

JESUS PERALTA (Ph.D., California at Davis), an archaeologist, is Chief of the Anthropology Division of the National Museum of the Philippines. His publications include *Iwak: Alternative Strategies for Subsistence* (1982) and *Tau't Batu Studies* (1983). He made a two-day field visit to the Tasaday in 1971, and another one-week trip to visit them in April 1986.

LAWRENCE REID (Ph.D., Hawaii) is a Research Professor of Linguistics at the University of Hawaii. He has been doing fieldwork for over thirty years, primarily in the Philippines, but also on the Austronesian languages of Taiwan and Thailand. He is currently involved in an extensive comparative study of the languages spoken by Negritos in the northern Philippines. His publications range from ethnographic, ethnobotanical, and linguistic studies of Bontok and a number of other Philippine languages to studies of the reconstruction and development of the morphology and syntax of Proto-Austronesian and other early stages of Philippine languages. He spent eight days with the Tasaday in March of 1990, collecting language data from them.

AMELIA ROGEL-RARA is currently an ethnographer with the Tasaday Community Care Foundation, Philippines. A graduate in anthropology from the University of the Philippines, she conducted anthropological, museological, and applied linguistics research among various Philippine hunting and gathering bands, swidden cultivators, and landless peasant farmers for two decades. During this period she worked as Panamin Foundation researcher and development officer (1967–73), Philippine National Museum ethnologist/museologist (1973–83) and as nongovernment organizations consultant/researcher on participatory development and educational programs for Philippine tribes (1983 to date). She is married to a Higanon tribal datu. She first visited the Tasaday with the Panamin team in 1972, and later conducted several lengthy periods of fieldwork among the Tasaday from 1987 to May 1989.

ZEUS SALAZAR (Ph.D., Sorbonne) is Professor of History and Anthropology and Dean of the College of Social Sciences and Philosophy, University of the Philippines, Diliman. He has taught at the Ecole de Hautes Etudes en Sciences Sociales in Paris, at the Dipartimento di Studi Asiatici of the Instituto Universitario Orientale in Naples, Italy, and at the Inter-University Center for Post-Graduate Studies in Dubrovnik, Yuguslavia. He was also Visiting Research Professor at the Institut für Ethnologie of the Universität Köln, Germany, in 1985–86. A recipient of the French decoration ''Chévalier des Palmes Académiques,'' Salazar was the first to question the authenticity of the Tasaday in two extensive "footnotes" published in 1971 and 1973.

LESLIE SPONSEL (Ph.D., Cornell) is an Associate Professor of Anthropology and member of the Institute of Peace at the University of Hawaii. A specialist in human ecology in tropical forest ecosystems, from 1975 to 1981 he made many trips to Venezuela to conduct fieldwork among several indigenous societies in the Amazon including the Sanema, a northern group of Yanomami. Since 1986 he has been comparing the cultural ecology of adjacent Buddhist and Muslim communities in southern Thailand. Sponsel has published numerous articles, including "Amazon Adaptation and Ecology" (1986) and "Farming and Foraging: A Necessary Complementarity in Amazonia?" (1989), and is currently writing a monograph on human ecology in tropical forests.

Foreword

In 1988 the American Anthropological Association (AAA) asked Thomas Headland to organize a special session on the "Tasaday Controversy" for its 88th Annual Meeting. The symposium was held in Washington, D.C., on November 16, 1989, and eighteen distinguished speakers presented papers. In my capacity as Editor of the Scholarly Series of the AAA's Special Publication series, I invited Professor Headland to publish the essays as a volume in this series.

The volume shows that no simple resolution of the controversy has emerged. The evidence available regarding the Tasaday is incomplete, sometimes equivocal, and is subject to varying interpretations. The principal researchers of the Tasaday and their neighbors, as well as other interested scholars, have made their views and interpretations clear in the papers collected here. What is also manifest in these essays is the importance of future research, when the political situation permits it. Whatever occurs in the future, however, it is vitally important that the existing evidence be made available for scrutiny and debate. This is a major priority of this collection.

At the time of the original presentation of these papers, Fred Eggan, Professor of Anthropology (Emeritus) at the University of Chicago and a dedicated scholar of the Philippines, had agreed to write a report for the Association concerning the Tasaday. It was subsequently hoped that such a report could form a concluding chapter to this volume. Sadly, Professor Eggan died in the spring of 1991 before he completed his evaluations, but his notes indicate his commitment to the knotty issues raised here. In a preliminary report to the AAA Executive Board, Eggan stated his hope that eventually he and other specialists might be able to "settle the issue, so far as anthropology is concerned." It is in this spirit, and in memory of Fred Eggan's distinguished anthropological career, that the American Anthropological Association publishes this important collection.

TERENCE E. HAYS
SERIES EDITOR

1

Preface

Thomas N. Headland

In 1971 a band of cave-dwelling people called Tasaday were discovered living in a remote area of rain forest in the Philippines. These 26 individuals were reported to be following a paleolithic lifestyle, surviving solely on wild foods, and wearing leaves for clothing. Throughout 1972 and 1973 there was an almost continuous stream of outsiders who were flown in to visit the Tasaday people. They included politicians, movie stars, journalists, filmmakers, and about a dozen scientists. In 1974 all visits were stopped by the government. After the international flurry of articles and TV films by the news media in the early '70s, no further word was heard about the Tasaday for thirteen years.

Then, suddenly in 1986, immediately after the fall of Philippine President Marcos, reports broke into the international press that the whole story had been a hoax. In the following months hundreds of articles appeared in newspapers all over the world.

By 1988 the public and media alike were turning increasingly to anthropologists for advice in trying to solve the mystery of this so-called Tasaday hoax controversy. In late 1988, the American Anthropological Association asked me to organize a symposium on the topic for its 88th Annual Meeting to be held in Washington, D.C., in November 1989. The chapters presented in this volume are revisions of the papers that were presented by the panelists at that symposium.

All of the scientists still alive who had visited the Tasaday in the early '70s and who had published reports of their research there were invited to present papers at the symposium. These included David Baradas, Richard Elkins, Carlos Fernandez, Teodoro Llamzon, Carol Molony, Jesus Peralta, and Douglas Yen. (Robert Fox and Frank Lynch were deceased.) All except Baradas and Fernandez presented papers. Four other ethnographers who did fieldwork in the Tasaday area after 1985 were also invited: Levita Duhaylungsod, Oswald Iten, Sean Mc-Donagh, and Amelia Rogel-Rara. These four also presented papers in Washington. Clay Johnston, an American field linguist who spoke Cotabato Manobo fluently, was invited because he had lived for ten years in Manobo communities just a few miles west of the Tasaday caves, and he understood the Tasaday speech when he heard it on taped recordings. Nine other scholars presented papers as "discussants" to the topic. They were carefully chosen because each has an area of special expertise that was needed in evaluating the papers of the other panelists

3

in the symposium. These were Gerald Berreman, John Bodley, Robert Carneiro, Thomas Headland, Richard Lee, William Longacre, Lawrence Reid, Zeus Salazar, and Leslie Sponsel. Their chapters are also in this volume.

Although McDonagh presented a paper at the symposium, he declined for personal reasons to submit a chapter for inclusion in the present volume. Baradas and Fernandez, who were unable to participate in the Washington symposium, were later invited to submit their papers to the volume. They also declined for reasons of their own. Douglas Yen submitted his chapter for this volume in 1990, but then withdrew it in September 1991, after the volume was in press. Barry Fankhauser is the only senior author in this book who was not on the symposium panel. His research was, however, presented there by Yen as an appendix to his paper. We have published it here as a separate chapter. David Hyndman and Emmanuel Nabayra are coauthors of two of the present chapters. They were indirect participants on our original panel, invited to coauthor the chapters by Duhaylungsod and Rogel-Rara, respectively.

All of the chapters review the controversy surrounding the Tasaday, and assess the ethnographic, archaeological, linguistic, historical, and botanical evidence for degree of isolation. In Chapter 1 (Introduction), Headland reviews the historical background and recent developments concerning the whole Tasaday hoax controversy. This is followed by Part I: The Skeptics, in which the theses by the four members of the Washington panel who are most skeptical of the original 1971–72 reports are presented. Berreman opens this section (Chapter 2) by examining claims made about the 26 Tasaday as isolated, Stone Age, cave-dwelling, nonhunting, nonfishing, rain-forest foragers. Theories discussed here concern how or whether this culture existed in Mindanao in 1971, and how or whether they changed to the way of life observed in 1986. Berreman presents evidence that led him to conclude that the original description was a hoax, perpetrated in self-interest by the then-Presidential Assistant on National Minorities (Panamin), through supervised control of brief, rare contacts between hand-picked observers and Tasaday. Berreman argues that the Tasaday were actually nothing more than typical house-dwelling swidden farmers whose dialect was entirely comprehensible to Manobo neighbors, with whom they have, in fact, intermarried. The Tasaday were, he says, persuaded to their command performances by threats and promises. He concludes that with the overthrow of the Marcos regime in 1986, outsiders finally met the Tasaday in unmanaged circumstances, which unmasked the hoax.

In Chapter 3, Oswald Iten displays the importance of the media in the Tasaday affair. Far more journalists than scientists visited the Tasaday in the 1970s. When, more than ten years later, serious questions arose about the cave-dwelling, Stone Age character of the Tasaday, some of the press that formerly had reported so uncritically became actively involved in what Iten calls a cover-up operation aimed at face-saving and salvaging reputations (mainly on the part of American publications).

In Chapter 4, Duhaylungsod and Hyndman present the Tasaday hoax in the context of competition over Tboli resources. The different interest groups and the extent of resource expropriation are discussed from a historical perspective that traces back to the pre-Panamin period and continues up to the present. This competition has made the indigenous peoples in the area, including the Tasaday, susceptible to the influence of these groups. Evidence gathered by these authors from local people further substantiates the continuing manipulation and exploitation of the Tboli and reveals that the more alarming issue is militarization and eventual loss of their homelands. This chapter argues that the Tasaday hoax can be fully understood only within these ecological and political realities.

In Chapter 5, Salazar reviews two data sets: the Panamin-sponsored publications on the Tasaday from the 1970s, and the reports and analyses of the hoax-thesis skeptics in 1986–88. Salazar, the first and almost only skeptic to go public before 1986 (Salazar 1971, 1973) reviews in this, his "third footnote," his analyses in support of the hoax thesis. These concern borrowed words in Tasaday speech and the early reports concerning their claimed isolation, use of stone tools, and lack of knowledge of agriculture. Most important, he presents here his data on the Tasaday genealogies, arguing how these show that several Tasaday are related by blood to Tboli or Manobo farmers living a few miles away.

In Part II: Supporters of the Early Reports on the Tasaday, the authors of the next three chapters take an opposite view. They respond to the skeptics, arguing in support of the early reports. Amelia Rogel-Rara and Emmanuel Nabayra (Chapter 6) present the results of their in-depth genealogical study of the Tasaday and their neighbors. Their findings, they argue, support and verify the genealogical descriptions published by the original ethnographers in the early '70s. Their genealogical data add three more generations domiciled in the Tasaday habitat to the four previously recorded. They also present data indicating that the nearby Blit Manobo agricultural people are newcomers to the Tasaday vicinity.

In Chapter 7, Molony reviews the Tasaday language data that she collected in 1972. She points out that a few of their plant names were lexemes borrowed from the nearby Tboli language, but that otherwise the Tasaday language appeared to be lacking the myriad words found in surrounding languages that were borrowed from Sanskrit, Chinese, Spanish, and English. Furthermore, she argues, the Tasaday language did not exhibit the great complex of terms associated with agriculture in other Philippine languages. She asserts that these data imply that the Tasaday had had only minimal association with speakers of other languages in recent times.

In Chapter 8, Elkins asserts that a comparison of the Tasaday language data with Cotabato Manobo dictionaries suggests that the Tasaday people represent a separate speech community, one that has developed differently from the main body of Cotabato Manobo speakers. He shows that the Tasaday speech in its development has been less conservative with regard to the retention of phonological reflexes and meanings of the reconstructed forms of the Proto-Manobo language. Also, instances of semantic skewing between Cotabato Manobo and Tasaday cognate lexemes seem to reflect the relative isolation and simple lifestyle that the original researchers claimed for the Tasaday back in the early 1970s.

In Part III: New Perspectives on Some Old Data, four more authors present some new perspectives on some of the early data. In Chapter 9, Fankhauser presents his findings that the nutrition provided by the Tasaday diet (as recorded over a five-day period by Douglas Yen) is inadequate, providing only 42% of energy requirements. He points out that casual eating during hunting and gathering activities could make up for the deficit, but this is not calculable because the types and amounts of food eaten during forays were not recorded.

In Chapter 10, Headland reviews the hypothesis that tropical moist forests in general, and the South Cotabato rain forest of the Tasaday in particular, lack sufficient wild foods to sustain a population of hunter-gatherers living independently of produced foods. If his hypothesis is correct, it does not mean that the Tasaday were fakes, but only that they were at least seasonally dependent upon cultivated plant food, and thus would not have been the pure (i.e., agriculturally independent) hunter-gatherers they were claimed to be.

In Chapter 11, Johnston reports that the language spoken by the Tasaday in 1972 is about 90% the same as the language known as Cotabato Manobo, spoken by some 12,000 people who live 25–50 km west of the Tasaday caves. He bases this conclusion on the reaction in 1989 of speakers of Manobo to a tape recording made by Carol Molony in the caves in 1972 and to a word list taken at the same time by Richard Elkins. Johnston includes here his notes about the words of Elkins's list, as well as his transcription and translation of a portion of Molony's tape recording. He concludes that Tasaday and Cotabato Manobo are mutually understandable dialects of the same language.

One of the unique features of Tasaday culture was their possession of stone tools. No other historic Philippine group had such implements, even in the 1500s. Thus, central to the issue of the Tasaday's authenticity is whether their stone tools were genuine. Two chapters focus on these tools. In Chapter 12, Peralta tells of his experience with the Tasaday in 1971 and during his recent field trip there again in 1986. He then describes the three stone tools found in use by the Tasaday when he was there in 1971.

Finally, in Part IV: Comments from Outside Scientists, six outside experts present their evaluations of the controversy. Richard Lee begins this section with an essay (Chapter 13) that draws together several themes and currents in the Tasaday debate. He first reviews the lines of evidence that lead to his conclusion that the Tasaday could not be what they were claimed to be, and considers the contrasting perspective afforded by placing the Tasaday within the context of the regional and national political economy of the Philippines. Finally, he looks at the way that the Western media—with fine impartiality—have packaged both the up- and the down-sides of the Tasaday story. Lee cautions anthropologists to treat all cases critically but at the same time not to dismiss soundly based ethnographies of foraging peoples elsewhere in South and Southeast Asia.

In Chapter 14, Carneiro presents the second of this volume's two chapters concerning the stone axes question. He examines the evidence available and concludes that the axes were too crudely made to be authentic. Rather, he concludes, they represent an attempt by the Tasaday to make an artifact not previously part of their culture in order to pass as a Stone Age group.

In Chapter 15, Reid examines the linguistic data recorded by the first researchers, assuming that if an attempt at a hoax had been perpetrated, evidence of it would almost certainly have come to light in the forms of the words that were elicited. He concludes that the apparently unsophisticated nature of the responses strongly suggests that there was no complicity to deceive the researchers as to the nature of the Tasaday language. They were clearly not Tboli people speaking Blit Manobo as a second language. Reid furthermore concludes that the differences (in intonation and lexicon) between Tasaday and its closest Manobo relatives could have resulted from a relatively short period of isolation, perhaps 150 years at the most.

In Chapter 16, Longacre briefly addresses the archaeological question. He suggests that if archaeological investigations could be undertaken at the Tasaday rockshelter sites they would quickly reveal if the caves had been occupied over generations or not. Longacre cautions, however, that while such fieldwork would lend weight to one or the other of the competing hypotheses addressed in this book, it would probably *not* result in a total solution.

In Chapter 17, Bodley points out some of the problems involved in the use of such concepts as "isolated," "Stone Age," and "contact" in the Tasaday debate. These terms are often poorly defined and difficult to apply in specific situations, yet they have well-established popular connotations and can be misused by policymakers concerned with indigenous peoples. A special problem with these concepts is that they underrate the vitality of tribal culture and obscure the importance of their political autonomy and territorial integrity. In Bodley's view, it is more critical to establish the validity of the self-identification of tribals as culturally unique, territorially based, self-sufficient groups than it is to determine whether such traits represent Stone Age continuity or contemporary devolution.

In Chapter 18, the editor invited Sponsel to explore the more general question, Why are we so fascinated with the Tasaday? While other chapters are primarily concerned with what the Tasaday *are,* Sponsel analyzes what they *represent.* He usefully places the Tasaday in the broader context of anthropology and history in Western civilization. The first part of his essay discusses what he calls "the Tasaday phenomenon" in terms of anthropological images. Based on an analysis of the Tasaday literature, Sponsel argues that they represent a complex symbol with multiple meanings relating to evolution, ecology, politics, and peace. The second part of his essay explores the Tasaday in relation to images of anthropology constructed by the media *and by anthropology,* and calls for more attention to media anthropology as a major route to reconcile the discrepancy between anthropology's self-image and public image. His essay concludes with a discussion of the meaning of the Tasaday for the 1990s, emphasizing the distinction between extrinsic and intrinsic values.

In the final chapter (Chapter 19), Headland summarizes the findings, presents some little-known facts, and proposes a hypothesis of how he thinks the

Tasaday were living before they were discovered in 1971. He also attempts to give his answer to the most often-asked question: Was the story a hoax or not?

On behalf of all the authors in this volume, I want to thank the two sponsors of the special Invited Session on the Tasaday, held at the 1989 AAA Annual Meeting, where the papers in this book were originally presented: the AAA Program Committee and the General Anthropology Division. We acknowledge also with thankfulness grants from the General Anthropology Division and the National Geographic Society, which helped cover transportation costs of some of the panelists who came from the Philippines. Finally, I am personally grateful for the professional editorial assistance I received on this volume from Betty Eastman, and for helpful editorial suggestions from Robert Bailey, Henry Bradley, Shirley Fiske, Bion Griffin, Janet Headland, Lou Hohulin, Richard Hohulin, Carol McKinney, Stephen Walter, Annette Weiner, and two anonymous peer reviewers of this book chosen by the AAA Special Publications Scholarly Series Editor, Terence Hays.

THOMAS N. HEADLAND

● *chapter one*

Introduction

Thomas N. Headland

Background: A Historical Review

In 1971 the news story broke of the discovery of a band of cave-dwelling people called Tasaday, who were said to be living in a secluded area of rain forest in the Philippines. These 26 individuals were reported to be following a Stone Age lifestyle, surviving solely on wild foods, and wearing leaves for clothing. They reportedly knew nothing of the outside world, or of the large village just a three-hour walk from their cave home; and they had no knowledge of the sea, just 20 miles away. They knew neither how to hunt nor how to grow food, but ate only what they could forage: roots, wild bananas, grubs, berries, and crabs and frogs fished by hand from small streams. They did not hunt or eat the deer, monkeys, or wild pigs that roamed throughout their area. Reports said that they had no pottery, no cloth, no metal, no art, no houses, no weapons, no dogs, and no domestic plants. Their only tools were small stone hammers, simple wooden digging implements, and sticks for making fire. One article stated that "the Tasaday regarded themselves [until 1966] as the only people on earth" (Jones 1989:67; see also Nance 1988a:471).

The story gained worldwide attention mainly through the National Geographic Society, both from the publication of the two famous articles on the Tasaday in their magazine (National Geographic 1971; MacLeish 1972) with its 8 million subscribers, and from their film on them (National Geographic 1972). Their film was shown first by CBS on US television on January 12, 1972, followed by repeated showings on TV worldwide. NBC also produced a TV film on the Tasaday, entitled "Cave People of the Philippines" (NBC-TV 1972). The fame of the Tasaday spread further with the publication in 1975 of the best-selling book *The Gentle Tasaday* by American Associated Press reporter John Nance.

Politicians, movie stars, journalists, and filmmakers were flown in to visit the Tasaday for short periods in 1972 and 1973. In addition, several scientists were invited by Panamin (the government agency then in charge of affairs concerning Philippine tribal peoples) to visit the site, though only one, Douglas Yen, was able to stay for more than a few days. (Yen's two periods in the area totaled 38 days). Most of these scientists published articles in local Philippine academic journals (e.g., Baradas 1972; Fernandez and Lynch 1972; Robert Fox 1976; Llamzon 1971b; Molony with Tuan 1976; and Yen 1976a, 1976b). Manuel Elizalde, Jr., the man who headed Panamin and who led the discovery of the Tasaday, also wrote an official report (Elizalde with Fox 1971a), dated July 1971, after the Panamin team's few hours of contact with them at the edge of the forest on June 7, June 8, and June 16, 1971.[1]

Then, in 1974, all known contact with the Tasaday was stopped by the Panamin authorities (but cf. Nance 1988a:456). A blanket of silence fell over the Tasaday, which lasted for 13 years, until the termination of the Marcos government in 1986.

In the intervening years, and up to the present, hundreds of thousands of university students have been taught in anthropology courses that the Tasaday were an extremely primitive stone-tool-using culture living in virtual isolation from other peoples, a viewpoint reflected in many anthropology textbooks and encyclopedias that discuss the Tasaday.

Almost immediately after the fall of Marcos in February 1986, sensational reports on the Tasaday again hit the international press. Although rumors in the Philippine academic community had quietly circulated for years that the Tasaday were not all they had been made out to be, independent researchers and reporters alike had refrained from investigating these rumors. This was due in large measure to Presidential Decree 1017 (PD-1017 1977), which threatened imprisonment or deportation for any social scientists entering the Tasaday forest without the permission of Panamin.

With the fall of Marcos, circumstances changed. In the chaotic month following Marcos's departure, foreign journalists, for the first time in over 15 years, were able to slip into the area with little fear of arrest. The first was Oswald Iten. In March 1986 he found the Tasaday living in houses and wearing regular clothes. This shouldn't have been much of a surprise—a plausible consequence of acculturation. But a week later the German magazine *Stern* sent in their reporters. They photographed the same Tasaday man that Iten had photographed, this time wearing leaves, but with underwear showing underneath the leaves! It is ironic that the rising of this news story to the level of an international scandal can probably be blamed on a pair of underwear.

Most of these accounts, beginning with Iten's (1986a), and followed by 1986 articles in *Newsweek* (April 28, p. 51) and *Asiaweek* (June 15, pp. 28–38, and August 31, pp. 60–61), argued that the Tasaday story was a complete fabrication. One of the more sober academic statements on the Tasaday published that year in the Philippines was by M. Lopez (1986). Later in 1986 an ABC documentary, "The Tribe That Never Was" (ABC-TV 1986), was shown on international TV, attempting to prove that the Tasaday story was a deception. In 1987 Central Independent Television produced their documentary, shown on NBC-TV, entitled "Scandal: The Lost Tribe" (Central Independent Television 1987). It also claimed the story was a hoax. In the following three years, hundreds of articles appeared in newspapers and magazines all over the world discussing the controversy.

Today the issue remains far from settled. Newspaper articles continued to appear into early 1990, and three encyclopedia articles were written or published in the same year (Grumet 1990; Headland 1992; Illustrated Encyclopedia 1990). Four important academic articles appeared: one in 1987 (Peralta 1987), two in 1988 (Dumont 1988; Molony 1988), and one in 1991 (Yengoyan 1991), and at least three major magazine articles (Berreman 1991; Hyndman and Duhaylungsod 1990; Jones 1989). In early 1989 I published a statement in *The Sciences* (Headland 1989c) critiquing Molony's (1988) argument on the Tasaday. Later in the year *Science News* published a cover story titled "The Strange Case of the Tasaday" (Bower 1989b), which was reprinted in the October 1989 issue of the *Anthropology Newsletter*. And an essay criticizing me on the issue was written by an American anthropologist in the Philippines (Olofson 1989), to which I wrote a response (Headland 1990a). Finally, the BBC released a new documentary film on the Tasaday, shown in March 1989 on public television in England and Europe. Entitled "Trial in the Jungle" (Lerner 1989), the opening words of it state:

> This group of 26 people, the Tasaday, may have pulled off the most elaborate hoax in scientific history. If they were able to fool every anthropologist who ever saw them, how credible is the science of anthropology?

Startling headline reports have appeared from both sides of the issue: The case has been referred to repeatedly in the press as "the most elaborate hoax perpetrated on the anthropological world since the Piltdown Man" (Mydans 1988). On the other side, *National Geographic Magazine* set forth the official position of their Society with the statement in their September 1988 issue, that "Recent stories that the Tasaday were a hoax have been largely discredited" (McCarry 1988:304).

For the public, the issue seems to have been simplistically reduced to just two possible polar alternatives, which have been stated in various ways. They are reflected in the subtitles of two recent articles: "Are they a primitive tribe—or a modern hoax?" (Molony 1988), and "Were they primitive hunter-gatherers or rain-forest phonies?" (Bower 1989b), as well as by a statement published in *Asiaweek* (November 25, 1988) that the Tasaday discovery is either "one of the major anthropological events of the century" or "the hoax of the decade" (p. 35). A statement on the cover of an official 1988 periodical of the University of the Philippines also reflects the public's view of the controversy by referring to it as "Media Circus and Science-Fiction" (Azurin 1988).

Three scholarly symposia have been held to debate the issue. The first was in Quezon City, Philippines, in August 1986; the second was at the International Congress on Anthropological and Ethnological Sciences in Zagreb, Yugoslavia, in July 1988. The issues were not settled at either of those meetings. The third symposium was held as a special Invited Session on the Tasaday controversy held at the 88th Annual Meeting of the American Anthropological Association (AAA), in Washington, D.C., in November 1989. Papers on which the chapters in this volume are based were presented at that symposium. The topic was a lively one at that AAA Annual Meeting, judging by the many anthropologists in the audience and by the media attention it drew. News reports on the symposium were published in the November 25 issue of *Science News,* the November 29 issue of *Chronicle of Higher Education,* the December 1 issue of *Science,* the January 8 issue of the *Los Angeles Times,* the February 19 issue of *U.S. News & World Report,* in London in the February issue of *Anthropology Today,* and most recently by the Encyclopaedia Brittanica, Inc., in their 1990 *Book of the Year* (Grumet 1990). Brief articles also reported on the symposium in three Manila newspapers on November 18, 1989, just one day after it was over; and two of the symposium panelists published short papers on the issue soon after that meeting (Molony 1989b; Sponsel 1990b). A longer cover story entitled ''Romanticizing the Stone Age'' appeared in a 1991 issue of *Cultural Survival Quarterly,* with a feature article on the Tasaday by a third panelist (Berreman 1991). Finally, an essay on the Tasaday by a fourth panelist will appear in the forthcoming *Encyclopedia of World Cultures* (Headland 1992).

Genesis of the Controversy

It is beyond the scope of this Introduction to try to analyze here why or how the Tasaday case has developed into such an international sensation. But let me mention six factors I believe led so many to question the credibility of the story: (1) the restrictions put upon Panamin-invited scientists to the area, both to brief stays of no more than a few days, and to limited time allowed with the Tasaday during those stays; (2) the strict forbidding of access to the area by *independent* scientists; (3) the conflicting evidence that raised skepticism (e.g., disagreements in the genealogies collected); (4) the heavy-handed political interventions that were almost constant even in the 1980s and even interfered with the planning and carrying out of the 1989 Washington, D.C., symposium; (5) the media blitz—first in the early '70s and then again in the late '80s—which sensationalized this case to the point where it is impossible to conduct an independent scientific study of it today; and (6) the overall question of plausibility—whether or not the early Panamin accounts were exaggerated, anthropologists, at least, find it difficult today to accept without question that the Tasaday were as primitive and isolated as claimed. Finally, as an anonymous AAA reviewer for this volume stated in his written review, ''The controversy arose in the first place because the Tasaday never had their own 'real' ethnographer to authenticate and legitimize them to the scientific community. They were stuck with [reporter John] Nance, who . . . even by journalistic standards, got an awful lot of mileage out of very little digging.''

Statements from Two Anthropological Organizations

In 1987 the Department of Anthropology at the UP (University of the Philippines 1987) wrote a formal statement entitled ''The Tasaday Controversy,'' which was later published in the February 1988 issue of the *Anthropology Newsletter,* the official publication of the AAA. This statement said, in part:

> We, faculty members of the Anthropology Department, wish to clarify what we perceive to be the issues [concerning the Tasaday controversy]. . . . We feel that

the integrity of the entire Philippine scientific community is at stake [if we are not allowed academic freedom to speak our view on the Tasaday]. . . . But voices of dissent were suppressed. . . . There have been attempts to discredit our colleagues. . . . [They] were [not] allowed to publish their views. . . . The longer we delay a resolution, the more we are bound to lose in terms of the Filipino scientist's credibility. . . . Our calls for an inquiry seek to test democracy, particularly our right to search for the truth.

Nine months later a second statement, in the form of a resolution, was presented at the 87th Annual Meeting of the AAA (in November 1988). This resolution was made in support of the UP anthropologists' statement, as well as because of concern for alleged human rights problems revolving around the Tasaday controversy. That "Resolution on the Tasaday Controversy" (printed in the *Anthropology Newsletter*, 87th Annual Meeting Edition, November 16–20, 1988, p. 8) said:

> Resolved that the membership of the American Anthropological Association supports the statement on "The Tasaday Controversy" by the Department of Anthropology of the University of the Philippines. . . . This Association further urges that a full-scale anthropological study of the evidence bearing on the question of the nature and authenticity of the people called "Tasaday" be undertaken by competent scholars. . . . Finally, this Association expresses its concern for the welfare of Philippine cultural minorities and the freedom and integrity of anthropological inquiry regarding these peoples, especially in the instance of the Tasaday.

The resolution went to a written vote of the entire AAA membership in March 1989, and passed with a vote of 94% in favor (*Anthropology Newsletter*, May 1989, pp. 17, 44).

This AAA vote did not deny the legitimacy of the Tasaday people, and it should not be so interpreted. Neither was it an endorsement of the so-called hoax thesis. Rather, the resolution was made for three other reasons: (1) in reaction to the reported intimidation of some Filipino anthropologists who tried to question the original reports on the Tasaday, some of whom have been sued in court, and others threatened with arrest and prison sentences if they tried to enter the Tasaday area;[2] (2) in reaction to more general human rights issues surrounding the controversy; and (3) "to support free enquiry."[3]

One response to the AAA resolution was the AAA Executive Committee's 1989 commissioning of a Panel on the Tasaday Question. Chaired by Fred Eggan, the Panel's objective was to provide the Association with "a summary of the evidence and an objective assessment of the Tasaday issue, and to offer its conclusions and recommendations to the Association . . . in 1990" (*Anthropology Newsletter*, October 1989, p. 36).[4] Another response to the resolution was, of course, the AAA sponsorship of the November 1989 AAA Tasaday symposium, where the material in this volume was first presented, and the AAA publication of this volume.

What the Main Question is *Not* About

For anthropologists, and for the authors of this book, the debate is not concerned with whether or not the Tasaday exist. None of us are suggesting that these are plastic mannequins we are arguing about.

Some reporters, then, are fighting a straw man by writing treatises arguing that these Tasaday actually do exist. As reporter John Nance (1988a:453, 454) recently argued,

> I want to say one thing with certainty. That is, simply, this: The Tasaday were and are a genuine people; they are real, *they exist.* There are those who claim otherwise. . . . A few . . . journalists and academics . . . [are] proclaiming the Tasaday don't exist now and never did. [emphasis added]

Further, it is less than honest when another reporter tells hundreds of thousands of people in a newspaper editorial that "The Tasaday are under attack by anthropologists . . . who claim they never existed" (*Globe and Mail,* July 3, 1989).

On September 21, 1989, Antonio Cervantes (a close associate of and spokesman for Manuel Elizalde, and the administrator, under Elizalde, of the Tasaday Community Care Foundation in Manila) stated in a letter to Richard Elkins, "No matter what distracting side issues the other side raises, the main question is whether the Tasaday are real or a hoax." This again is an attempt to circumvent the real question, because the opposite of "hoax" among the debaters in this volume is not "real," but degree of primitiveness and isolation.

The question debated by the Philippine Congressional Committee in 1987–88 also missed the point when it deflected the debate into an argument concerning existence versus nonexistence. No scientist to my knowledge could disagree with the Committee's conclusion, that the Tasaday "exist and are an authentic cultural minority group" (Committee on National Cultural Communities 1988:4, 16, 19). There are at least a hundred authentic cultural minority groups in the Philippines today. Anthropologists are neither claiming nor trying to prove that the Tasaday do not exist. Anthropologists are seeking to validate whether or not they were pure foragers, not whether or not they exist. And most of the authors in this book, I suspect, reject both extreme viewpoints ("absolute paleolithic isolation" versus "paid actors").

What This Book *Is* About

What, then, are the scientific issues regarding the Tasaday? What is being debated among anthropologists? Why are anthropologists so interested in the Tasaday case? We are not engrossed in a simplistic controversy about whether these people do or do not exist. For anthropologists, the core of the argument centers on whether or not the Tasaday people were pristine foragers; that is, to what degree they were living a Pleistocene-like foraging subsistence until the middle of this century? Were they living in caves, and for how long? To what degree, if any, were they following a lifestyle close to what we would call paleolithic? That is, to what extent were they living without iron tools, independently of cultivated foods, and with no interaction with farming peoples?

A Proposed Working Hypothesis

In researching these questions, we need a target upon which to focus our attention, one which is scientific, not journalistic. An overall working hypothesis that crystalizes the issue and is testable can provide such a target. At the Washington, D.C., symposium I suggested the following as such a hypothesis:

> a small band of people known as Tasaday lived in caves in the southern Philippines following a stone-tool-using foraging mode of subsistence, without iron, eating only wild foods, and having no contact with agricultural peoples until the 1960s.

The Immediate Scientific Questions

Following upon this hypothesis, a number of corollaries or minor working hypotheses could be proposed. I will not attempt to develop them here, but they would be formulated from the obvious immediate questions generated by the main hypothesis, some of which are

> What is their origin?
> Where did they live during the first half of this century?
> Did they live permanently in the caves?
> To what degree did they make and use stone tools?
> For what purpose?
> What was their relationship to the outside world in the 1950s? 1890s?
> Did they have any contact with farmers before Dafal met them?
> If not, why not?
> What kind of outside contact did they have after Dafal?
> From which parent Manobo groups did they break off? When?
> How did they survive as a viable group over a long period of isolation?
> Where did they get their spouses?
> Does their gene pool show heavy inbreeding?
> How did they make their living?
> What is the nutritional viability of wild foods in the area?
> What was the range of their foraging activities?
> What is their midden content?
> What was the nature of their language?
> When did Manobo farmers first move into the area?

Still other working hypotheses may of course be generated from the main hypothesis that I have proposed—ones relating to Tasaday demography, ethnobotany, cave archaeology, questions of social structure and kinship, etc. Several of these are, in fact, addressed by the authors in this volume.

In my view, anthropology as a social science can best approach the main hypothesis by establishing and testing corollaries (minor working hypotheses) to the main hypothesis. The authors in this book followed this procedure by addressing themselves to the implicit corollaries in an attempt to reach conclusions that speak to the main hypothesis proposed. Ultimately, in this manner science will bring us to a general understanding of the validity or lack thereof of the main hypothesis.

The Significance of the Topic for Anthropology in General

The controversy concerning the Tasaday must be dealt with not only because of our interest in the Tasaday debate itself, or the specific questions already mentioned, but because of two more general areas of interest: (1) human prehistory and (2) human adaptation to tropical forests. First, the subject of the Tasaday is of concern to those of us interested in human prehistory and hunter-gatherer studies; for if the descriptions of the Tasaday from the 1970s are correct, then we may indeed have here what some have referred to as the anthropological find of the century—data with which we can test hypotheses concerning how *Homo sapiens* may have lived in the tropics during the Upper Pleistocene, a chance to test, for example, Rousseau's noble savage idea or Marshall Sahlins's (1972) Original Affluent Society concept.

Over the last decade archaeologists and cultural anthropologists alike have struggled with whether or how the Tasaday case might be used to modify our theoretical models of how humans lived during the Paleolithic. It is vital to our discipline that we find out to what degree the Tasaday in the 1960s are a reflection of how our prehistoric ancestors may have lived at the end of the Pleistocene. This is not just so we can solve the Tasaday mystery, but so that we can interpret this ethnographic example correctly in our scientific efforts to understand human life and behavior in the past. In the last few years the anthropological pendulum has swung away from the view that small foraging bands can be treated as if they exist in a pristine state of prior evolutionary time.[5] But this does not mean that we cannot make generalizations about the past based on the Tasaday culture, or the culture of any other group, *if* we can first learn enough about that culture. Unfortunately, we still know almost nothing about the Tasaday culture.

Second, we are interested not only in reconstructing the past, but, increasingly important for the 1990s, in understanding the present and the future for humankind in the tropical world. Thus, the Tasaday are of keen interest to those of us who are spending our professional lives researching what we refer to as *human adaptation to tropical forest ecosystems*. In the last decade hundreds of thousands of landless people around the globe have migrated into tropical forest areas to attempt a new life. For most, the move has been an economic and ecological failure. As applied anthropologists are called upon by development planners for help in the next decade, we turn for answers to studies of traditional peoples who *have* lived successfully in such ecosystems for many hundreds of years. As the ecological spoiling of our planet accelerates before us in the next decade, groups like the Tasaday may provide us with unique insights and answers found nowhere else.

Notes

1. The Presidential Assistant on National Minorities (Panamin) and Manuel Elizalde, its director, are major players on the chessboard of this whole controversy, and the interested reader should refer to two important sources (Griffin 1988; Rocamora 1979), to grasp the significance of the role they played. Panamin, roughly the equivalent of the Bureau of Indian Affairs in the United States, functioned from 1968 until it was dissolved in 1984. In August 1989 the Tasaday Community Care Foundation, Inc., was officially registered at the Securities and Exchange Commission in Manila. Antonio Cervantes is its administrator and official Treasurer, while Elizalde is reportedly the real head. The TCCF address is the same as the address of Elizalde & Co., Inc. (141 Ayala Avenue, Makati, Manila).

2. This threat is quite real, and is still enforced by the powerful Presidential Decree No. 1017 (PD-1017 1977), entitled ''Prohibiting persons from entering into unexplored tribal grounds and providing penalty therefor.'' This decree, signed into law in 1976 by former President Marcos, states that it ''shall be unlawful for any person, especially . . . social scientists, without prior . . . recommendation of [Panamin] . . . to enter unexplored tribal grounds . . . for the purpose of conducting studies of their customs. . . . The penalty shall be prison.'' The ''Tasaday Reservation'' is listed in the decree as one of four forbidden areas.

3. As the President of the American Anthropological Association explained to reporters in an unpublished letter in June 1989, ''The intent of the AAA resolution was to support free inquiry.''

4. Unfortunately, this panel's report was never completed, due to Professor Eggan's untimely death in May 1991.

5. Indeed, this new view of Holocene hunter-gatherers as societies living in *interdependence with* rather than *independence of* surrounding state societies is today the major issue among hunter-gatherer specialists. Referred to as the ''Hunter-Gatherer Revisionist Debate,'' it is even being referred to as a ''new paradigm'' shift (Gordon 1991:49; Lewin 1988:1148) in hunter-gatherer studies. By the end of the 1980s such peoples were no longer seen as isolated, or as reflections of how prehistoric humans once lived. Instead, the revisionists argue that such peoples exist not in spite of but because of their contacts with the outside world, with long histories of trade and interaction with the dominant societies around them. This revisionist movement was probably conceived by the writings of Keesing (1981) and Wolf (1982), then brought to bear specifically to hunter-gatherers by chapters in Leacock and Lee (1982) and Schrire (1984), by Hoffman's (1986) study, and now moved to the point of major debate by Wilmsen's polemical book (1989). (Several reviews of this revisionist movement are now in print: Bower 1989a; Brownlee 1990; Headland 1990b; Headland and Reid 1989; Lewin 1988; Solway and Lee 1990; and Wilmsen and Denbow 1990.) This movement keeps pushing the Tasaday to the forefront in anthropology studies because they appear as *the* paradox to the revisionists' ideas.

PART I

The Skeptics

● *chapter two*

The Tasaday: Stone Age Survivors or Space Age Fakes?

GERALD D. BERREMAN

In order to adequately understand the Tasaday controversy, one must be clear on the argument—on what is at issue and what is not—for there has been a noticeable tendency to shift the grounds of the debate in the process of pursuing it. Some of those who were privileged to visit the Tasaday during the nearly two and a half years of access to them, and who have described them to us, began the post-Marcos debate by swearing to the accuracy of their original startling descriptions and inferences. Then in the face of contrary evidence or implausibility they have retreated to a new, quite different, largely noncontroversial position, which they present as a successful response to the challenges directed at their original stance. That position seems to be that *whatever* the nature of their culture and society, whatever their history, whatever the circumstances and evidence of their 1971–72 encounter with their "discoverer," Manuel Elizalde and his associates and guests, the "Tasaday" are after all real people, deserving of respect and social justice. As Elizalde is quoted as having said, "In this whole case, the truth becomes insignificant. Whether the Tasaday are fake or not is really incidental" (Mydans 1987:6).

The actual and persisting argument before us is simply and directly an argument over whether the people "discovered" in 1971, and termed "Tasaday," were as they were described by those who reported upon them at that time and in the ensuing few years. Did they at all have the culture (the social organization, the political organization, the economy, the religion, the language, the technology, the diet) they were described as having? The issues being debated are the accuracy of the characterizations made of the Tasaday and their way of life, the nature of the evidence upon which those claims were based, and how believable the evidence and the characterizations are. Following upon that argument is the one joined in 1986 when, after Marcos's overthrow, the Tasaday were revisited. Then the question was raised whether the present-day Tasaday are those same Stone Age people after fifteen to twenty years of intensive contact and consequent astounding change. Or is their present style of life, including agriculture, houses, complex technology, and the other accoutrements of contemporary life in the back-country of Mindanao, essentially that which they were living two decades ago, differing primarily in that now, in the absence of Elizalde's close supervision as cabinet-level head of Panamin (Marcos's Presidential Assistant on National Minorities), the pose of primitivity has been dropped except for brief performances acknowledged as such?

If the answer is no, they were and are not as originally described, then we might want additionally to know who they "really" were/are and what they were/are "really" like. This would be a subject for careful anthropological research.

We might also like to know, with what motives and by whom and through what means were we—or some of us—misled? These, it seems to me, are important but not strictly anthropological questions. I will therefore mention them only briefly here. I have addressed them at some length in the context of the entire debate in another place (Berreman 1991).

The Making of the "Tasaday": 1971–72

The earliest firsthand account of the Tasaday was that by Elizalde in collaboration with Robert Fox (Elizalde with Fox 1971a). This was followed by the reports by anthropologists Carlos Fernandez, Robert Fox, and Frank Lynch (Fernandez and Lynch 1972; Fox 1971b, 1976; Lynch et al. 1973; Lynch and Llamzon 1971); ethnobotanist Douglas Yen (Yen 1976a, 1976b; Yen and Gutierrez 1974; Yen and Nance 1976); linguists Teodoro Llamzon, Richard Elkins, and Carol Molony (Elkins 1971, 1972; Llamzon 1971b; Molony with Tuan 1976); journalists Kenneth MacLeish, John Nance, and an anonymous writer for the *National Geographic* (MacLeish 1972; Nance 1975, 1981; *National Geographic* 1971). All of these observers were selected, briefed, and escorted by Elizalde.

Most of the basic claims that have been made about the Tasaday, nineteen of which are listed in Table 1, appeared in these publications. Many of them were immediately identified and critically assessed by Zeus Salazar (1971, 1973).

These 19 assertions characterize the Tasaday way of life as it was described from the time of their discovery in 1971 until they were revisited after 13 years of isolation under martial law. Repeatedly they were so depicted in the words and photographs of mass and professional media.

Or were they?

On closer inspection the photographs and descriptions prove not to show exactly this—or even this at all. The claims were not what they appeared to be. Rather, the claim was that this was the way the Tasaday *had* lived before they met Dafal, a neighboring farmer and gatherer of forest products who discovered them, transformed them, and ultimately introduced them to Elizalde. Soon after Elizalde and his entourage first saw them, he introduced them to journalists, scientists, and other observers in a major media presentation at the edge of the forest (on July 20, 1971). Among those present were John Nance (Associated Press), Jack Reynolds and his three-man television crew (NBC-TV 1972), a National Geographic crew, Christopher Lucas of *Reader's Digest,* as well as anthropologist Robert Fox, a Yale anthropology student spending the summer with Panamin, Edith Terry, archaeologist Jesus Peralta and artist Manuel Santiago, both with the Phil-

TABLE 1
Basic claims made about the Tasaday in the 1970s by scholars and journalists who visited them

1. The Tasaday had been isolated for hundreds of years at least.
2. They comprised a distinct social unit called "Tasaday," composed of 25 people.
3. They were unaware of other people except for two groups similar to their own, called Tasafeng and Sanduka (or Tasanduka), with whom they had had marriage and other kin relationships but whom they had not seen for several decades.
4. They comprised a distinct linguistic community whose language was not easily or at all mutually intelligible with related languages of the region (i.e., other Cotabato Manobo dialects) or elsewhere and was free of loan words from other languages.
5. They had no words for war, weapons, conflict, violence, nor for processes, implements, or products of domesticated plants or animals, nor for structures of any kind, nor even for some natural phenomena such as the sea (just 22 km away and which could be viewed from less than a 3-hour walk from the caves).
6. They had lived since time immemorial in a series of streamside water-formed rock shelters or "caves" on a mountainside deep in the rain forest of South Cotabato, Mindanao.
7. They wore clothing made only of fresh leaves.
8. They derived their livelihood solely from foraging in the neighborhood of their caves. Of the eight edible varieties of tubers in their immediate vicinity they knew only one, the yam called *biking* (*Dioscorea* sp.) and depended heavily upon it. They were unaware of the edibility of both the nutritious pith and the starch of the plentiful palms in their area, or how to extract it or leach it. They also foraged fruits, nuts, and small animals such as frogs (the largest creatures they had ever eaten), crabs, fingerlings from the nearby creek, grubs, and the like, but excluding mammals and birds.
9. They manufactured extremely crude, weakly hafted stone tools made of soft, coarse, river pebbles ground to a rough edge in a few minutes on the spot. There is one disputed high-angle, pressure-flaked flint scraper, seen too briefly to be photographed or even adequately drawn, and subsequently lost, which, if authentic and of contemporary manufacture, would be unique in the Philippines. It was identified by one informant as having been part of a trade-goods strike-a-light kit rather than of local manufacture (Fox 1976:4–5).
10. They were without weapons of any kind, without technology for hunting (such as bows and arrows or blowguns, spears, clubs, or traps), nor for fishing (such as hooks, spears, nets, weirs, traps, or poisons).
11. They were without carrying or storing technology of any kind such as baskets, boxes, pottery, nets, or bags.
12. They made fire with a spindle whorl (reportedly the only case thereof in the Philippines).
13. They built no structures of any kind.
14. They possessed, and knew of, no domestic plants or animals of any kind.
15. They had no knowledge of farming peoples, including those of villages demonstrated to be a 3-hour walk from their own (Yen 1976b:170).
16. They were without political or religious organization or specialists of any kind.
17. They believed in a supreme being known as "the owner," who rewarded good, punished evil, and owned and protected the immediate environs of the caves from human depredations.
18. They had no rituals of any kind.
19. They had no songs or music of any kind.

ippine National Museum, and others (Nance 1975:48–49). The Tasaday were then quite different from the Stone Age image projected of them, for they had already had the benefit (if that is an appropriate word) of the remarkable effect of Dafal's example, instruction, and propensity to bestow gifts upon them. Nance quotes Charles Lindbergh as having commented that "[Dafal] brought the apple and they bit it, no question about that," and he notes that "Robert Fox had once talked of Tasaday history as falling in the phases B.D.—Before Dafal—and A.D.—After Dafal" (Nance 1975:136).

Indeed, by the time they encountered Elizalde, the Tasaday had acquired virtually *all* of the very artifacts, skills, and knowledge whose alleged absence among them (as announced by Elizalde and his associates) had led to their public renown, their scientific interest, and finally to the present controversy. That is, when Elizalde met them, they *had* cloth garments (in which all of them were scantily garbed in his initial photographs [Elizalde with Fox 1971a]), brass jewelry, metal bolos and knives, bows and arrows, spears, clubs, a variety of animal traps, a diet including large animal meat (deer, monkeys, birds) obtained throught the use of the allegedly newly acquired technology (accompanied by a hearty appetite for it and skill in butchering and cooking it), fishing and the technology to do it, baskets in which to carry and store things, and brooms with which to sweep their caves (thereby preventing a floor midden from accumulating). (How post-Dafal sweeping was supposed to have achieved this ex post facto effect after more than 500 years of occupation mystifies me!) They also had major dietary dependence upon the previously (pre-Dafal) unknown palm pith *(ubod)* and palm starch *(natek)*—the latter made possible only through the elaborate technology and skills required to extract and leach it, "the whole . . . process" taught them by Dafal (Nance 1975:138), although puzzlingly—one of many such puzzles—Elizalde himself in an initial publication (Elizalde with Fox 1971a:6) mentions that Dafal "was emphatic that . . . when he first contacted [the Tasaday] . . . their staple food was the pith of wild palms." He follows this with the information that "on his first trip into the Tasaday area, Dafal accidentally came upon a group of men . . . who were preparing the pith of wild palms" (1971a:7). It seems that among the most difficult features of this myth was keeping the stories straight.[1]

Be that as it may, at the time of Elizalde's first visit the Tasaday were also reported to be using, allegedly as a result of Dafal's efforts, seven previously unknown varieties of wild tubers (including one that requires leaching before it is edible). They exhibited a craving—even demand—for rice. They used "strike-a-light" (flint and steel) fire-making technology; they had abandoned (if ever they had engaged in) the manufacture of flaked tools and the highly implausible, evidently technologically useless, geometric stone objects called "heirloom tools" in descriptions of Tasaday technology. They were playing the characteristic Philippine bamboo "Jew's-harp," and singing the tunes it produced. All of these, and more, were in the Tasaday's cultural inventory when scholars and journalists first saw them in 1971–72. Most of them are documented in photographs, some of them contradicting by their presence the accompanying text! *Every single one of these features* is contrary to or inconsistent with the reports of their uniquely primitive, Stone Age, cave-dwelling, foraging (nonhunting/nonfishing) economy and technology, and accordingly those who announced or chronicled the discovery of the Stone Age Tasaday attributed *every single one of these features* to introduction by the amazing Dafal.

Dafal, a man to ponder: a peripatetic individual with ties marital, parental, and residential to the three main ethnic groups and their villages in the adjacent lowlands—Manobo, Ubo, and Tboli. He was the first outsider the Tasaday had ever met, and he revolutionized their way of life (reportedly without learning to speak their language, or they his), in the five years of his association with them. (Or was it 3? Or was it somewhere in between? It depends on which account you read, as Yen 1976b:176 and Molony with Tuan 1976:17 make clear.) This all happened before he brought them to the attention of Elizalde, whom he had met through the latter's activities in the region with Panamin.

Those to whom Elizalde first introduced the Tasaday promptly joined him in identifying them as isolated, Stone Age cave dwellers. Upon seeing them, Charles Lindbergh, for example, intoned: "That is cave man" (Nance 1975:135). It was announced that their language (and therefore, their persons) separated from others of the region 571–755 years ago. Evaluations of their scientific importance were extravagant: "Fernandez felt that few scientists would quarrel with his belief that the Tasaday were the most significant anthropological discovery of this century— 'and I think we could say centuries' " (Nance 1975:134). An unidentified Filipino scientist was reported to have described the discovery as more significant than man's landing on the moon (Nance 1975:348). Upon revisiting them in 1986, Peralta announced that "the Tasaday are absolutely authentic," and added, "I don't know of another people like them anywhere in the world" (*Asiaweek* 1986:38).

Rationalizations and Challenges

How could such a small society have persisted so long with the sort of economy, technology, and diet attributed to them, especially in view of social isolation from, and geographic proximity to, agricultural villages?

Accounting for Primitivity

Two alternative explanations were immediately proposed by those who were convinced of the Tasaday's extraordinarily primitive way of life (Elizalde with Fox 1971a:16–17):

1. They were cave-dwelling survivors of a paleolithic preagricultural society and culture which had for unknown reasons persisted in the rain forest unchanged in language and culture from its primeval origins (Elkins 1971; Llamzon 1971b). Lynch speculated that the people of Blit represented a group that had split off from the same stock to become agricultural, while the Tasaday remained as before.

2. They were rain forest refugees from a formerly lowland swidden-farming, hunting, trapping, foraging society who had lost or relinquished that way of life,

and the language that had gone with it when, presumably to escape epidemic, enemies, or some other threat, they took refuge in the caves of the mountain rain forest, there to remain in isolation, relinquishing and then forgetting their former way of life, and ultimately forgetting their origins and neighbors—until the fortuitous encounter with Dafal (Elizalde with Fox 1971a; Olofson 1989:22, 27). Molony reports that Elkins later adopted this view (Molony with Tuan 1976:14).

Some of those who disbelieved the accounts altogether articulated a third explanation:

3. The Tasaday were swidden farmers typical of the region, living in one or more settlements and comprising a speech community (within the Cotabato Manobo language group) located near the forest, recruited through threats and promises (including the suggestion, frequently attributed to Elizalde, that apparent primitivity would elicit sympathetic gifts and aid from outsiders) to enact an occasional well-coached performance as Stone Age, leaf-wearing, nonhunting foragers, living in rock shelters in the forest. That portrayal was not entirely unfamiliar because of the proximity of the forest and the caves to which they made periodic forays for useful products, ritual activities, or refuge (cf. Salazar 1971, 1973).

A fourth explanation, essentially a variant on the third, constitutes something of a compromise between it and the first two:

4. The Tasaday are descended from people who long ago migrated from the lowland to the periphery of the forest—or even into it—where they cleared land, built houses, and followed their traditional swidden agricultural economy while coming to know and rely upon the forest environment as well. In their relative isolation they developed a distinct variant of the swidden-farming society and culture from which they had come, entailing major utilization of the adjacent forest—resulting in an economy, technology, and diet suited to that environment. These changes were manifestations of environmental adaptation, combined with cultural drift resulting from relative isolation (cf. Berreman 1960). In the process the Tasaday did not abandon the ways of their lowland forbears and neighbors nor become entirely isolated from them. Neither did they disappear into the forest. Their use of the caves was limited to ritual activities and occasional shelter. Their leaf-wearing, cave-dwelling appearances in 1971–72 were brief forays—publicity stunts—performed for the benefit of outsiders, at the behest of Elizalde, portraying a way of life they had never known, but in an environment and utilizing resources familiar to them.

A fifth explanation of the Tasaday is a logical possibility:

5. They were hunter-gatherers of the rain forest (with the expectable trading relationship with neighboring swidden farmers) when discovered by Elizalde, who then induced them to pose as the uniquely primitive, isolated cave dwellers he introduced to the world as "Tasaday."

In my view, the third explanation, namely that the "Tasaday" comprised a group of the local swidden-farming folk recruited to act as cave men in the nearby forest, is the most likely of the five, with perhaps a 66% probability. Its variant, number 4—that the Tasaday were swidden farmers unusually close to, involved with, and adapted to the forest—is less likely but plausible, with a probability of something like 33%. The fifth explanation—that the Tasaday were hunter-gatherer recruits to Tasadaydom—is very, but not entirely, improbable, at a level of no more than 1%. The first two scenarios—the authentic "Stone Age Tasaday" of disparate histories—are so improbable in my view as to be totally implausible.

Accounting for Change

In the summer of 1986 following Marcos's overthrow, journalist-scholar Oswald Iten visited and reported on the Tasaday (Iten 1986a, 1986b), followed in quick succession by teams from *Stern* (Unger and Ullal 1986) and *Asiaweek* (1986) magazines, and then by an American Broadcasting Company television news team (ABC-TV 1986). All four reported witnessing a very different, or drastically changed, Tasaday fifteen years after they had been "discovered" and twelve years after they had been last observed. All reported that the Tasaday appeared at the caves, dressed in leaves, when forewarned of the visitors' coming; otherwise they now lived in conventional village settings and dressed in clothes common to such villages.

But not everyone reported change in the lifestyle of the Tasaday. Mai Tuan, Elizalde's trusty lieutenant and self-described "official interpreter," who is also a Tboli headman and mayor of the local municipality, announced on Central Independent Television (1987): "They're still living in the caves, even up to this time. For fifteen years we know them. They've never changed. The same way we first saw them—the same way until this day." He must have lost his script, for no one but he has made this claim.

The other observers—those who saw change—generated at least three propositions to explain and interpret what they had seen:

1. Since their discovery the Tasaday had moved away from the caves in which they had lived, to the periphery of the forest where they were in contact with swidden agriculturalists who lived in houses built on stilts, cultivated root crops, tubers, bananas, vegetables, and some grains (not including rice, which, if used, had to have been acquired from the lowlands), raised chickens, pigs, and dogs, dressed in clothing common to peasants throughout the island and nation, and spoke a Cotabato Manobo dialect mutually intelligible with others of the region. There the Tasaday learned and adopted some of the lifeways of their neighbors while retaining some of their old ways suited to the rain forest.

2. The Tasaday had, in the fifteen years since their discovery, moved from their caves to join or establish the swidden agricultural village situated on cleared land where they are now found, adopting fully the culture and social organization of their new-found neighbors. They now rarely enter the forest, but live instead in the village, in houses on stilts, engage in swidden agriculture, raise chickens,

pigs, and dogs, dress in the clothing conventional among other people of the region, share fully in their technology and lifestyle, speak with them freely in the
local Cotabato Manobo dialect, and in fact have married among them to the extent
that their numbers have increased, as reported by the *Asiaweek* team, from 26 to
61 (and now, I am told, over 70).

Archaeologist Peralta of that team is quoted by John Nance in *Asiaweek* (*Asiaweek* 1986:38) as follows:

> This is "rare—very rare—to see a group at this level of development and
> change . . . from gathering to trapping to hunting—and soon, I expect, to plant-
> ing—all in a single lifetime. Traditionally such changes span many centuries.
> The whole process is being contracted here before our very eyes." Fernandez
> agreed.

3. The Tasaday were, at the time of their "discovery," simply lowland,
house-dwelling, agricultural villagers, speaking, as does every other local speech
community, their dialect of the regional language, Cotabato Manobo (the third
scenario of the five given above—or, optionally, scenario number 4, if one finds
that more convincing). In either case, they were induced by Elizalde to leave their
houses and fields for occasional brief periods, and under his direction to take the
walk to the caves (which they knew as a place with religious significance and/or
as a place of temporary refuge) and there to dress in leaves and mimic the paleolithic troglodytic way of life as Elizalde imagined it to be, for the benefit of journalists, curiosity seekers, scientists, and other visitors during brief, carefully supervised visits announced well in advance.

I am convinced this last explanation is accurate, and therefore that the image
of the Stone Age Tasaday is without doubt an artifact, a deception—in short, a
hoax.

The Hoax vs. the Hoax Busters

Some commentators have found the implausibilities of the Stone Age Tasaday
scenario easier to swallow than the probability of a hoax, suggesting that to have
succeeded as well as it did, a hoax would have to have been impossibly elaborate
and ingenious. I think not.

I believe that in fact it would have been a very simple hoax. How? One must
recall that the Tasaday were called upon to perform at the caves only briefly and
infrequently. They were free to go where they wished in their off-hours, that is,
at night, when they frequently disappeared until morning—the villages from
which they probably came were only a three-hour walk away. They were already
familiar with the forest and the caves as previously mentioned. All visitors were
required to be *invited* and *closely supervised* by Elizalde, abiding by his rules (including a prohibition upon following or asking about the Tasaday's nocturnal forays). All visitors were well briefed in advance as to the nature of the Tasaday, as
to what they could expect to see; so they did expect it, and to a significant extent
did see it. All, even linguists, had to depend entirely upon Elizalde's appointed
staff interpreters for their communication with the Tasaday. Nance says that fol-

lowing the first encounter with the Tasaday (and later encounters were no different in this regard), "It was impossible to know to what extent information from the Tasaday had been colored or changed by translators" (Nance 1975:26). The primary translators were Elizalde's close associates and employees Mai Tuan and his young brother Dad Tuan.

The issues of language and mutual intelligibility are crucial to the plausibility of a hoax; so crucial, in fact, that four of the chapters in this volume (by Elkins, Johnston, Molony, and Reid) speak entirely to this issue. It has been asserted from the first reports that the Tasaday spoke a language that, while clearly Malayo-Polynesian and related to Cotabato Manobo, was not mutually intelligible with neighboring languages and dialects: "no one could be found—Tboli, Ubu, or Manubo [sic] Blit—who could understand their language well enough to obtain detailed information," and the bilingual Manobo Blit/Tboli woman who interpreted "estimated that she understood less than half of the Tasaday's usually hesitant responses to her many questions" (Elizalde with Fox 1971a:4). Molony has repeatedly asserted the irrefutable scientific basis for determining the distinctiveness of the Tasaday language, citing the word list she gathered via David Tuan in her two weeks of fieldwork in 1972 as supporting the lexicostatistically determined figure of 571 to 755 years reported by Llamzon (1971b) (or as Molony has also put it, "several hundred years") for separation of the Tasaday language from that of their agricultural neighbors. Actually, the calculation's authority and precision is evidently rather less than it is cracked up to be, given that during the symposium at which these papers were presented, Molony revised her estimate for time of separation to 125 years—30 generations reduced to 6! She has based her case against "the hoax theorists" (I prefer "hoax busters") not only on her firsthand fieldwork and the scientific nature of linguistic (notably glottochronological) evidence (Molony with Tuan 1976; Molony 1988, 1989a, 1989b), but most especially on the premise that hoaxers could not have created and taught (especially to children) the unique language she claims her informants spoke.

According to Molony (1989a:1), "the crux of the hoax theory . . . is this: that adults and children from surrounding tribes, speaking as their first language more than one language, were coaxed to masquerade . . . as monolingual speakers of a theretofore unknown language, or dialect of a known, nearby language" (Molony 1989a:1). She concludes,

> Logically it is very difficult to imagine that Elizalde or anyone else was clever enough to: (1) create a new language, with all the complexity of a real language . . .; (2) to coerce children to never use their first language with their parents (or adults to never lapse into their usual language); (3) to choreograph this language hoax with the complex of other cultural traits they displayed; and (4) to coach these adults and children so thoroughly that they never slipped in their presentation to different investigators over a period of 1½ years. [Molony 1989a:8]

In a slightly earlier article she said, "No one has ever suggested exactly who might have been clever enough to design a phony Tasaday language and then teach Tboli and Blit Manobo actors to use it exclusively," and "the notion that a small group of Philippine natives, ignorant of modern linguistic techniques, could have designed or used a language that would so thoroughly fool the trained ears of linguists is preposterous'' (Molony 1989b:55). But it is Molony and her co-believers in Stone Age Tasaday who make the claim that the Tasaday speak a language not mutually intelligible with any of those of their neighbors, and it is she who says on the same page, "there is simply no getting around the linguistic evidence for their authenticity." These statements bear investigation.

Several scholars have noted that the Tasaday are in close communication and in fact intermarry with their swidden-farming neighbors (Hyndman and Duhay-lungsod 1990; Salazar 1988). In the television production "The Tribe That Never Was" (ABC-TV 1986), Lobo (surely the most widely photographed Tasaday) tells the interviewer that "we speak both Manobo and Tboli" and intermarry with neighboring people. "As for me," he remarks, "my mother is Manobo and my father is Tboli"—hardly characterizations of an isolated people.

Let us consider the words of Clay Johnston, another linguist, this one's ears trained to *understand* the Cotabato Manobo language of which Tasaday is said to be a dialect, and his tongue trained to speak it. In a letter of 1988, he wrote that he had listened to a tape of Tasaday speech Molony recorded in 1972. He recalled that he had "lived in Mindanao from 1963 to 1968, and from 1973 to 1978," and "during this entire period I was assigned by SIL [Summer Institute of Linguistics] to learn the Cotabato Manobo language, to analyze and write papers [about it] . . . and to produce written materials [in it]." He says that "my opinion, based on what I heard on the tape, is that the language being spoken is identical to Cotabato Manobo in the following features: verb affixation and sentence structure, phrase structure, pronoun sets, kinship terms and terms of address, directional and locational words, pronunciation and intonation. Recognizing that the speech on the tape represents only a small sample of the total language, I estimate that I understood at least 90% of the words as identical with the Cotabato Manobo lexicon I had studied." And, "If I had not known there was some question about what I was hearing, I would have said without hesitation that they were speaking the language called Cotabato Manobo" (Johnston 1988; cf. 1989 and this volume). Defining "a language" in terms of mutual intelligibility (entailing a shared vocabulary of roughly 75% or more), and defining "dialect" differences as those noticeable to groups of speakers of a language, he concluded that to the question, "Is Tasaday the same language as Cotabato Manobo? . . . The answer is Yes" (Johnston 1989:6; cf. also Johnston this volume). In other words, if there was indeed a hoax, no one had to be taught another language—no linguistic deception was involved, all they had to do was speak their own first language. To the extent that language facilitated the hoax, it did so because the "trained ear" of the linguist was not trained to recognize what language, much less what dialect, was being spoken—or what was being said! If there was deception it was not in the language spoken, but in what the listeners in 1972 reported (Molony with Tuan 1976).

So, what is preposterous turns out to be not the suspicion or claim of a hoax, but the idea that someone who could not recognize the language would make authoritative and erroneous pronouncements about it. If Johnston's knowledge had not been available, another—no doubt unintentional—element in the hoax would likely have been firmly fixed in place. Given his knowledge and the experimental evidence he thereafter produced (by playing the tape for other Cotabato Manobo speakers), the linguistic errors of what we might term "the Stone Age authenticity theorists" have been conclusively exposed and the structure of the hoax further revealed.

Motives for a Rain Forest Watergate

The motives for the hoax are more complex, less amenable to explicit verification, than its probability and the means employed. I address them here because they are by far the most frequently asked-about feature of this entire scenario, and are crucial to its understanding. What might they have been? I believe the following three factors, in inextricable combination, are the primary sources of the hoax.

1. The most widely suggested motive for the Tasaday story is that Elizalde and his associates promoted it in order to make available, to themselves and their cronies, the natural resources of the 46,299-acre Tasaday-Manubo Special Forest Reserve established by Marcos in 1972 following the Tasaday "discovery." The area was then closed to access except with Elizalde's permission; hence the popular pun on Panamin, "Pana-mines" (cf. Duhaylungsod and Hyndman 1989; Hyndman and Duhaylungsod 1990). It is frequently noted that exclusive rights to these resources went to Elizalde and Marcos and their associates in the form of mines, timber, hydroelectric sites, and plantations—and in the persons of tribal peoples, the men as laborers and as soldiers to combat insurgents or to ward off competing timber and mining operations, the women as servants, prostitutes, and concubines.

2. Many say Elizalde used the Tasaday to promote himself and his political ambitions. (He ran for the senate shortly after the discovery). Perhaps he was seeking to promote Panamin and the Marcos regime (as well as himself) as heroic champions of the downtrodden tribal people rather than the exploiters and destroyers many believed them to be (cf. Razon and Hensman 1976; Rocamora et al. 1979).

3. In a related vein, observers of Elizalde often attribute the Tasaday episode, and his role therein as *Momo Dakel Diwata Tasaday* ("great man, god of the Tasaday," an honorific used by the Tasaday to refer to Elizalde—at his insistence, it is said), to his craving for acclaim, or, more broadly, his widely remarked strange personality (cf. Central Independent Television 1987). Nance cites "one particularly caustic Filipino [who] had argued that the Tasaday were mainly an 'ego trip' for Elizalde, a chance to indulge his vanity and flex his muscles, play God" (Nance 1975:310).

The inducements for the Tasaday to participate in the hoax were, presumably (as confirmed on several occasions by Tasaday themselves and their close relatives), promises that goods, money, and other desired rewards (reportedly including guns and a helicopter) would be forthcoming from sympathetic visitors and other outsiders once they had witnessed the poverty-stricken primitivity of the Tasaday. These were likely accompanied by threats and dire predictions, enhanced by vivid indoctrination concerning the dangers said to be awaiting residents of the region who remained unprotected by Panamin from land-hungry peasants, ruthless loggers, and violence-prone opponents of Marcos's government from other parts of Mindanao and the Philippines.

"Evidence": Stone Age Knee-Slappers

At the 1986 International Conference on the Tasaday Controversy in Quezon City, Philippines (Bailen n.d.), anthropologist Florante Henson of the Philippine National Museum gave a paper entitled "The Unmasking of a Hoax: The Tau't Bato" (Henson 1986). In it he described the Tau't Bato, a group similar to the Tasaday, as having been "initially portrayed [upon their 'discovery' by Panamin, under Elizalde, in 1977] as another newly discovered [primitive] group of people, in southwest Palawan [Philippines]" (Henson 1986:1). Eight months later they were visited by Marcos and a few days thereafter their territory was declared a reservation.

Several incidents gave Henson "an inkling of Elizalde's rather dubious motives" and led him to ask, "What are the implications of [this] on the Tasaday controversy?" (p. 3). He answered his own question:

> I believe that in the Tau't Bato case, Elizalde tried to pull a hoax but fortunately failed [because] the National Museum research was able to stay in the area continuously for six months without interruption. . . . The Singnapan valley, unlike the Tasaday area, is physically more accessible and less easy to control. . . . I strongly think that had Elizalde allowed serious scholars to do more extensive work among the Tasaday instead of sealing off the area and refusing to issue clearances to interested and qualified scientists, a lot of the issues raised in this so-called Tasaday controversy could have been scientifically resolved a long time ago. As it is, 15 years after the Tasaday discovery, and with very limited solid empirical data on hand, we are left with nothing much to do but to conjecture on what could have been. [pp. 3, 4]

The implausible claims made about the Tasaday are many and will be obvious, I think, to almost any anthropologist who takes the trouble to consult such accounts as the following: Elizalde with Fox 1971a, Fernandez and Lynch 1972, Nance 1975, Yen and Nance 1976, and the critiques by Salazar (1971, 1973, 1988, 1989, n.d.).

I will here briefly recall some of these claims, confining myself to the most preposterous of them—the real "knee-slappers." To test their believability I would challenge anthropologists to read the claims as written by their authors, and try to believe them. To do so requires staggering imagination.

1. Imagine people living in a cluster of rock shelters for hundreds of years during which the floors remain devoid of accumulated debris: no living floor, no midden. When pressed, advocates of this archaeological miracle contend that there is probably a midden somewhere yet to be discovered, as if such an accu-

mulation were not a pervasive and inevitable consequence of continued residence in a confined space—as if it were a situated structure like an outhouse, whose location may be obscure but discoverable with diligence and luck. Alternatively they propose that there is, or may be, a midden at the lip of one of the caves, as if such an accumulation is some sort of household convenience resembling a dustbin or dispose-all. In support of this wistful notion, they assert the tidy nature of the Tasaday, who are said to have regularly swept the cave floors bare. Perhaps those arguing thus forget that brooms were announced to have been among the artifacts unknown to the Tasaday until they were introduced by the ever-helpful Dafal, less than a decade or so before their "discovery" by Elizalde (Fernandez and Lynch 1972:285, 300).

2. Imagine the cave dwellers dressing daily in fresh green leaves: G-strings for the men, skirts for the women (tied around the thighs when pregnancy rendered the angle at which they depended immodest), supplemented in recent years by leaf brassieres for the women, with even a narrow masculine model sported by one modest cave man in a photograph by the *Stern* team (Unger and Ullal 1986:23). This, like several other features attributed to the "Stone Age" Tasaday, sounds like a neophyte's idea of what "primitive" culture might entail.

3. Imagine these foragers living within a three-hour walk of farming villages, yet totally unaware of them and their way of life; and in spite of being no further than that from a view of the sea, they were unaware of the sea to the extent of having no word for it (Elizalde with Fox 1971a:3).

4. Imagine them foraging and consuming a single variety of edible tuber in their forest, but failing in over 500 years to have discovered the other seven tubers that abound there.

5. Imagine them having had no technology for hunting the abundant game, or fishing the stream, or transporting or storing the food they gathered until Dafal taught them, and then virtually instantaneously developing remarkable hunting, trapping, and butchering skills, a hearty appetite for the results of their efforts, and the routine use of baskets.

6. Imagine them subsisting on the scanty rain forest diet described for them, which qualified scientists—believers and skeptics alike—agree is unlikely (Clark 1989; Headland 1987, 1989a, 1990a; and Yen 1976b:174–175 [cf. Nance 1975:270–271]). That is, it appears that they would have to have had another food source. No such source is identified by the advocates of Tasaday isolation, despite the fact that their overnight excursions away from the caves are repeatedly mentioned and their taste for both rice and game is often remarked. Headland (1989b) has compiled a list of 27 mentions of rice consumption in Nance 1975, and two in Yen 1976b.

7. Imagine them manufacturing and using stone tools (for what purpose?) of soft, crystalline river pebbles, ground (but not shaped) to a rough edge and shakily hafted in no more than 15 minutes (Nance 1975:140–141). These are amateurish tools such as seventh graders might be expected to invent in response to a classroom assignment, rather than the products of a stone-tool-using society skilled in their manufacture, a point Robert Carneiro has made independently and from far

more sophisticated knowledge than mine (Carneiro 1988, 1989, and this volume; see also Clark 1989). In his 1988 letter, after carefully examining photographs and videotapes, Carneiro referred to the "axe heads" (his quotation marks) as "bogus" specimens, and concluded that he "strongly suspect[ed] that when the Tasaday made their stone axes they were merely doing what someone told them to do" and "thus, to the extent that Tasaday stone axes bear on the matter, I would say that they point to a hoax. . . ."

The more symmetrical "heirloom tools" are no less doubtful in form, function, and authenticity, if in fact they are manufactured at all rather than being naturally formed cobbles. In any case, they are reported to be no longer made, and most of the examples depicted in the reports have been lost. It is noteworthy that the Tasaday are said to call metal knives by their term for "striker," while stone ones, implausibly, are called by a modified, presumably derivative term "stone striker" (Carneiro 1989 and this volume; Fernandez and Lynch 1972:294; Salazar 1971).

8. Imagine the Tasaday being only 25 in number yet in contact with—aware of—only two other, reportedly similar, groups of people, the Tasafeng and San-duka (or Tasanduka), who have not been seen by the Tasaday or anyone else for over 50 years, and whose existence has not been in any way verified (Nance 1975:352, 447). And compare this claim to Lobo's, quoted previously, that his mother was Manobo, his father Tboli.

9. While on the subject of population, consider the case of the "missing boy" of July 1972, described by Nance (1975:286–298, 285). From photographs, it seemed evident to Panamin anthropologist David Baradas, and finally to Nance as well, that a boy who had been among the Tasaday was no longer there, but another boy of similar age and appearance was now there. Nance ponders the fate of the missing boy: "What had happened to him? Had he joined another group? Run away? Died? Been traded? . . . killed?" (1975:287). An obvious answer did not occur to him: I would guess that in dispatching people into the forest to pose as cave men for the occasional batch of visitors one boy chanced to be unavailable or disinclined, and another of similar age and description seemed to whomever rounded up the cast to be a suitable substitute. Little boys, they probably reasoned, look pretty much alike to strangers. But when one is perpetrating a charade, one must pay attention to detail—otherwise, one may give it away, and it seems to me that this was a slip that did exactly that.

10. Imagine the Tasaday—or anyone—having engaged in the spontaneous conversations reported in chapters 8 and 11 of Nance's book (1975:149–168, 198–211), which were translated into English somehow by Mai Tuan, despite his claim to only a tenuous grasp of the language.[2] These conversations are said to have been secretly recorded by Elizalde with a tape recorder concealed in the caves during the hours when outsiders were prohibited. There is no way of verifying them, for the tapes are reported to have been lost. We will leave the questionable ethics of this procedure aside and simply point out that the conversations are ludicrously improbable. For example, one man announces flatly to his fellows out of the blue, in apparent reference to a rock protrusion in the caves that gen-

erations of children are said to have worn smooth by playfully sliding on it, "Our rock is very shiny" (Nance 1975:160). This seems to me analogous to an urban American announcing to friends over drinks, "Our streets are made of concrete." A bit later in the transcript, a man (Balayem) is quoted as spouting a paean of praise for Elizalde, and concluding, " 'We'll always be happy now that we have *Momo Dakel Diwata Tasaday* with us—not like before when he was not with us. Have you all heard what I said?' [He then calls to each person by name, and each answers 'yes']" (Nance 1975:167). That is, he calls roll to his audience of eleven to assure that they heard his remark—a remark that is spontaneously echoed hundreds of times daily, according to this account.

If these two inanities are not enough to exceed one's tolerance for conversational implausibility, note that in the 1001 lines (of approximately 14 words apiece) of alleged translation of natural conversation presented in these two chapters, the four-word honorific referring to Elizalde (usually abbreviated in the book as "MDDT") appears 439 times, an average of nearly *every second line,* comprising therefore about one eighth (12.5%) of the total number of words in the entire transcript! Even if the four-word honorific were to be calculated as only a single word, it would constitute 3.5% of the text. If pronoun references to him were included in the calculation, the incidence of references to Elizalde in these purported conversations would be more than double that reported above. If the transcriptions are authentic, the Tasaday must have been hard up for conversational fare.

11. The loss of the tapes, especially when combined with the loss of irreplaceable evidence for other exciting discoveries in various of Elizalde's enterprises, suggests a pattern amounting to a rain forest "Watergate." In addition to the loss of the crucial Tasaday tapes, there was the loss of stone tools crucial to assessing the claims for a Tasaday lithic technology. There was also the inexplicable loss or disappearance of the two tribes (the Tasafeng and Tasanduka) with whom the Tasaday are said to have intermarried and without whom they could not have functioned socially or persisted demographically—lost forever in this circumscribed region laced with trails wherein it would be hard to hide anyone for long. And finally, though perhaps trivially, there was the loss of a unique tarantula specimen Elizalde claimed to have discovered.[3] The pattern of losses exemplified by these elusive "four Ts," as I like to call them (tapes, tools, tribes, tarantula), three of which are central to authenticating the Tasaday, seems to me unlikely to have been purely coincidental.

In the "Afterword" to a new edition of *The Gentle Tasaday,* Nance says that Elizalde claims now to have found the tapes (Nance 1988a:469). If so—and as of May 1992 they have not appeared—we will be interested to learn what they contain and in what language (and whether, if produced, the ones "found" in fact date from March–April 1972).

12. Hard to believe as the conversations and the disappearances are, the epitome of incredibility is achieved by the mysterious Dafal. Upon him—upon the authenticity of the accounts of his contribution to Tasaday culture—rests the entire case made by those who advocate the authenticity of the Tasaday discovery,

their isolation, their technology, their knowledge, and their entire alleged way of life. In short, upon Dafal's role as much as upon the claims about their language, depends the believability of the Tasaday story.

One could hardly imagine—or invent—a shakier, more inconsistent, and implausible linchpin for these claims. For the claims to be authentic, Dafal would have to have been the source of every bit of knowledge, skill, and technology in the Tasaday cultural inventory at the time of their "discovery" that was inconsistent with the accounts of their pristine primitivity and isolation as reported by Elizalde, his associates, designated scientists, and journalists. That is, he would have to have provided them with virtually their entire 1971 cultural inventory, from music to technology and the supporting economy. And if he did so, he did it, according to all accounts, without having learned their language sufficiently to be able to speak it or interpret it to others—a remarkable feat if, as the authenticity theorists insist, it is not mutually intelligible with the Tboli and Blit Manobo spoken by Dafal and their other neighbors.

Of course, we have now learned that in fact the people called "Tasaday" were speaking a dialect entirely mutually intelligible with the language of the nearby swidden farmers. As already noted, Johnston (1989 and this volume) has told us that he and the swidden-farming people he has lived among understand the Tasaday on tape and film because the Tasaday speak, with minor dialectal variations, the language they themselves speak.

13. Imagine anthropologists, or anyone else, claiming the description of the Tasaday as the product of research. Contacts between Tasaday and the many observers—few of them scientists and even fewer anthropologists—were few, brief, and closely controlled. Fernandez and Lynch (1972:281) were the first to report the scanty opportunity for observation, and Nance (1975:318) followed. That this was a major problem can be seen by anyone reading the accounts. Figures will vary because reports and definitions of contacts vary, as they must when they are so brief. How does one tally a visitor who arrives by helicopter one evening, stays the next day, and leaves the following morning: three days (as Nance does), one day, a day and a half? But the orders of magnitude of the observations reported are consistent in all reports. Moses (1988), whose paper is both recent and succinct, reports that 50 Panamin employees, cronies, guests, and celebrities (plus 26 outside tribesmen brought in to build a helicopter landing pad, and a group of school children) were chosen to visit the Tasaday in the 15 years prior to Marcos's overthrow. Forty-one journalists were similarly honored, and only 12 scientists. Of the scientists, 4 were with the Tasaday for 2 days or less apiece, 2 for 3 or 4 days, 2 for about 10 days, 2 for 12 days, one (Fernandez) for about 18 days and one (Yen, an ethnobotanist) for 38 days. This constitutes, or includes, anthropological research?

14. Finally, imagine such a group practicing a religion uninfluenced by others, focused on a single, all-powerful, moralistic, paternalistic male deity called the "Owner," who owns and protects the caves in which they live (Nance 1975:277, 445)—or the mountain (ibid:62), or the forest (Nance 1981:13)—and who punishes wrong behavior and rewards good (Nance 1975:62, 445). "When

The Owner was happy—sunshine . . . when he was angry—storms!'' (Nance 1981:13). Compare this to Garvan's statement (1931:197–198) in his classic ethnography of the Manobo: the "Tagbuana or lords of the mountains and the valleys . . . [comprise] a class of local deities each one of whom reigns over a certain district . . . [and] is assigned the ownership of the mountains and the deep forest." "Respect must be shown, . . . his territory must not be trespassed upon, . . . his name . . . in no wise be mentioned. A violation . . . would be followed by a storm." Can one imagine these two sets of beliefs to be independent? The further we look, the more similarities we discover. The evil spirit *busaow* of the Tasaday (Nance 1975:178) is clearly the hideous demon *busau* described for the Manobo (Garvan 1931:195). Nance's report (1975:99, 132; 1981:13) that the Tasaday regard the behavior of a species of bird as an omen, together with their practice of taming such birds, is surely related to similar beliefs reported in more detail by Garvan (1931:212, 221, 223). And so it goes.

By these accounts, Tasaday religion sounds like someone's idea of a "primitive" version of Judeo-Christianity—simple manifestations of monotheism, moralism, paternalism, patriarchy, concern with property—plastered over a smattering of beliefs and practices found among their Manobo farmer-neighbors, rather than the integrated tradition of an isolated foraging society.

As these fourteen knee-slappers suggest (many others could be cited as well—for a substantial list see Salazar 1971, 1973, 1988, 1989, n.d.), we are asked to believe an anthropological "Just So Story," in the true Kipling tradition—an imaginative juvenile version of a "primitive" society and its culture. But it is not simply the inventory of implausible cultural items that renders the account of the Stone Age Tasaday incredible. The totality—the overall pattern of the culture—is far more incredible than any of its constituent elements. Ruth Benedict was among the first to urge anthropologists to recognize the universality and significance of cultural patterning whereby every culture is more than the sum of its parts. In this case we are confronted with an ostensible culture made up of implausible parts in utterly dissonant relationship to one another, constituting an anthropologically incredible configuration. How *could* we believe it?

But didn't BBC-TV (Lerner 1989) ask its audience in tones of irony, "If [the Tasaday] were able to fool every anthropologist who ever saw them, how credible is the science of anthropology?" And haven't others claimed or implied that everyone who has actually seen the Tasaday has affirmed their authenticity? The answer is, of course, that most have not been fooled, at least not for long. Robert Fox, Frank Lynch, and David Baradas—the only Ph.D. social/cultural anthropologists to have been allowed to see the Tasaday during the Marcos era—were enthusiastic about them to begin with but soon had second thoughts, and each soon resigned from Panamin. As Oswald Iten put it in response to the BBC film:

> It is untrue that all anthropologists who visited the Tasaday remain firm on their authenticity. There have been four anthropologists at the caves. Lynch and Fox split over the nature of the Tasaday but both recoiled in disgust. [Actually, Fox never visited the caves; he resigned before he or anyone else had done so. Lynch replaced him, until he too resigned.] David Baradas, [who had been] accom-

panied by Carlos Fernandez, withdrew from the research after having realized
the extent of the manipulation. Thus Fernandez today remains the only anthropologist sticking with the old story. [Iten 1990; Berreman 1991:32, 39, n.3.; cf.
Fox 1976:3; Nance 1975:102, 169, 267–268, 270, 288–289.]

Baradas has confirmed this in two television interviews: on ABC News when he
was interviewed by Tom Jarriel (ABC-TV 1986), and on Central Independent
Television (1987) by Adrian Wood. He recently did so again in a personal interview with me and two mutual friends not involved in the controversy on August
23, 1991, wherein he asserted, ''There were three—*three!*—Chicago anthropologists—three Ph.D.s—in the Panamin Tasaday project: myself, Frank Lynch and
Robert Fox, and *all three resigned* because of our suspicions and disgust with the
project.''

Conclusion: The Politics of Truth

The evidence leaves no doubt that the entire Tasaday episode has been a deliberate
deception, a hoax—not complex but simple, not clever but crude—perpetrated
by Elizalde through his agency, Panamin, backed by the authority of Marcos's
martial law (for all but the first year). It was carried off more or less successfully.
(Salazar and a few others recognized and exposed it at once, but to an inattentive
or disinterested audience.) It was possible because of Elizalde's nearly total control of the situation in his role as government administrator, manager, and bene-
factor—''great god''—of the vulnerable villagers who were induced to cavort in
their leaves as cave people before outsiders during the latter's brief, preannounced
visits. At the same time, he selected all outside observers and decreed when, for
how long, with whom, and under what circumstances they would visit. Through
advance briefing he defined for them what to expect, and through constant supervision in the field he controlled what they would ask and limited what they would
see. Thus, through what students of the psychology of deception have termed
''misdirected attention'' and ''controlled expectations,'' he created ''the invited
inference'' (Hyman 1989:136–137). Ultimately he created ''true believers'' in
his deception (Hoffer 1951).

Psychologists of deception point out that direct observation can be a contrib-
uting or even necessary part of successful deception (ibid.:145–149). Scientists'
''normal mode of operation makes them especially vulnerable to deception''
(ibid.:149) because they tend to be so trusting of researchers and their reports as
to be inattentive to intentional misdirection and misrepresentation. In fact, ''otherwise competent scientists'' are sometimes willing (or can be persuaded) in their
trustfulness to make inferences under less than ''rigorous, fraud-proof conditions,'' thereby leaving themselves open to deception.

Unaware of these possibilities, those who scoff at us skeptics for never having
seen the Tasaday overlook the fact that, in a very real sense, neither have they.
At least we *know* we have not; the believers think they have when in fact what
they have seen is a charade. They had an opportunity to see and discover the truth,
but only saw what they had been led to expect to see. Others, denied the opportunity to see, discovered the reality the conjurers had concealed from their audi-

ence. We are all nevertheless indebted to that audience because their reports revealed to others the truth they themselves failed to see. Those others, beginning with Zeus Salazar, who understood the evidence, were able to distinguish the plausible from the implausible. They thereby pieced together the implications of the seen and the unseen to reveal the truth behind the deception, which constituted surely the most successful hoax yet discovered to have been perpetrated on social/ cultural anthropologists. I believe that this volume and the conferences, papers, discussions, and publications that led up to it, demonstrate this fact beyond a reasonable doubt.

The exposure and dissemination of the truth of this matter is a significant achievement in what C. Wright Mills aptly termed "the politics of truth." As he put it, "in a world of widely communicated nonsense, any statement of fact is of political and moral significance" (Mills 1959:178). The Filipino participants in the unmasking testified from the frontier of the controversy. To do so required great personal courage as well as perspicacity.

Tribal peoples the world over are misunderstood and misused to an intolerable extent as it is. This cruel hoax perpetrated on the Tasaday and their neighbors has created not simply a vacuum of information but a morass of misinformation, prejudice, exploitation, harassment, and violence that has compounded malicious insult with grievous injury to them. To my mind, there has been no more telling statement of the significance of the Tasaday controversy in the Philippines—and by extension, to the situation of minority and tribal peoples everywhere—than that issued by the Department of Anthropology, University of the Philippines. I close with its brave and humane concluding sentences:

> . . . The Tasaday incident is a microcosm of many other problems we have in Philippine society today. We fear for the people of South Cotabato, including the alleged Tasaday. We fear for other minority groups similarly situated elsewhere in the country. We fear for the entire nation, where academic integrity and democratic process continue to be sacrificed for the powerful. [University of the Philippines 1987]

Notes

1. Fernandez and Lynch (1972:299, 305, 311) state in three different places in their report that wild palm pith *(ubod)* was introduced to the Tasaday as a food by Dafal in 1966 or later.
2. In his interview for Central Independent Television (1987), Mai Tuan remarks that "[the Tasaday] have their own language. We do not understand the dialect because they speak different from our tribe so we have to be there with them, stay with them, and speak by sign until we get a few words from each other. Even now I do not speak fluently yet their dialect—they have different words from us." Nance reports that another interpreter (Igna) had to be secured because Mai Tuan, a Tboli, could not communicate with the Tasaday (Nance 1975:12–14).
3. "Elizalde jumped up, shouting 'Look at that! Look at that! Who ever said there were no tarantulas in the Asian tropics? That's one. That is a tarantula!' He sounded delighted about it" (Nance 1975:358). But the specimen was lost en route to the museum to which it had been dispatched and where it could have been determined whether it was the unique specimen he claimed.

● *chapter three*

The "Tasaday" and the Press

OSWALD ITEN

What Made Me Investige the Tasaday?

In 1985, I prepared a report for the *Neue Zürcher Zeitung* on the attitude of the tribal peoples of Kalinga-Apayao Province on Northern Luzon toward the New People's Army. I remember, when I interviewed President Marcos's Foreign Press Secretary for that report, that I felt the government policy of protecting the Tasaday from intruders was an example of positive action. Never would I have dared to disturb the last two dozen Stone Age cave men of the world.

Some months later, however, I met the Catholic Bishop of Marbel, South Cotabato, Monsignor Dinualdo Gutiérrez. By chance, I mentioned the Tasaday. Gutiérrez laughed and exclaimed: "Don't you know the story was faked? Some of my priests know the so-called Tasaday personally."

No, I did not know, and I did not believe the words of the bishop. So I reviewed all the publications on the subject. To my surprise, I found that very little material of scientific substance had been published. One would have thought that the world's foremost Philippine specialists in the field of anthropology and archaeology would have jumped at the opportunity to study the world's last Stone Age cave men. But even those few scientists who did go to see the Tasaday published little in the scientific press. It seemed that many of them preferred to publish their findings in the mainstream media or in the Panamin publications. Moreover, most of the scientists were forced to compete with the endless clicking of photographers' cameras. The unprofessional working conditions they had accepted should not have been tolerated.

When we now examine who of these scientists spent how many days with the Tasaday, we see that the average number of days is very few (see Nance 1975). Six of the twelve scientists who visited the Tasaday were there for four working days or less, some for only a day or two. And even in those few working days the number of hours they were allowed to spend with the Tasaday each day doing fieldwork was restricted.

From the beginning the Tasaday were a media affair. (The press in 1971 outnumbered the scientists seven to one, and later four to one, roughly speaking).

Flocks of journalists courted Manuel ("Manda") Elizalde (the Filipino million-aire politician who "discovered" the Tasaday in 1971), for the favor of a heli-copter ride, seeming to leave their analytical minds behind, even as cries of hoax emanated loudly from the scientific community at large. NBC in exchange for $50,000 was rushed to the head of the documentary line. If one includes the myr-iad visitors—movie stars, VIPs, Marcos cronies, and schoolchildren—the ratio of scientists to other visitors is between one to ten and one to twelve.

Medical studies from different parts of the globe (e.g., Neel 1979, Scrim-geour 1979, and Tyrrell 1979) indicate that any people long isolated from the rest of the world would be killed off by diseases to which they were not immune if an overwhelming stream of visitors were to come their way. But the Tasaday were not harmed by such exposure. This fact was a key ingredient in my decision to drop some of my scruples and visit them without government permission.

My Visit at the Caves

I chose the end of the 1986 election for my attempt to trespass into the Tasaday Manobo Special Reserve. Marcos had just been deposed when I arrived in South Cotabato. My first surprise was that so many people were now openly expressing their opinion that the "Tasaday discovery" had been a hoax orchestrated by Eli-zalde. Some, like the mayor of Surallah, claimed to have precise knowledge of how the affair was fabricated. So, on principle, I ruled out sneaking in with some member of the old boy network, such as the Manobo hunter Dafal or the Tboli Mayor Mai Tuan; for if the story of the Tasaday really was a hoax, I did not expect them to help me shed light on the affair.

I decided to seek assistance from the Passionist Fathers of the Santa Cruz Mis-sion at Lake Sebu. That was when the second surprise came. Father Sean Mc-Donagh told me that he considered the Tasaday to be a separate ethnic unity, even though back in 1984 he had expressed the opposite point of view in writing about the "dubious claims that the famous Tasaday are in fact a separate group" (McDonagh 1984:147). Both he and Father Rex Mansmann seemed annoyed by the inquiry into the Tasaday matter, and they expressed their profound opposition to any such attempt. I wondered why this change of mind. Was it sheer coinci-dence that after Elizalde had fled the country the mission has used the Tasaday in a successful 1984 grant application for USAID funding (USAID 1984)? Had the Tasaday become a convenient bit of Panamin's legacy that might now be used to trigger the imagination of American donors? USAID did come up with $750,000 for the Santa Cruz Mission, and the mission, in fact, became the most potent po-litical and economic institution in the area, filling the power vacuum left when Elizalde fled the Philippines in 1983. (In 1986 the mission successfully ran its administrator for mayor of Lake Sebu.)

So, finally, I turned to the priests whom Gutiérrez a year earlier had referred to. One of these priests, who told me that he had occasionally seen some of the Tasaday when they came to the Lake Sebu market, put me in contact with some families where the Tasaday used to stay when in town. Two families, one Muslim and one Tboli, agreed to take me to the Tasaday houses. They said the Tasaday could be reached in just a day's walk. I could hardly believe this, since the earlier reports had led me to believe that they must have lived in one of the most remote, inaccessible places in the entire Philippine archipelago.

On Monday, March 17, 1986, I set out on foot from Surallah accompanied by a group of eight people. With me was Joey Lozano, a correspondent from the bishop's weekly newspaper, and some Muslims and Tboli who served as guides and watchdogs against armed bands of the Moro Islamic Liberation Front (MILF).

First, we crossed the hip-deep water of the Allah River. Then we followed the valley of its tributary, the Lawa River. We spent the night in a farm belonging to Muslims. Early the next morning we reached the compound of Datu Galang, an important Tboli *datu* ("chief"). The *datu* said he knew some of the so-called Tasaday. In fact, he said, some were his relatives, but they did not live in caves. They stayed at nearby caves only when foreigners would come, as they had been instructed by Elizalde, Dafal, and Mai Tuan to do routinely. As a reward Elizalde gave them rice and knives. (Since their own area was not suitable for growing rice, they eagerly accepted such gifts.) Originally, Galang continued, Elizalde had also urged *him* to participate in the cave-man group. Elizalde had offered him Garand rifles if he would take part. Datu Galang said he could easily take us to his Tasaday relatives the next day, and he pointed to a mountain about ten kilometers away.

Early the next morning we started out with a group of Datu Galang's relatives, all of them with the long hair typical of Tboli men. They served as hunters along the way and looked out for tadpoles and wild fruit, which became a staple of our touring diet as it had for the Tasaday in the early reports. The area was heavily sloped, dotted here and there with little gardens for the principal foods: corn and root crops. There was also forest, but most of it appeared to be secondary forest such as results from slash-and-burn agriculture, which the local Tboli and Manobo of the area practice. If a reservation had ever been established, it certainly had not protected the forest. We came to nipa huts every few kilometers, where we would stop so that our Tboli guides could chat with their Tboli and Manobo friends. (In this area both ethnic groups routinely intermingle and intermarry).

After an easy four-hour walk from Tobak, Datu Galang's settlement, we arrived unannounced and unexpected at the foot of Mount Tasaday. Galang led us straight to a nipa hut where we made the acquaintance of Lobo, Lolo, and Natek (Figure 1), three brothers whose faces were familiar to me from the countless photographs I had seen in the past. Their family was tending its own garden (see Figure 2). The clothing of the three brothers, especially their shabby T-shirts, differed in no way from those of the other inhabitants of the area. They described themselves as half Tboli and half Manobo. Their father, Bilangan (Figures 1, 2, and 3), who was also familiar to me from previous reports on the Tasaday, is a first-degree cousin of Datu Galang.

Presented with photographic reports from the early 1970s, the three brothers recognized all the people in all the pictures (see Figure 4). (They were seeing the pictures for the first time.) Before their father arrived, they revealed that Elizalde,

FIGURE 1
Bilangan (second from left) and his sons (from left) Natek, Lobo, and Lolo (photo by Oswald Iten, March 1986)

Dafal, and Mai Tuan had instructed them to do lots of climbing around on jungle vines for the benefit of photographers (Figure 5).

When their father Bilangan joined us, he introduced himself as a Tasaday and answered our initial questions, just as Elizalde would have wished. Only when he spotted Datu Galang did he drop his reserve, for he knew nothing of the fate of Elizalde, who had fled in 1983, reportedly taking Panamin's millions with him. Nor was he aware of Marcos's downfall, which had occurred just three weeks before our encounter. "We didn't live in the caves, only near them, until we met Elizalde," he told us.

These men went on to tell me that it is the *mountain* that they call Tasaday, not themselves. The caves have ritual significance for them, and they had tried to keep its existence secret. The hunter Dafal was the one who had revealed the existence of the caves to Elizalde.

"Elizalde forced us to live in caves," Bilangan continued, "so we'd be called cave men. Before that we wore regular clothing, though very shabby. Before Elizalde came I lived in a nipa hut on the other side of the mountain, and we did *kaingin* farming" (i.e., slash-and-burn agriculture).

Lolo, Lobo, Natek, Bilangan, and Gintuy (another Tasaday who had by now joined us, shown in Figure 6) related how Elizalde had promised them a great deal of aid and wealth if they would remain in the caves. Before each visit from an

FIGURE 2
Bilangan (lower right), working his garden with his wife, in front of their house (photo by Oswald Iten, March 1986)

outsider, Elizalde or his aides would fly out to the Tasaday to make sure that everything was as it should be. Datu Mafalu, a son of Datu Dudim of the Manobo farming village of Blit (both described by Nance 1975), now joined our group and detailed how he had sometimes maintained a radio transmitter in Blit for Elizalde. He also described how he was in charge of transporting rice and other foodstuffs to the Tasaday. He said he was fully aware, from the beginning, that the whole thing was a swindle.

For years Elizalde was the mightiest man these people had ever met. He appeared as master of life and death. Even though Elizalde had not shown up for a number of years, the Tasaday continued to live in fear of retaliation should they do anything contrary to his orders. The guards Elizalde left to keep outsiders away remained in place. "Commander Machine Gun" (named after his weapon), who was Panamin's chief guard, did not withdraw from the Mount Tasaday area until after Elizalde had fled the country.

The following morning we walked for an hour until we reached the fabled caves. This stretch could still be called a tropical rain forest, the *only one* we had encountered on our journey so far. By now our number must have been nearly thirty, for many people living nearby had joined us. Most of the trail was a small riverbed that passes just below the caves. For the short slope from the river up the caves our path had to be cleared with machetes. The trail had obviously not been in use for some time.

FIGURE 3
Bilangan (with hand over mouth), sits surrounded by relatives from the Tboli and Manobo tribes in the cave which provided the locale for the Tasaday fraud in 1972; Lobo and Lolo are seen perched in smaller caves at the right (photo by Oswald Iten, March 1986)

We found the caves completely abandoned. There were no middens, no hearths. In the lower cave, the scaffolding that had been constructed by the Tasaday in the 1970s after they could no longer bear to sleep on the humid rock was now rotten (see Figures 7 and 8). With apparent delight, Lobo climbed up a tree and into the middle cave as he had done as a child for photographers fifteen years earlier (Figure 5).

These former "Tasaday" were pleased that our visit had broken the conspiracy of silence imposed by Elizalde, and that they would now be able to restore the caves to their original ritual function. Bilangan explained their belief to me: Their ancestors had originated in these caves. His people still present offerings to their forefathers before harvesting or hunting.

All the Tasaday confirmed that Manda Elizalde had instructed them to call him *Momo Dakel Diwata Tasaday*—"Great Man, God of the Tasaday." This term was referred to so frequently by Nance that he coined the abbreviation MDDT for it in his 1975 book. It allegedly derived from a Tasaday myth that prophesied the arrival of a foreigner who would bring them everything they needed, but only if they never left the caves. This story (borrowed in part from the legendary Mexican Quetzalcoatl) was fabricated in order to explain why the Tasaday had chosen to remain in their humid caves for centuries, since living in such quarters was neither appealing nor healthy.

FIGURE 4

Lobo, who was about 10 years old when the Tasaday first made headlines, looks at a photograph of himself taken in 1972 by American photojournalist John Nance (photo by Oswald Iten, March 1986)

To reach the caves from the nearest major airport had taken me only about 1½ days of easy hiking. I wondered why no scientists had ever asked to do the same thing. It would have helped them had they become acquainted with the neighboring communities. Probably Elizalde, by claiming that the only means of access was the helicopter, intended to prevent their becoming aware of the Tasaday's proximity to other Manobo and Toboli swidden agriculturalists. If a scientist, a fine ethnobotanist like Douglas Yen, for instance, had *walked* in, I am sure he would have realized that the presumed gatherers he was studying were inhabitants of an area populated by settlements, hamlets, and even a town (Surallah)—good sources for "gathering." (If the gatherers did not, in fact, get their food from such settlements, the only other way they *could* have gotten it without coming upon these places would have required walking around in tiny circles.) Hiking in would have provided an explanation of Yen's observation of a small Tasaday child's familiarity with rice as food but not with an unthreshed rice stalk. The fact that the Tasaday were so eager to eat rice when Yen was there, when they allegedly had neither seen nor tasted it before, should in itself have made Yen suspicious. It is not common for people, tribal people in particular, to be eager to give up their traditional staple and eat an unknown food. My studies in the Sudan showed that it is not easy to introduce a new food even to victims of starvation, and this has

FIGURE 5
Lobo, Natek and Gintuy demonstrate how they used to clamber up to the caves for the benefit of photographers (photo by Oswald Iten, March 1986)

been the experience of aid agencies operating in famine-stricken areas all over the world.

If any of the researchers had used their good solid legs and common sense and *walked* to the caves, Elizalde's plan would have met with disaster. That no doubt is why he prevented investigators from walking in. If anyone *had* ventured to do so, they would have assuredly met with an armed attack. Elizalde did not want any hiking scientist to observe that the other people of the area were just like the Tasaday. The local tribesmen also had long hair, knew how to utilize forest produce, possessed tattered or little clothing, and knew how to make fire by friction, as do tribal people throughout the Philippines.

It really did not take a genius choreographer to stage the hoax. What it took was Elizalde's ability to be the almighty power in the area. He had a helicopter at his disposal and possessed unlimited numbers of firearms. (Elizalde's family was the Philippine licensee of Colt Firearms.) He was able to parcel out patronage and power to his loyal followers and gifts to his faithful subjects. This continues today, since his return to the Philippines in 1987 after his four-year absence.

It was not a matter of paying *actors* for a role in a difficult-to-learn Stone Age play. It was easy to get a few local tribesmen to exchange their shabby clothes for orchid leaves and have them sit around in caves or gather food (as they normally would) in the forest, all the while smuggling rice into the camp to fill their bellies.

FIGURE 6
Gintuy, with his two wives, dressed as found by Oswald Iten in March 1986 (photo by Oswald Iten, March 1986)

The individuals selected for this role did it with a gun to their head and rice at their mouth. They were not sneaky "imposters"; they were helpless local tribesmen intimidated by Elizalde.

The only trick in maintaining the fiction was to make sure that no scientist was able to investigate independently. This was accomplished by Elizalde's helicopter shuttle service, the disturbing flow of journalists and hordes of other visitors, and by imposing highly controlled conditions for fieldwork. No language had to be invented and taught to 24 individuals, since most communication between the scientists and the subjects of their study was carried on with the aid of one interpreter (a brother of the Tboli co-organizer Mai Tuan), who could have easily been instructed not to use terms for "agriculture," "war," or "enemy." Under this restriction no outside linguist conversant in Tboli or the local South Cotabato Manobo dialects could go in to investigate the supposed new language.

Questions soon arose about the language, but the tapes were never made available to inquiring scientists such as Frank Lynch. To this day, John Nance and Manda Elizalde have failed to provide them with tapes, and all but one of Carol Molony's tapes have gone astray.

The Tasaday I met were the poorest Filipinos I have ever encountered. Their area has been completely neglected by government and nongovernment agencies alike. The declaration of a Special Tasaday Reserve had the net effect of sealing

FIGURE 7
The lower cave on March 20, 1986; note the unswept debris on floor and remains of old wood drying rack (photo by Oswald Iten)

the area off from all social services. There was no medical care, no schooling. Not even essential trade items were available. This lack of basic services and commodities affected the 24 Tasaday and the nearby Tboli and Manobo equally. We paid our guides not in money but with salt, tobacco, rice, and dried fish. When I hear cries that the destruction of the Tasaday myth will mean the destruction of the Special Reserve, I shed no tears. The Special Reserve sealed off an area of several thousand inhabitants without offering them the rewards of an undisturbed life. Instead, it made them exploitable by those solons who controlled access to it.

The Experience of *Stern* Magazine

I had hardly arrived back in Surallah from my trip to Mt. Tasaday when I learned that Walter Unger and Jay Ullal, German reporters working for *Stern* magazine, had also just gone to the caves. (Neither of us had knowledge of the other.) They used the Manobo hunter, Dafal, who lives about a day's hike from the caves, as their guide. It was a mistake for which they were to pay a high price.

Before taking off with these German reporters, Dafal had gone to "scout the path" in order (as he claimed) to bring back a list of gifts the Tasaday would expect from their visitors. On his return, then, the group set out together. When they reached the caves, they met two Tasaday men and some women and children.

FIGURE 8
The upper and middle caves on March 20, 1986; the cave floor did not have the polished appearance one would expect if humans had inhabited it for centuries (photo by Oswald Iten)

The rest of the Tasaday were said to be "out hunting." Indeed the Tasaday man Balayam didn't arrive until 48 hours later. This coincided with my own experience and a week earlier, when the Tasaday said it would take two days to send for Balayam and bring him from his house to the caves.

This time the Tasaday, having been warned by Dafal of the approaching reporters, were wearing leaves. The German reporters observed, however, that some Tasaday were wearing colored underpants beneath their leaf G-strings. In addition, some women had added orchid leaf brassieres to their Stone Age outfit. Finally, 49 Tasaday gathered at the caves—probably everybody living nearby— since gifts could be expected. Among them were the five Tasaday men (and their wives) I had photographed a week earlier (see Figures 1–8). But instead of wearing jeans and T-shirts as in my pictures, they posed for *Stern* in their cave-man outfits.

At night, Unger and Ullal were left practically alone at the caves. When they asked where the Tasaday would go to spend the night, the explanation was that everyone, including women and children, were out hunting. But despite the nightly hunting sprees, the Tasaday had no food at the caves. The "cave men" had to rely on the reporters' provisions! So Dafal was sent away for more supplies.

He never returned. Instead, some mysterious bandits led by a certain "Commander Kris" appeared and took the two Germans prisoner. Kris spoke the same language as the Tasaday—fluently, as can be seen on the *Stern* videos.[1] He released the Germans only after a hefty ransom had been paid. In their report Unger and Ullal (1986) left no doubt that they considered the Tasaday a fraud, a fairy tale, and a Stone Age sideshow. What the *Stern* reporters had experienced was a hoax attempt like the original one in the 1970s; in the absence of Elizalde/MDDT, however, it turned out to be even sillier than the original.

Reaction of the Exponents of the Earlier Media Hype

Back in Switzerland I immediately phoned the *National Geographic Magazine*. Apart from the *Neue Zürcher Zeitung,* the National Geographic Society was the only institution informed beforehand that I would attempt to visit the Tasaday. In December 1985, I had personally informed the magazine about my suspicion of a hoax. Since this was considered highly speculative, I agreed to give them all the material from my trip no matter what the result. A representative of *National Geographic* expressed profound interest in the fate of the Tasaday since the magazine had made several unsuccessful appeals to Elizalde to let its staffers return to the caves.

But the day following my call, I received a telegram stating that the *National Geographic* had no interest whatsoever in a follow-up ŝtory about the Tasaday, nor did it want to look at any of my field material. I then wrote the editor a letter, but it was never answered. Almost two years later the *National Geographic* finally did a follow-up of sorts in its centenary issue (McCarry 1988:304), stating that recent reports of a hoax had been "discredited," without however, specifying by whom.

Unlike the *National Geographic, Asiaweek* did want to see my material. But after seeing it, they did not return it to me. Instead, they extended me an invitation to contribute to their letters-to-the-editor section. This is the publication with which the reporter John Nance is formally associated. Nance had spent more time with the Tasaday in the early 1970s than any other foreigner, and had identified completely with the Tasaday story. For many years it was the focus of his life work. Either Nance knew about the fraud or else he was simply not capable of grasping it. Neither conclusion is flattering.

Nance received a platform in *Asiaweek* about this time (*Asiaweek* 1986). Using a helicopter, as in the good old days, he returned to the Tasaday in April (1986), a month after my visit and just days after the *Stern* reporters had been kidnapped at the caves. He traveled in the company of Jack Reynolds, who had done the earlier 1973 film for NBC, and scientists Carlos Fernandez and Jesus Peralta, both veterans of the Tasaday affair. (Fernandez had been Panamin's Director of Scientific Research starting in 1974.)

Once again the scientists' findings were published in the mainstream press rather than as scholarly papers. While we still wait for Peralta's scientific findings of the 1970s,[2] his conclusions based on his 1986 trip were published in 1987 in a journal, and at length in the *Manila Standard,* a newspaper owned by Elizalde (Peralta 1987). Nance alo reported the conclusions of the four days of research that they did together at the caves. Nance's report was published in *Asiaweek* (*Asiaweek* 1986).

Nance's party found the Tasaday just about as the *Stern* people had found them. "Most were topless, although some . . . covered their breasts with leaf brassieres and others uneasily crossed their arms over their chest" (ibid.:30). Since I had met them only 34 days earlier in quite different apparel (of which Nance was not yet aware at the time of his visit), *Asiaweek*'s text later accounted for the embarrassing and bizarre photographs by explaining that the pseudo-Stone Age outfit was worn "because they thought it pleased visitors and [would] thereby bring the Tasaday economic benefits" (ibid.) It seems the Tasaday did not want to please *me*. In an interview with the *New York Times* (Mydans 1986a), Nance explained that the Tasaday's recent preference for clothing was natural progress. "If leaves would be better, we'd all wear leaves." Fair enough. But then, why did the many Blit Manobo women who had recently married into the Tasaday population forget about their clothes and start to wear leaves? Never short of an explanation, Nance quotes a Tasaday woman: "Cloth is good, leaves are good. Both are good" (*Asiaweek* 1986:37). When Nance told the Tasaday "that wearing clothes was perfectly agreeable" to his expedition, the "Tasaday increasingly appeared in garments" (ibid.:32). But where did Nance's Tasaday store their textiles when not wearing them? There is no wardrobe storage visible either in *Asiaweek*'s photos nor *Stern*'s. Were the garments stored in tree tops? Nance has not provided us with a plausible explanation for this.

Nance did not find the caves in the same condition that I had the month before. I had found the scaffold-like furniture constructed in the 1970s rotten. Nance found new scaffolding. According to Nance's report (1988b:29), he found just what he did in the 1970s: The "lower cave, the inner chamber, held latticed platforms for sleeping, racks for drying wood. . . ."

The earlier use of this type of furniture will be recalled from the 1972 reports. The women had been observed originally having to pass their babies to the men when they wanted to climb into the upper cave, which then served as their main living quarters. (Did the mothers throughout the centuries have to call for assistance each time they desired to get to the upper cave? Why had no steps ever been cut into the slippery rock?) Later in 1972, the Tasaday unexplainably had given up living in the upper cave and moved to the lower one. And still later that year, this lower cave had been outfitted with sleeping platforms and racks for drying wood, as in a local nipa hut.

There is only one possible explanation—*if* the Tasaday were authentic as portrayed in the 1970s—for why neither the *Stern* reporters nor I found the furniture intact. The Tasaday must have come to dislike the comfort of sleeping on wooden platforms and gone back to sleeping on bare rocks! But then why did new scaffolding suddenly appear—after 13 years—between my March visit and Nance's April visit? We might easily conclude that the Tasaday were preparing for a long new siege at the caves and did not want to wait too long for a minimum standard of comfort.

One entirely new enlightenment struck Nance and his accompanying scientists on their April 1986 trip: "The scientists also suggest that the caves may never have been a permanent, year-round shelter, contrary to previous reports" (*Asiaweek* 1986:32). In an interview with a Philippine newspaper (Malayang 1986), Nance also deprives us quietly of the Stone Age illusion: "They are real people but definitely not Stone Age" (Malayang 1986, p. 10 of the fourth article in the series). Nobody had ever claimed they were *not* real flesh-and-blood human beings.

To get their heads out of the noose, Nancy, Reynolds, and a good number of scientists fed increasingly weird explanations to an eagerly awaiting press, the same press that had already been taken in by the Tasaday fantasy years earlier. The most mind-boggling was the miraculous population boom the once-near-extinct Tasaday had undergone between 1974 and 1986.

When last heard from in 1974, the Tasaday were said to have numbered 26 (sometimes 24 or 25). In Nance's latest account in *Asiaweek,* 6 had died, reducing the original population to a mere 20—in and of itself a miracle of demographic viability. Now, following his April 1986 trip, Nance brought back news that 17 women and 2 men immigrated to the caves from Blit, the neighboring agricultural village. This brings the number of "Tasaday" to 39. This influx took place mainly during the last five years, according to Nance. Yet now, according to the scientists of the 1986 expedition, the Tasaday number 61 (*Asiaweek* 1986:32; Peralta 1987; and chapters in this volume). Remember, this population explosion from 39 to 61 took place in just five years in the complete absence of any medical care, which—if it were true—would make it a unique phenomenon in demography.

A decade ago the Tasaday were said to have run out of wives because they had lost contact with two other mysterious populations of cave dwellers. Earlier, these phantom cave people had always been kind enough to supply the Tasaday with a sufficient number of wives. But now, no matter how far the Tasaday ventured into the forest looking, the two kind groups of women suppliers had vanished—so it was claimed in the 1970s.

But why venture so far if the agricultural settlement of Blit is only three hours' walk away? Miraculously, the Tasaday always seemed to have missed Blit when venturing forth to gather food and look for wives. When, according to Nance (*Asiaweek* 1986) (and Fernandez and Peralta), a contact with Blit *was* finally established, it remains unclear whether it was the Tasaday who stumbled onto the Blit Manobo or vice versa. Nance remains uncommitted on this issue. In the same article we read that the Tasaday saved their clothing "for visits to the Manobo Blit, where the men had courted women and now visited their in-laws" (ibid.:32); but further on Nance quotes the Tasaday man Balayam, whom he met at Blit, as saying, "This is the largest number of Tasaday ever to come out here together. We have not met some of our in-laws yet" (ibid.:37).

If the story of the miraculous multiplication of the Tasaday were true and the original Tasaday authentic, the Blit Manobo—not the Tasaday—would indeed be an extraordinary subject with which to study basic human behavior. For, as a general rule, everywhere in the world, women tend to marry into a socially equal or advanced status, possibly forwarding material benefits to the families they leave. This is especially the case with hunter-gatherers (Bailey 1988). But at Blit the opposite holds true: Girls in large numbers are said to have married into an unfamiliar tribe of cave dwellers, trading the better diet of agriculturalists and animal breeders for the forage of simple gatherers; and the Blit men, for their part, did not seem to mind the exodus of their daughters and potential brides to unknown forest people with whom they could not even negotiate compensation for the loss of wives and manpower. Such generosity is all the more strange when we remember that the Blit Manobo are polygynous and could easily absorb any surplus of women if such were ever to occur.

Are these the kind of facts that made the *National Geographic* declare that the hoax reports had been discredited? The quotes from Nance in *Asiaweek* are clearly no more than a cover-up that attempts to portray the Tasaday as a separate tribe as originally reported—now stripped of Stone Age cave-man status and acculturated to their neighbors. Such a stunning impossibility contradicts common sense and the experience of anthropological sciences. This tack is the sad last line of defense on the part of those scientists who, even now, claim that the Tasaday speak a separate language, a thesis supported by questionable scientific standards.

Though the arguments used in the 1986 cover-up attempt have added important knowledge about the Tasaday, it is wishful thinking for the advocates of authenticity to now claim the *original* literature of the 1970s stands until refuted by new research. Surely they know that independent and extensive new research cannot be carried out in the violent atmosphere created by Elizalde and his local warlords. But even if new studies could be carried out and the original Tasaday story successfully refuted, would not the proponents of the original merely say that the situation of the 1970s cannot be recalled in 1990? One is reminded of scientists, publishers, and reporters who prefer to have Carlos Castañeda's Don Juan continue living, rather than abandon the fiction of years past (De Mille 1980).

The Reaction of the U.S. Print Media

In Europe, news of recent Tasaday developments has been reported fairly and honestly (even by papers that ran "Stone Age" stories in the 1970s). But in the United States, most publications that had reported the old Tasaday version have kept quiet about the recent developments. The only large magazine that published an article on the recent claims of a hoax was *Newsweek,* which gave its readers a summary of the hoax claims, though softening the blow with the statement that "confirming them will be difficult" (Begley and Howard 1986). Following the *Newsweek* article, the *Wall Street Journal* presented the findings of the first Tasaday Symposium at the University of the Philippines and the tangled business interests of the Elizalde family (Kronholz 1986).

But other major U.S. publications, such as the *National Geographic* and the *New York Times,* decided to actively uphold the old story. Following the 1986 hoax revelations, the *New York Times,* in an article by their correspondent Seth

Mydans (1986a), sided with Nance, Peralta, and Fernandez. Mydans relied solely on their material for quotations. By calling the Tasaday "a textbook case of change," he fully subscribed to the fantasy explanations put forth by Nance (in *Asiaweek* 1986). Mydans never bothered to go to Mindanao. His uncritical attitude was maintained in two later articles (Mydans 1986b, 1986c). The final one of these is a masterpiece of journalistic sloth. Mydans interviewed the Tasaday woman Dul in Elizalde's mansion after she had been plucked from the mountains and brought to Manila in 1987 to help shore up the old story (and participate in legal proceedings outside her frame of cultural reference). Not once did Mydans ever mention the many reports in the Philippine press referring to the coercion and violence surrounding the Tasaday's several trips to Manila, including reports that the tribesmen were forcibly held in Elizalde's custody. A complete blackout was imposed by the *New York Times* on the public statements of the Anthropology Department of the University of the Philippines.[3] Nor did Mydans report other critical voices. Of the slew of critical letters sent to the *New York Times* editor, only one was ever published, and then it, too, was refuted by two advocates of authenticity, including yet another statement by Nance (1988b), who already enjoyed an information monopoly in Mydans's earlier articles.

At least Clayton Jones (1989) of the *World Monitor* went to Mindanao. Jones recalled a tribal exhibit he visited in Lake Sebu where "the [Santa Cruz] Mission staff had invited the Tasaday to help them show the world they are real" by having them sit in a "cave, constructed of crumpled gray paper and decorated with forest vines," where "they appeared to be right at home, like the bears in the San Diego Zoo." Jones was revolted. Yet not many weeks later, he, too, interviewed the Tasaday in Elizalde's Manila mansion (in his combined living-room roller-skating rink). And, predictably, they towed the Elizalde/Nance line. Did they have any choice? (Articles like these are particularly frightening because they fully encourage Elizalde to increase his pressure on critics in the Philippines.) All in all, not one U.S. paper found the case worth investigating extensively and independently; and, apart from Jones, none took the trouble to go to South Cotabato to do original research.

The Television Documentaries

The Tasaday case got more attention from broadcasters than from the printed press. (It will be remembered that the first television report, done by NBC in the early 1970s, presented the Tasaday as authentic cave dwellers.) In 1986 ABC's *20/20* sent a research and film expedition to Mindanao. The *20/20* team is, to date, the only TV crew that cared enough about the story to *walk* into the area and form its own opinion by actually living with the people in question. The resulting documentary, produced by Judith Moses (ABC-TV 1986), was called "The Tribe That Never Was."

Then a British company, Central Independent Television (1987), spent many months researching Panamin and the Tasaday story in Mindanao and other areas of the Philippines. They reported firsthand from the Tasaday reserve, and their interviews with the Tasaday were gripping.

Later the BBC did an armchair job *without* going to Mindanao at all (Lerner 1989). Their report reviewed the issues put forward by the "pro" and "anti" exponents, which by then were well known. Following the line of advocates of authenticity, the BBC's story started from the wrong assumption. It asked whether the Tasaday were *able* to pull off the most elaborate hoax in history of anthropology. None of us who doubt the original Tasaday story ever claimed that. It was *Elizalde* who pulled it off, and it was all too easy to do. Like all other advocates of the original story, the BBC's producer refused to discuss the implausibilities or acts of violence that had surfaced during the cover-up operations. (And, interestingly, the BBC strengthened the arguments for authenticity, whether consciously or unconsciously, by bestowing upon one scientist a Ph.D. while depriving an opposing journalist of his rightful academic title.)

The conclusion of the BBC piece was that each journalist found the Tasaday as he wished to find them. This is a proposition that does not withstand even superficial scrutiny, though it *could* be applied to my own journey! After walking to the caves and having met the "neighbors" along the way, I certainly did not expect to see the Tasaday any different from how I in fact found them. But the *Stern* reporters expected to find the Tasaday in jeans and T-shirts, and they found them in orchid leaves and G-strings. And Nance, together with Fernandez and Peralta, met them once in one wardrobe and once in another.

The Philippine Press

In 1986, hundreds of articles on the Tasaday appeared in Philippine newspapers at the time a hoax was purported to have been orchestrated. Then, all of a sudden in 1987, arguments seeking to prove the hoax claims practically vanished. What happened? Elizalde had just returned to his home country!

In 1986 Elizalde, who had been living in Costa Rica, was forced to leave when the Arias government responded to reports that he was corrupting minor girls and engaging in prostitution rackets (*La Nación* 1986a, 1986b; *Tico Times* 1986). He fled to Miami, but his U.S. visa was not extended beyond February 1987, so at that time he went back home to the Philippines. The new government dropped all charges of graft and corruption against Elizalde; for, after he had fled the Philippines, his family had become one of the early financial supporters of the Aquino campaign.

Overnight, hoax claims became very dangerous. Mr. Elizer Bon, a relative of some of the Tasaday who testified before the 1986 symposium in Manila, was murdered. My colleague, reporter Joey Lozano, narrowly escaped a murder attempt by a sharpshooter of the Philippine Constabulary, who recently confessed to the crime while under the influence of alcohol. Who hired this law enforcement official to kill a man he didn't even know?

To silence his toughest opponents, Elizalde launched the largest libel suit in Philippine history against the *Philippine Daily Inquirer*—which had done the most vigorous reporting on the Tasaday scandal—and against Jerome Bailen and Zeus Salazar of the University of the Philippines. Plainclothes goons began harassing and intimidating them. The net result was to inhibit a key dissenting scientist who had done fieldwork among the Tasaday in 1972—David Baradas, a Ph.D. in anthropology from the University of Chicago—from any further public discussion (after he spoke his conviction that the original story was absurd in ABC's *20/20* television documentary [ABC-TV 1986]).[4]

In the mountains of South Cotabato armed men convinced everybody who had made a "wrong" statement to recant. One of Datu Galang's brothers was shot dead. Then, shortly after Datu Galang at a public meeting of five thousand people in Surallah had urged solidarity for the purpose of stopping the Tasaday affair, he appeared in Manila recanting. Supervised by Elizalde's cohorts, he was a victim deprived of his freedom, fed helplessly to a steady stream of selected American journalists. That abusive practice continues to the time of this writing. Certain Tasaday are routinely flown to Manila by Elizalde. Like Datu Galang, they are routinely led before American reporters. Unfortunately, none of the journalists find the opportunity to interview the Tasaday privately through an independent speaker of Tboli or Manobo, the local trade languages.

Recently, uncritical journalists were provided opportunities for safe visits at the caves where former Tasaday awaited them, dressed like anybody else in the area now that the mock Stone Age outfits are an object of ridicule. Most of the tribesmen of Tasaday fame appear to be settled in nipa huts one hour's distance from the caves in order to facilitate more frequent visits by sympathetic members of the press.

Manda Elizalde has not only silenced the Philippine press by means of libel suits, he has recently started a PR offensive in the U.S. He hired a Washington-based publicist named Suzanne Hurley to generate favorable press prior to the November 1989 Tasaday symposium. She also tried to harass ABC's Tom Jarriel and persuade him to reconsider the earlier *20/20* report. An employee of the same firm lunched with some *National Geographic* staffers in order to persuade them to do another major story.

From the safety of distance we must not forget that for some of our colleagues in the journalistic and scientific professions—not to mention the tribesmen who have to continue to live as Tasaday—the affair has more than academic face-saving importance. It has become, for some, a matter of life or death.

Notes

1. Besides taking photographs, Jay Ullal also recorded video sequences. These are unpublished but may be requested from the magazine.
2. [Editor's note: Peralta's findings of the early 1970s appear in his chapter in this volume. Iten wrote his chapter before he knew this. —TNH]
3. [Editor's note: This formal statement of complaint came from the Department of Anthropology at the University of the Philippines. It was first circulated underground in typescript form in the Philippines in 1987, then published in a Philippine newspaper, and finally by the American Anthropological Association in their *Anthropology Newsletter* (see University of the Philippines 1987). —TNH]

4. Thomas Headland (the organizer of the Washington, D.C., symposium in 1989 where the chapters in this book were first presented) formally invited Baradas—as he did all of the scientists still alive who had studied the Tasaday in the early '70s—to present papers at the symposium. Baradas never responded. Likewise, Headland sent him several invitations in 1990 inviting him to write a chapter for this volume. Again, for personal reasons we can only surmise, Baradas never answered those letters.

● *chapter four*

Creeping Resource Exploitation in the Tboli Homeland: Political Ecology of the Tasaday Hoax

Levita Duhaylungsod and David C. Hyndman

The Tasaday scandal illustrates Fabian's (1983:143) argument that "relationships between anthropology and its object are inevitably political." When we embarked on our investigation in February 1989 our 13-day presence spread like an underground broadcast that spanned several South Cotabato municipalities; and yet we were traveling almost incognito and for the primary purpose of visiting kin. The visibility of military men, uniformed and undercover, was a formidable obstacle. It was only the local family links of one of us (L.D.) that allowed us to even survive the trip. Since our trip that February, the Duhaylungsod family in Maitum has been threatened, and those in Manila and Los Baños have been visited by emissaries of Manuel Elizalde, Jr. (the millionaire politician who "discovered" the Tasaday in 1971).

This chapter goes beyond academic debate because it poses additional threats to the already beleaguered individuals involved. The names of many of the Tboli that we spoke with are withheld, and we identify only those with a modicum of security. To say that the local political volatility of the controversy has become much more serious than writers, journalists and anthropologists alike, have described, including our earlier writing (Hyndman and Duhaylungsod 1990) is an understatement. More than ever, we are convinced that it is Tboli society and history that is important, and precisely because it enhances our understanding of their struggle today to empower and take control of their communities and resources.

Pre-Panamin Resource Competition at the Frontier

It is not hard to recognize that there are "peoples without history" (Wolf 1982) in South Cotabato when such peoples are viewed through the achievements of the powerful, as proudly written by the Provincial Planning and Development Office (PPDO) in 1988 (Figure 1). According to this reading of history, South Cotabato was "nothing to start with," the "virgin lands of promise" to be "carved" into a province that now "functioned as a regular government" under a capitalist mode of production "ushered in big investments from both foreign

60 DUHAYLUNGSOD AND HYNDMAN

WHAT IT WAS......THEN.

WHAT IT IS..... NOW!

Before the turn of the 20th century, the area to which South Cotabato would be carved, was sparsely inhabited by Muslims, B'laans, Manobos, Tagabilis, and other ethnic groups, who probably came to this part of Mindanao before the birth of Christ.

From 1939 until after the Japanese occupation, an exodus of settlers from Central Luzon and Visayas poured into the virgin lands of promise, longing for a place in the sun, and seeking for pieces of land they could call their own. These people undauntedly faced the challenges of nature and the vagaries of politics.

In the early 50's, population and investment swelled in this southern part of Cotabato, the mother province, and at this stage – a louder voice arose in the management of the local government. After countless appeals and petitions, R.A. 4849 was passed and approved on July 14, 1966, separating South Cotabato from its mother province. Nevertheless, it was not until the local elections on November 1967 did the province elect its first set of officers. Finally, on January 1, 1968, South Cotabato functioned as a regular province. It had only 11 municipalities then, but it had slowly transformed into a new and bustling province, from practically nothing to start with, in terms of basic facilities.

Tboli

Ubo

Maguindanao

South Cotabato today, is one of the most progressive provinces in the entire country. Four (4) years after its creation, it was able to provide facilities for provincial and national offices, built a capitol building and a provincial hospital, and equipped its motor pool with heavy equipment and vehicles.

Years ushered in big investments from both foreign and domestic sources. Highly mechanized farming came of age; ranches and livestock farms have been developed; fishing projects gained grounds in both domestic and foreign markets. Other large, medium and small scale industries are very well rooted. All these have continuously paved the way for a sophisticated system of trade and industry in the province.

Today, South Cotabato has already 18 component municipalities and one (1) city.

Manobo

FIGURE 1
What it was then . . . what it is now (Source: PPDO 1988a)

and domestic sources.'' The obvious gaps are the histories of the indigenous peoples whose powerlessness in fact made it possible for the colonial invaders to lead their easy lives. History, like anthropology, is always written within political formations (Benterrak et al. 1984). Our multivoiced reading of the pre-Panamin frontier contextualizes the resource competition between invaders and invaded as the clash between kinship and capitalist modes of production (Wolf 1982).

The Five Original Peoples of South Cotabato

The Manobo live primarily in Sultan Kudarat province, but about 50,000 live across the border in South Cotabato. The Kalagan live in the south of the province on the border with Davao del Sur province. The Tiruray-Upi are primarily located in North Cotabato. The B'laan live in South Cotabato and across the border in Davao del Sur province. The Tboli are entirely located within South Cotabato; about 150,000 are in the municipalities of Kiamba, Maitum, Maasim, Lake Sebu, Tboli, and Surallah. The two groups of the Tboli include the Tboli Mohen (coastal) and Tboli S'bu (Lake Sebu mountains). [George Tanedo interview 1989][1]

George Tanedo identifies himself as a Tboli, the most numerous of the indigenous peoples at the time of the first frontier invasion. His father, Alfredo Tanedo, an Ilocano government surveyor, was the first colonial to come into the coastal area. He arrived in 1919 and married one of the daughters of Datu Kaka and settled in what is now known as Maitum. This region is the location of the Tboli Mohen people, who live principally in the municipalities of Maitum, Kiamba, and Maasim. The Tboli S'bu live in the mountains of Lake Sebu and other Tboli municipalities (Figure 2).

Tboli Encounter on the Frontier

Tboli sociopolitical structure resembles the Muslim sultanate. Maitum was the home of Sultan Walih, a leader of both the Tboli Mohen and the Tboli S'bu when I arrived in 1947. Sultan Walih rode a horse, carried a 45-caliber sidearm and had a 50-man guard each armed with bow and arrow and sword. The Tboli Mohen were wet-rice cultivators in the coastal lowlands, which then were covered in rain forest. The Tboli S'bu practiced dry-rice *kaingin* [shifting cultivation] in the rain-forested mountains. In 1947 Sultan Walih passed his authority to his brother Datu Alas, who changed his name to Datu Alas Boone. Alfredo

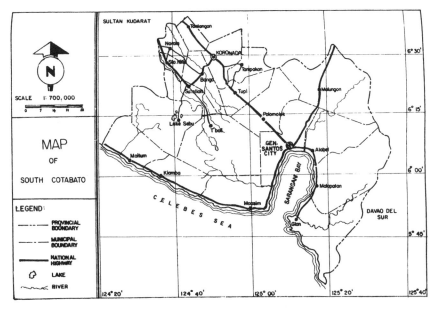

FIGURE 2
Municipalities of South Cotabato (Source: PPDO 1988b:18)

Tanedo married a Boone, and their children, George, Franklin, and Romarico, were among the first to attend Edenton Mission College which opened in 1947. [Virgilio Villanueva interview 1989][2]

Virgilio Villanueva identifies himself as an Ilocano. He was one of the frontier colonial migrants of coastal South Cotabato. When he became mayor, the Tanedo brothers were among the few educated Tboli, and it was Villanueva who introduced the Tanedos to Panamin officials.[3] George Tanedo and he are key figures representing the indigenous Tboli and the colonizer Ilocano in coastal Maitum.

That the Tboli "functioned as a regular government" well *before* the time of the colonial frontier in the early 20th century is an established fact. At least one chief among the Tboli Mohen is known to have risen in importance over the others. Present-day Maitum was the seat of one such hierarchical political confederacy. (As invasion advanced, the political significance of that confederacy gradually diminished, but its cultural and religious importance was retained. One example: the Tboli S'bu always ritually purify themselves with sea water on their trips to coastal Maitum.)

Religion

> . . . it has been the common assumption that Roman Catholics dominate the scene . . . The next largest group are the Protestants, segmented into several sects, which include the Baptist, Alliance, Wesleyan, United Church of Christ in the Philippines (UCCP), and Presbyterian. Protestant missionaries were responsible in the conversion of some of our highlander brothers like the Tboli. Some Protestants are likewise active in charismatic movements within the province. The Iglesia Ni Kristo (INK) is another big group . . . There are many other sects existing in the province, although these are only represented by a minimal percentage, to mention some, Seventh-Day Adventist, Aglipay, Jehovah's Witnesses and Mormons. Furthermore, Paganism is still believed to be practiced by a few, particularly by the highlanders who have not been converted to Christianity by any missionary group. [PPDO 1988b:20]

This reading indicates that, although Catholics dominate in the province, the Protestants are converting their "highlander brothers," such as the Tboli, from "paganism" to Christianity, and that all will eventually convert.

Edenton Mission College

> Edenton Mission College opened in 1947 by acquiring Tboli land by deception. Amado Chanco, the founder, promised free education for Tboli in exchange for 54 hectares turned over to the church as part of the Christian Mission in the Far East (CMFE). Actually the land was titled to Amado Chanco and not the church for many years after the initial transfer. He and his family lived in luxury and he schooled his children in the United States. No free education was provided to the Tboli, and Amado Chanco drained the wealth from Edenton Mission College for evangelical expansion and personal gain. [Fabian Duhaylungsod interview 1989][4]

Protestant missionaries among the early colonial invaders in Maitum considered that they had sufficient justification for this deception. They were making

Christianity available to the Tboli, and the Tboli were in turn relinquishing some of their lands. Of course, with their kinship mode of production the Tboli could not afford the tuition fees (which according to the promise of free education should not have been charged in the first place).

Fabian Duhaylungsod has managed to sustain a small congregation administratively independent from this mission, but he has not succeeded in integrating the few Tboli converts into the colonial migrants' parish. Decades of cultural resistance to conversion by the Tboli is perceived by the mission and the colonial community as primitive backwardness. It is not primitive backwardness, however; it is the persistence of a cultural identity system.

"Political advancement" and "social awakening" in South Cotabato are attributed by the PPDO to the American colonial attraction policy (PPDO 1988b:12). But the Americans never did "attract" the Muslims or the Tboli through this social laboratory policy imposed under the late President Quezon. They succeeded only in attracting thousands of Visayan and Luzon colonists to the frontier of what was to become South Cotabato.

With Alfredo Tanedo's arrival at Maitum in 1919 and the Kiamba colonizers in 1920 (ibid.), the Ilocanos dominated along the coast (Figure 2). Then with General Paulino's arrival at Sarangani Bay in 1939, the Visayans dominated in the expansion up the Surallah valley (ibid.) (See also Figure 2). Finally, in the immediate postwar period of the 1950s following President Magsaysay's "land of promise" campaign, there was a massive exodus of Ilocanos and Visayans to South Cotabato.

It should be noted that during the pre-Panamin frontier period the population in South Cotabato grew more than tenfold in just 52 years, from 42,787 in 1918 to 466,110 in 1970 (PPDO 1988b:23). The Tboli Mohen, who could already speak Manobo, started speaking Ilocano in this period, and the Tboli S'bu started speaking Ilongo. By 1980 Tboli speakers accounted for only 5% of the population in South Cotabato, whereas Ilocano speakers comprised 6%, Ilongo speakers 37%, and Cebuano speakers 31% (PPDO 1988b:19). The pre-Panamin frontier became "multivoiced," and competition for resources was intense.

As land became titled to colonial invaders, the underpinning legal arrangements failed to recognize the aboriginal land rights of the Tboli. To the Tboli, the land and its owners are not subject to a single higher authority (the state), nor is land vested in someone's proper name or quantified over a given period or area. In their view, ownership is circumscribed by extensive and intimate knowledge of place, and the right to use the land is established by membership in clan groups identified with the names of their cultural landscape.

The Tboli still remain marginal to the system that is harnessing South Cotabato export resources to the cause of the world capitalist system. It is the Ilocanos on the coast and the Visayans in the interior lowlands who are providing the food commodities—rice, copra, cotton, and pineapples (Figure 3). The Tboli, in their remaining homeland, still control their own means of production, but the food, goods, and services that they produce circulate reciprocally within their commu-

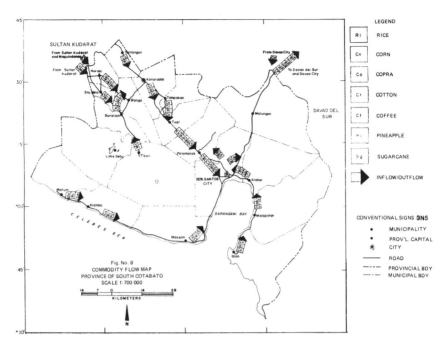

FIGURE 3
The flow of commodities in South Cotabato (Source: Land Resources Evaluation Project 1989:112)

nity. To the colonials, the Tboli system is backward; they believe that unless people develop a commodity orientation they will never progress.

The clash between the kinship and the capitalist modes of production in South Cotabato started with the arrival of the settlers, but it eventually penetrated into the mountains with the granting of logging concessions. The American transnational Weyerhauser operated one of the earliest logging concessions out of Pulimbang in Sultan Kudarat Province and adjacent Maitum municipality in the early 1960s. This company left the concession in 1964, but it was purchased by George Hofer, a German naturalized Filipino married to a Tboli—he is related to the current Vice-Governor Thomas Hofer (Samuel Duhaylungsod interview 1989).[5]

Logging Concessions

During the 1960s logging concessions were found throughout the Tboli S'bu homeland, much of the Tboli Mohen forests were already cleared by the Ilocano migrants and what remained was taken by the Basilian Lumber Company (Basilco), later to become Mindanao Lumber Development Company (Miludeco) owned by the family of Gaudencio Antonino, who was a senator in the 1960s. What was to become the Tasaday reserve was already under a logging concession to Borja and Bautista (B&B). To the west of their holding was the Hofer concession. Northwest of B&B was the Habaluyasa logging concession and northeast was the Crisotelo Montalban concession. The latter is now presently operated by

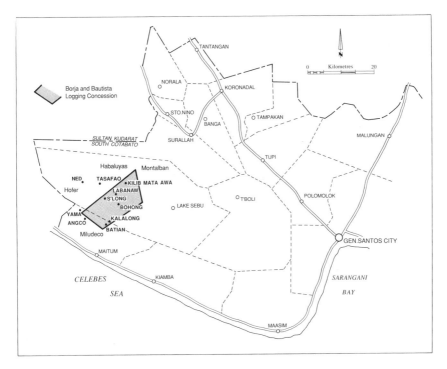

FIGURE 4
**Pre-Panamin logging concessions in the Tboli homeland (Source: Field notes of
Duhaylungsod and Hyndman, February 4–16, 1989)**

the Bayanihan Company, whose manager is also a previous partner of Habal-
uyas. The Bayanihan Company is believed owned by a Chinese businessman.
[George Tanedo and Tim Duhaylungsod interview 1989] (See Figure 4)[6]

In view of such development, Elizalde's (Elizalde with Fox 1971a) initial
surprise that the Tboli rain forests could be inhabited was a gross illusion. And
logging was not the only development. Panaminization introduced resource competition in general, which has continued to intensify.

Panaminization: Resource Exploitation Advances

When Panamin arrived in South Cotabato in the 1970s, competition on the
resource frontier was already well established. Still under contention was the
mountainous homeland of the Tboli, which was increasingly squeezed between
the Ilocano and Visayan colonists. The steep forest lands of the Tboli had been
classified as suitable for lumbering (PPDO 1988b:12); and, in fact, the B&B
concession was already logging in the Tboli community of Barrio Ned (Figure 5)
when Panamin came on the scene.

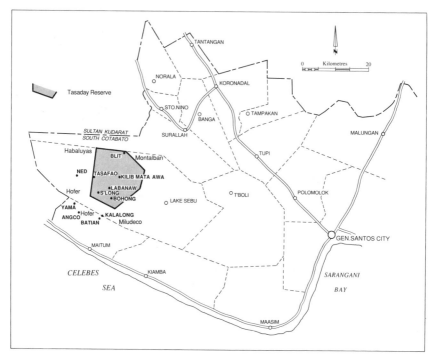

FIGURE 5
Tasaday reserve and logging concessions during Panaminization (Source: Field notes of Duhaylungsod and Hyndman, February 4–16, 1989)

Barrio Ned

Barrio Ned of the Tboli was recognized in 1963. By the time a reserve was set aside for the "Tasaday," there were eight *sitios* [small hamlets]. The *sitios* outside the reserve are Kalalong, Angco, Batian and Yama. At least 15,000 Tboli consisting of about 3,000 families continue to live in the four *sitios* of S'long, Labanaw, Tasafao and Bohong within the reserve. Kalibuhan northwest of Ned is Manobo territory and Blit is dominantly Tboli, not Manobo. [George Tanedo interview 1989]

Panamin's approach to competition was to recommend a presidential decree. Accordingly, Presidential Decree 995 of April 6, 1972, set aside 19,000 hectares for the 26 "Tasaday." Thus half of the B&B concession was immediately eliminated, and the remaining half sold to Hofer. The Tasaday reserve does not give recognition to the fact that it was already the homeland of 15,000 Tboli. A token 130,000 hectares allocated in 1974 through Presidential Decree 407 became Tboli municipality (Figure 2). (Mai Tuan, an important figure in the creation and perpetuation of the Tasaday, has been its mayor ever since.) But these 130,000 hectares were not set aside for the benefit of the Tboli. They were part of Panamin's countrywide routine use of forced primitivism, reservations, and "hamletting" (see following section) to insure their exclusive control over indigenous peoples' resources. This was merely a tactic to let agribusiness, prospecting, mining, and logging interests exploit Tboli lands and resources (Rocamora 1979). Creating the gentle, Stone Age Tasaday perfectly fitted Panamin's forced primitivism (Rocamora 1979:12). Even before Panamin created the Tasaday, a B'laan man had been forced to pose naked for photographs (Pastor N. Edralin interview 1989). They also had attempted a hamletting project in Angco *sitio* in Ned based on sweet potato gardens and doles of food. (When the food program ended, the scheme collapsed, and Angco has been under the influence of the Moro National Liberation Front [MNLF] ever since.) Panamin confined their efforts to non-Muslim indigenous peoples because they never successfully competed against the MNLF—it was the MNLF that kidnapped the German journalists from *Stern* at the Tasaday reserve in 1986 and ransomed them through Hofer.

During martial law under the Marcos dictatorship, state agribusiness and hydroelectric expansion required Panamin to deal with the indigenous peoples who were the victims of these programs. Panamin dealt with them through the use of reservations and strategic hamlets patterned on the CIA counterinsurgency Montagnard program in the pre-liberation Vietnamese highlands (Rocamora 1979:13).

Hamletting

Panamin's reservation program is basically a strategic hamlet program, probably imported from the Vietnam Montagnard program, and thus a military control program; it should not come as a surprise that there is little development, since military objectives may be considered to have been achieved. [Fr. Vincent Cullen in Rocamora 1979:20][7]

The first regional director of Bukidnon and Misamis Oriental in Mindanao was Oliver Madronial, a military officer with five years of experience in the Montagnard program (Rocamora 1979:19). Panamin attempted to grab the whole territory of the Dibabawon and Mandaya peoples by hamletting Malamodaw barangay in Mawab, Davao del Norte. That is, they required the people of a given area to move into the "hamlet," and by military force Panamin would become the constituted authority of the whole region. The people successfully resisted, but to this day the community is still nicknamed Panamin. In 1982 ex-convicts hired by North Davao Mines successfully defended its mineral rights against armed Panamin forces (Samuel Duhaylungsod interview 1989).

By the end of 1977 Panamin had organized 2,600,000 indigenous people on 400 reservations throughout the country, more than half of the then-estimated 4,500,000 in the Philippines. According to a Mindanao Panamin official, "We settle the natives on reservation land which we manage for them. From then on, any company that is interested in the land deals with us" (Rocamora 1979:17). Panamin policy secured reservations, which it administered as government property. Even though Presidential Decree 410 (1974) allowed indigenous peoples to acquire legal title over their ancestral lands, Panamin in no way encouraged this.

Counterinsurgency was the largest item in Panamin's budget (Rocamora 1979:19). According to a statement of Roque Reyes in 1977,[8] "Those minorities who pass our loyalty check are permitted to participate in the government's fight against subversive elements'' (Rocamora 1979:18). Out of a total of over 400 Panamin weapons to South Cotabato, over 300 were distributed among the Tboli (Artajo 1977). Panamin made the Tboli the most militarized indigenous peoples in the Philippines. Panamin also hired former Hukbalahap fighters, who had surrendered to Magsaysay in the early 1950s and resettled in Pangantukan, Bukidnon, and Talacogon, Agusan del Sur, for counterinsurgency operations at Lake Sebu (Samuel Duhaylungsod interview 1989).

The Tasaday proved to be Panamin's most self-contained scheme of forced primitivism, and the one to gain the most notoriety. George Tanedo and Mai Tuan, both schooled at the Edenton Mission College, are important "Tasaday" power brokers. When George figured in the 1986 International Conference on the Tasaday Controversy and other Urgent Anthropological Issues (ICTCUAI) in Manila, he was a key person in uncovering the hoax. His claim to the legitimacy of his position is based on his wife's kinship relation to Bidula, one of those who originally posed as a Tasaday. Moreover, he was himself used as a "Xerox Tasaday" during the Panamin-staged cultural parade for former President Gerald Ford's state visit to the Philippines (George Tanedo interview 1989).

The continuing contention that the "Tasaday" are authentic finds no credence among any of the interest groups in Maitum. The notion of "primitive" Tasaday is laughable to them, for one of the original 26 Tasaday "discovered" in 1971, Saay (Udelen), was a well-known Tboli man once resident in their community!

Saay Boone, alias Udelen (Figure 6), was educated at Edenton Mission College. During the late 1950s and early 1960s he lived in Maitum with a council-

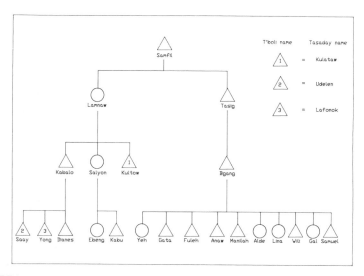

FIGURE 6
Kinship of Tboli from Maitum exploited to pose as Tasaday (Source: Field notes of Duhaylungsod and Hyndman, February 4–16, 1989)

woman named Felisa Narvaez. Datu Kaming, the grandfather of Bidula (another of the original 26 "Tasaday"), also lived in Maitum. The fact that Udelen and Bidula were known in Maitum gave the whole scheme away. It is the oft-repeated opinion of the people of Maitum that Panamin's big mistake was their choice of Udelen and Bidula to pose as Tasaday; had they chosen *all* of their recruits from among the Tboli living in the area of Barrio Ned and Blit, the secret might have been kept. In fact, except for two Manobo individuals (Balayam and Itut), all *were* Tboli who could speak Manobo, and *most* were from Barrio Ned and Blit.

Of course, Tboli involvement was evident from the very name *Tasaday*. According to George Tanedo (interview 1989), *Tasaday* is a Tboli place name for a mountain. Its caves, another place of cultural significance, are named *kilib mata awa* (Figure 5) in Tboli.

Clay Johnston (an SIL linguist whose chapter is elsewhere in this volume), when he saw the televised "first encounter," recognized the speech of the "Tasaday" as being no different from the Cotabato Manobo language. This does not disprove that they were Tboli, of course, since the Tboli are multilingual; speaking Manobo was a tactic the "Tasaday" used to draw attention away from the fact that the hoax was perpetrated in the Tboli homeland.

After the revelations of the ICTCUAI in 1986, Philippine congressional inquiry was initiated. Maitum local leaders, especially the Tanedos, arranged for Edenton Mission College to be the venue for the hearing that would take evidence from local witnesses. At this hearing Bidula was the main witness. The congressional committee itself met later at Lake Sebu. At both hearings Bidula clearly established that the Tasaday were a hoax. The testimony of Bidula and Saay (Udelen) was critical, since they were foremost "Tasaday" actors, and they have suffered the worst Panamin manipulation. However, since the time of their original testimony, they have regularly been with Elizalde in Manila, and together they have taken out a libel suit *against* those Filipino academics and journalists who have exposed the scandal.

Panaminization was already associated with enforced primitivism before the Tasaday case, but this extreme scheme was undertaken, no doubt, because resource competition was so intense on the frontier. The continuing effort to portray the Tasaday as primitive is motivated by the desire to control the reserve. More resources are at stake than just logging.

OSCC Takeover of a Militarized Frontier

The Office of Muslim and Cultural Communities (OMACC) succeeded Panamin in 1984. But following Panaminization's demise, militarization, land dispossession, and competition for Tboli resources only intensified (Tribal Forum 1985:25–28). Under OMACC, indigenous peoples continued to be compromised by export-oriented and foreign capital–dependent state development policies (Okamura 1987). OMACC's interest has not been the benefit of the peoples themselves, but their land.

Counterinsurgency was one of the agency's principal objectives: their 1987 budget specified that "OMACC as a civil agency can therefore be actively involved in the counterinsurgency program within the framework of the policy of attraction and reconciliation'' (Okamura 1987:14).

President Aquino abolished OMACC by Executive Order 122 in January 1987. In its place she created three new offices: an Office for Northern Cultural Communities, an Office for Southern Cultural Communities (OSCC), and an Office for Muslim Affairs. Their objectives, policies, and activities remain, however, the same as those of OMACC and Panamin (Okamura 1987).

OSCC and Its Role

The general functions of OSCC are assumed from the functions of the former OMACC and the defunct Panamin. As stated earlier, access to the Tasaday has been placed under the sole control of Panamin; thus, the OSCC, as the incumbent government agency responsible for the welfare of the southern cultural communities must likewise find out the real situation of the Tasadays.

. . . In OSCC's short visit to the Tasadays, an ocular survey was made and it was contended that based on their physical features the ''Tasadays really looked like primitive people'' and ''there is a genuine Tasaday tribe.'' [J. Lopez 1989][9]

''Tasaday'' are being recruited again in Maitum; some new ones had already disgustedly returned home from the caves in 1989. Rice and dried fish have reportedly been purchased from Maitum to feed the ''cave-dwelling'' cast. The Tasaday Community Care Foundation, a nongovernment organization headed by Antonio Cervantes, who is also comptroller of Elizalde and Co., Inc., is backing the recruitment drive. It is for the preservation of the persisting Panamin interest that the reserve is militarized. George Tanedo's brother Franklin, having been compromised over an illegal logging conviction, has been compelled to work as the Panamin front man in Maitum.

Logging and Militarization

Hofer lost their logging concession in 1988 due to militarization. In 1979 they had acquired an additional concession from B&B. They only got to operate their B&B acquisition for 10 years, although they had a 25-year lease. Their concession was suspended, on orders issued through the office of the Defense Minister Fidel Ramos, for allegedly supporting the MNLF. Hofer was accused of providing 250 bags of rice to the MNLF, but actually they were advancing rations to Muslims hired to work in their rattan concession. [Philip Musin interview 1989][10]

Clearly, logging concessions needed to be replaced by resource alternatives on the Tboli resource frontier because the forest had become so seriously denuded (PPDO 1988b:109a). Moreover, the population of South Cotabato had doubled since Panaminization. It had reached 985,674 by 1987, which represented the fourth highest annual increase of any province (PPDO 1988b:21). Yet the Tboli homeland has remained a reserve only for a handful of ''Tasaday,'' not for the 15,000 Tboli from Barrio Ned. The reserve is protected not because it is homeland to the ''Tasaday'' but because of its valuable potential for further advances in resource exploitation.

The value of the land now appears to derive from its gold resources. Gold prospecting is the latest assault. In Maitum, Fabian Duhaylungsod, Jr. (interview

1989), has had a gold assay confirmed of 6 gm per ton.[11] Heightened militarization on the Tboli frontier is certainly not over iron ore! Nor is it over the negligible
amount of gold acknowledged by the provincial government to be located in the
Visayan-dominated region of Polomolok (PPDO 1988b:17).

Commoditization of the South African gold mining frontier proceeded only
after the indigenous peoples were pacified and their kinship mode of production
was destroyed to provide African labor to the mines (Wolf 1982:350). The trajec-
tory of gold commoditization in South Cotabato has not yet forced the demise of
the Tboli kinship mode of production as occurred in the South African gold frontier. Nonetheless, the rapid commoditization of gold is clearly posing a critical
threshold to the Tboli.

Declaration of Location

The Bureau of Mines must be approached for a Declaration of Location (DOL).
The maximum DOL permitted to an individual is 81 hectares. A DOL is good
for one year and is renewable only to a new person. An application to survey is
good for two years. After the survey phase, a fee of P15,000 is required per
claim. With a technical description deputized by the Bureau of Mines a mining
lease of 25 years may be taken out, with the possibility of a further 25-year extension. A corporation can lease a maximum of 5,000 hectares per province and
the maximum to individuals is 500 hectares. There must be 60/40 Filipino/for-
eign equity. I am negotiating with Banahaw Mines with Australian equity in order to increase my lease to 5,000 hectares, the location of which is 22 km down-
stream of the Tasaday reserve. Only the President can authorize a lease within
the reserve. [George Tanedo interview 1989]

Prospecting around the Tasaday Reserve

There are 1,500 individual gold prospecting leases (DOL) of 81 hectares each in
seven municipalities, including Barrio Ned. In Maitum, Blucor is competing
with George Tanedo. As far as I am concerned, resources belong to surface
dwellers and any benefits derived should redound to them. [Governor Sueno interview 1989][12]

The Tasaday reserve is now virtually ringed by DOLs, but Mai Tuan and George
Tanedo are the only Tboli with significant holdings.

Currently, the gold rush is concentrated in Kemato, a *sitio* located only 3 km
from Tboli town (Figure 2). Since June 1989 some 8,000 miners, mostly from
Diwalwal in Davao del Norte, have dug 350 tunnels into the mountain at Kemato.
Over 35,000 miners including their families have invaded the neighboring town
of Tboli, which until recently was home to only 800 Tboli. Gold exploitation is
dispossessing the Tboli of their land and causing serious mercury contamination.
The Tboli have realized no benefit—the few Tboli incorporated into the commoditization of gold are merely gold ore "packers."

Dear General De Villa

The Santa Cruz Mission as a religious organization is part of the Diocese of Marbel. This Mission has been working assiduously for 27 years among the Tribal

people of South Cotabato. Its services in the fields of education, health, agriculture and religion are well known and admired both in South Cotabato, throughout the Philippines and in many parts of the world. [Gutierrez 1989][13]

To the Last Grain of Rice

Q. What can you say about your work with the Tasaday people?

A. Very challenging and fulfilling. In a period of 1½ years, we have been working with these peoples, we feel we have helped shaped their minds so they will recognize themselves better as human beings. We noticed, however, that the Panamin which worked with them before, have conditioned them to indolence. We are trying to erase that. We are trying to teach them dignity of labor so they could be self-reliant.

Q. Do you feel the people of Blit and Tasaday love you?

A. They show it by helping us build the schools or teachers' quarters. Rain or shine, they were there with us. When we ran short of food, they share their food, even the last grain of rice they have, even those reserved or stored for seeds. They also look after our security, always making sure that we are not alone. [interview, *Lunay S'bung* 1989][14]

OSCC Attacks SCM

The OSCC on Dec 2 directed Sta. Cruz Mission director Fr. Rex Mansmann to "immediately remove all your belongings from the Tasaday reservation area, otherwise they will be accused of illegal entry."

The Sta. Cruz Mission set up two schools and community centers in the Tasaday and Manobo Blit reservations three years ago upon the persistent request of the residents there.

The military, on the other hand, has been bombing the forested areas of the Tasaday reservation and recruiting and training unqualified tribal Filipinos into armed CAFGU members. [*Lunay S'bung* 1989][15]

Elizalde and OSCC Conspiracy

Three Santa Cruz Mission staff were arrested for trespassing on the Tasaday reserve and for being communist supporters. I feel they should have gone to jail because their charges would have been dismissed. Elizalde wrote Fr. Rex that SCM could remain on the Tasaday reserve as long as four conditions were met, but Elizalde, of course, no longer has any authority to make any demands concerning the Tasaday. [Governor Sueno interview 1989]

Philippine Information Agency

I was a member of the OSCC committee to investigate the activities of the Santa Cruz Mission. It took 18 months operating in the area before OSCC charged the SCM with exploitation and slavery. I am very much interested to visit the so-called Tasaday area but it is very difficult to conduct an independent inquiry into the Tasaday issue because of the various interest groups. Right now, the only way one could go there is through Mai Tuan. [Olivia Sudaria interview 1989][16]

Like the OSCC, the Santa Cruz Mission considers the Tasaday to be authentic and primitive. To them, the Tasaday, being without a capitalist mode of production, do not possess the dignity of labor and are barely able to recognize themselves as human beings. However, the Tboli do possess "self-reliance" in their kinship mode of production, enough, in fact, to feed themselves and the mission too—"to the last grain of rice." But as Tboli lands and resources are usurped, the PPDO (1988a) perpetuates the rhetoric of primitivism and portrays the Tboli as gaining their identity only through ancient crafts, costumes, and dance. Tourists are encouraged to experience the Tboli vicariously through the Koronadal supermarket or the Santa Cruz Mission. But the "Tasaday" are never mentioned as a tourist attraction because of war on the reserve in the Tboli homeland.

The Hamletting of Blit

There are enough reasons to conduct an operation. [I have] confidential reports on the area submitted to higher headquarters. As the military commander of the area, I decide where to conduct an operation and I am responsible for the actions of my men. [Soriano 1989][17]

Col. Orlando Soriano, Task Force Buayan commander, appeared before Bishop Gutierrez and the municipal mayors during a peace and order campaign. Soriano had authorized bombing of the Tasaday reserve. This had driven over 300 Tboli into Blit where they had to build their houses near the military. When we requested permission to travel to the reserve for the purposes of our present study, Governor Sueno could not encourage us to make the trip because he has no influence with Mai Tuan or Col. Soriano.

The power of Mai Tuan has now escalated to the proportion that even Governor Sueno admits to minimal influence in Tboli and Lake Sebu municipalities. In fact, Mai Tuan, according to Governor Sueno (interview 1989), is working on creating a separate Tboli province out of these municipalities. Distressed and displaced persons, which include "cultural and ethnic communities" and "rebel returnees," constitute the largest category of clientele catered to by provincial social workers as the Tasaday reserve becomes the focus of militarization in South Cotabato (PPDO 1988b:81).

Militarization manifests itself in various guises, from evangelists to members of the media. A radio announcer, who claimed he was a National Intelligence Coordinating Agency (NICA) agent deployed as a deep penetration agent (DPA) in the MNLF, promised us a videotape interview with Saay (alias Udelen) produced by Radio Philippines Network (RPN) in General Santos City. We paid him P160 ($7 U.S.) in exchange for a copy to be sent through RPN in Manila. It never reached us despite several follow-ups. Another media agent claimed to have in his possession a taped interview with Datu Galang. This interview was said to indicate that Judith Moses, the producer of the American Broadcasting Corporation Tasaday exposé "The Tribe that Never Was" (ABC-TV 1986), coerced Datu Galang into participating in the ABC production. The tape, however, was not made available to us. Our attempts to follow how the local press handles the scandal was rendered futile because the tag of communist or communist sympathizer, a pervasive pattern throughout the Philippines, is conveniently used to discredit those who have attempted to expose the hoax. Joey Lozano, the local journalist who broke the hoax story, was so accused during the Philippine Congressional proceedings on the scandal.

Clearly, the gold potential of the Tasaday reserve is a factor in the increasing militarization of the Tboli people. Although the early division of the Tboli by the Visayan and Ilocano colonial usurpers who disbursed power between the Tboli Mohen and the Tboli S'bu continues today, with George Tanedo competing for influence among the Tboli Mohen and Mai Tuan among the Tboli S'bu, the Tboli are beginning to deploy arms in the pursuit of their own independent interests. It remains to be seen if they will relinquish their social networks and hierarchies while actively participating in commodity production.

Tasaday Reserve: Crossroads of Indigenous and Invader

Academics are being used. If the Tasaday can be maintained as authentic, then Panamin/OSCC have exclusive access to the area. If they are proven to be a hoax, the Tboli, through their Kontra Moro Brigade (KMB) will fight to claim the reserve as their rightful homeland. The militarized contenders surrounding the reserve are at a stalemate as they position for access to the gold. The mayor of Kiamba is married to a Tboli and supplied arms to the KMB that secured the truce. The AFP are to the north of the reserve, the NPA to the east, the KMB to the south and the MNLF to the west (Domingo Non interview 1989).[18]

The "Tasaday" controversy, therefore, goes far beyond merely what they eat, speak or wear. For anthropologists to continually insist on determining the reality and degree of primitiveness of the "Tasaday" is to further contribute to the perpetuation of the "illusion of primitive society" (Kuper 1989). The Tboli of South Cotabato cannot be portrayed as being "encapsulated Time in culture gardens" (Fabian 1983:153). Rather, they are a people whose self-determination has been historically arrested and is still being prevented by the political ecology of colonialism. Unfortunately, their remaining recourse is to empower themselves through armed struggle.

Notes

1. The Tanedo family resides permanently in Maitum, South Cotabato. George Tanedo has been a leading figure among the Tboli and in the Tasaday controversy. During our intensive discussions, George impressed on us that by exposing the truth he is under increasing threat from the Panamin camp. Due to sociopolitical conditions in South Cotabato, individuals are virtually powerless in the face of veiled threats and intimidations.
2. Virgilio Villanueva is an important Ilocano power-broker residing in Maitum. He was the long-standing mayor of Maitum during the era of Panaminization.
3. Panamin is the name of the now-defunct government organization that was in charge of indigenous peoples in the Philippines during most of the Marcos era. Manuel Elizalde was the head of Panamin from 1968 to 1983.
4. Fabian Duhaylungsod taught at the Edenton Mission College for over twenty years after Presbyterian missionary work among several Muslim peoples. Although he is now retired, he continues his evangelistic work among the Tboli Mohen in the outlying *sitios* of Maitum.
5. Samuel Duhaylungsod is a forest ranger of the Bureau of Forest Development assigned to the Davao del Sur and Davao del Norte provinces of Mindanao.

6. Tim Duhaylungsod was manager of the Montalban logging concession during the era of Panaminization.
7. Fr. Vincent Cullen worked with the Manobo of the Bukidnon reservation during the era of Panaminization.
8. Panamin's two highest officials after Elizalde were José Guerrero and Roque Reyes, both military officers.
9. José Lopez is a lawyer and Undersecretary of the Office of Southern Cultural Communities and strongly opposes the Sta. Cruz Mission's presence in the Tasaday reserve. The document was made available to us from the files of Judith Moses.
10. Philip Musin is presently personal secretary to Thomas Hofer, Vice-governor of South Cotabato. He was formerly the manager of the Hofer logging operation until they lost their concession in 1988.
11. Fabian Duhaylungsod, Jr., was the municipal development officer of Maitum during the last years of Panaminization.
12. Ismael Sueno is the current provincial governor of South Cotabato. During the ICT-CUAI, he argued that the more fundamental issue of the Tasaday controversy is the impoverishment of the indigenous peoples of the province, more than their primitivism.
13. Bishop Dinualdo Gutierrez, DD, is the bishop of the Diocese of Marbel, which sanctioned the presence of the Sta. Cruz Mission in the Tasaday reserve. This is an excerpt from his letter to Gen. de Villa, Chief of the Armed Forces of the Philippines.
14. Sta. Cruz Mission interview conducted among the eight lay missionaries they assigned to the Tasaday reserve.
15. The *Lunay S'bung Newsletter* is published under the Sta. Cruz Mission Cultural Foundation. The title means "Torch-tree Gathering or the Community of Lords and Ladies of Lemlunay, the Tboli tribes' equivalent of King Arthur's Camelot—a mythical place of the Golden Age. Now, by extension, those who are laboring for a New Golden Age for Mindanao's beleaguered tribal peoples."
16. Olivia Sudaria, manager of the Philippine Information Agency in General Santos City, South Cotabato, was appointed member of the committee created to investigate the activities of the Sta. Cruz Mission in the Tasaday reserve.
17. Col. Orlando Soriano made the command decision to forcibly relocate the Tboli surrounding Blit. On November 15–16, 1988, the military bombed Datal Lewa, four hours' walk from Blit, from the air; they carried out an aerial reconnaissance mission on November 18 and on November 21 five helicopters and a Sikorsky gunship appeared over Blit firing two rockets and depositing 45 fully armed troops under Lt. George Cardos and 28 Tboli CAFGU's under Commander "Bong" from Tboli town (*Lunay S'bung* 1989).
18. Domingo Non is Professor of History and Vice-president of Mindanao State University in General Santos City, South Cotabato. He has lived in the province for over 12 years and is an expert on Tboli history. He delivered a paper on the local history of the Tasaday controversy during the International Conference on the Tasaday Controversy and other Urgent Anthropological Issues (ICTCUAI) in 1986.

● *chapter five*

Third and Final Footnote on the Tasaday

Zeus A. Salazar

In 1971, almost immediately after the first reports about the so-called discovery of the Tasaday by close associates of Panamin (Presidential Arm for National Minorities), I registered my doubts about their being an isolated, stone-tool-using and foraging (preagricultural) group before their alleged contact with a trapper called Dafal (Salazar 1971). This "footnote" was followed with a second more extensive one in September 1972 (Salazar 1973), written in reaction to reports that the people were cave dwellers and because the spate of "prehistoric data" concerning them came from the same Panamin sources. The whole matter subsequently escaped my attention, even when I found myself in the Tasaday environs while doing fieldwork among the Tboli people of Lake Sebu. I kept up with the "literature," however; and in the winter of 1984, while doing research in Germany, I was able to help a young student from the University of Munich, Gerd Unger, work out his proseminar paper entitled "Zum enzyklopädischen Stichwort Tasaday." Dr. Oswald Iten got ahold of this paper while toying with the idea of going himself to the Tasaday caves. Iten's exposé of the hoax in March 1986 (Iten 1986a, 1986b; Iten and Lozano 1986) then led to the convening of the International Conference on the Tasaday Controversy at the Philippine Social Science Center in Quezon City in August of that year. There I tried to summarize the evidence for the nonauthenticity of the Tasaday as an isolated, Stone Age, stone tool–using and cave-dwelling group and, at the same time, presented to the Conference three relatives of the so-called Tasaday. In this chapter, I would like to lay to rest the issues of the Tasaday—at least as far as my tired self is concerned.

Looking At Two Sets of Data

There are two sets of data available to anyone who would want to judge the Tasaday issue as an exercise in ethnological analysis. The first set consists of the reports, pamphlets, books, films, etc., made or issued by people associated with, hired, or invited by Panamin. Chronologically, these documents range from Fox (1971b), Elizalde with Fox (1971a), Llamzon (1971b), Lynch and Llamzon (1971), NBC-TV (1971), Fernandez and Lynch (1972), and MacLeish (1972), through Nance (1975), Yen and Nance (1976), and Fernandez (1977) to Nance (1981). Aside from this, Fernandez has mentioned a 250-page manuscript about his fieldwork with Baradas among the Tasaday.[1] It is probably, if it really exists, a longer version of his "inside story" published in *Filipino Heritage* (Fernandez 1977). Ending with Nance's "photo novel" on the *Discovery of the Tasaday* (1981), the whole set may be called the "Panamin corpus," particularly if we supplement it with the various attempts by the same group of people to counter Iten's exposé and other revelations subsequent to it.

Starting with Iten's investigative reports of 1986, the second set of data consists of independent inquiries into as well as testimonies by and about the Tasaday. In this corpus should also be included the ABC interview of the Tasaday (ABC-TV 1986), the deposition of three relatives (Elizir, Joel, and Blessen) of the Tasaday at the International Conference on the Tasaday Controversy in 1986, the interview of the Tasaday by a London TV company, the affidavits of people in the area concerning the Tasaday, the genealogies of the so-called Tasaday, and the deposition on the "Tasaday" Bidula before the Investigation Committee of the House of Representatives at the Santa Cruz Mission in Lake Sebu. All these data point to the actual perpetration of a hoax. That is, the so-called Tasaday were deliberately gathered together to pose as a paleolithic group that has survived into the space age.

The First Set of Data

We shall go back to this corpus after we have dealt with the first set of data. The best way to treat the Panamin data—and this is what I have done all along in my three previous papers (Salazar 1971, 1973, 1986)—is to view them in terms of their consistency with the supposed preagricultural and premetal level of development of the Tasaday before the advent of Dafal. The whole exercise cannot simply be dismissed by the oft-repeated argument, which is actually a *pétition de principe,* that we cannot really analyze or even comment on the significance of the data because we have never been in the area. It is not the *ethnographic* report as such that is being questioned but the *ethnological* meaning attributed to the data. In other words, the Panamin data cannot be made to support the thesis that the Tasaday are (or, at least, were before Dafal's advent) an isolated stone tool–using, cave-dwelling, and preagricultural ethnic group. The data do not, then, support the working hypothesis that Headland proposes in the introductory chapter of this volume.

The arguments for this have been sufficiently ventilated. Only the more important ones can be repeated here. A crucial point has something to do with the role assigned to Dafal. Serious doubt with regard to his testimony (or what he is made to claim) is indicated, particularly

> because . . . [no] real reason for . . . [his] benevolence toward the Tasaday has been established except that the Tasaday were giving him *bui,* a vine chewed with betel nut, which he could have procured for himself anyway. His "about five trips" or even ten to the Tasaday . . . do not appear sufficient in frequency or intensity to produce the kind of techno-economic and linguistic changes his supposed importations imply, even assuming he was capable and willing to carry them out. In this sense, a great number of the presently known Tasaday vocab-

ulary items would have to be dismissed as loan words from the Blit [Manobo] through Dafal, a phenomenon comparable in dimension to the Indianization of Indonesia or, why not, to the Americanization of the Philippines (with Dafal playing the role at once of the soldier, the banker, the businessman, the missionary and the Peace Corps volunteer). This should be emphasized in the face of the fact that, up to the time of Tasaday contact with Panamin and even beyond this, *Dafal did not seem to know much of the Tasaday language* since, according to Secretary Elizalde and Dr. [Robert] Fox, no one could be found, "either Tboli, Ubo or Blit, who could understand (it) to obtain detailed information" *except Igna* who said at the outset that "less than half" of what the Tasaday said was intelligible. He [Dafal] must have taught the Tasaday by sign language, the Tasaday learning thereby more proficiently Dafal's Blit than he their Tasaday! [Salazar 1973:109]

In fact, it is strange that Dafal was the least effective in precisely the area where he was really an expert—i.e., in hunting and trapping, although the entire array of terms related to these skills have apparently entered the Tasaday vocabulary because of him (Salazar 1973:107–108)! (Of course, we know now that Dafal helped organize the Tasaday and that it was he who came to tell the Tasaday to repair to the caves when visitors were signalled by radio to be coming from the outside. It was also he who organized the Tasaday for the *Stern* journalists in 1986, setting loose a bunch of armed men on the latter when he sensed they were suspecting a swindle.) If, therefore, Dafal himself was a put-on, what about the rest of the act (and the "scientific" speculation) built around his benevolence?

Were the Tasaday a preagricultural people who knew no metal before Dafal came and gave them some bolos? Quite early I asked why then it was that the bolo was called *fais,* the old term for the Tasaday stone axe which, as a result,

purportedly came to be known as *batu fais* or "stone *fais.*" If true, the phenomenon is linguistically a most quaint instance of a new object taking the generic name of an old one instead of being classified as just one specified type. In this sense, our *pan Americano* would be called simply *pan,* while the earlier known ones would be specified as *pan Filipino* or *pan Español. . . .* The point must be driven home, because the designation of the bolo as *fais,* instead of *"fais Dafal"* (in honor of this culture-bearer and on the model of *bulbul siko* and *bulbul laso . . .*) or simply whatever Dafal calls the bolo . . . may in fact be normal in the light of an earlier knowledge of metal or even the bolo itself. [Salazar 1973:104]

In the subsequent publications of Panamin, the bolo was no longer simply *fais* but (what else?) *fais Momo Dakel,* in honor of Elizalde. The truth of the matter is that *fais* really has something to do with metal and, in fact, iron. Among the Blaan (an ethnic group close to the Manobo), *fais* refers to a steel sword. It means the same thing among the Tboli and the Manobo. Among the Tiruray, *fais* is nothing else but 'a slashing bolo'. It is in fact cognate (by metathesis to Malay-Indonesian *besi* 'iron', Western Bukidnon Manobo *wasey* 'iron axe' and even Ilokana *wasay* 'iron axe'). It is no wonder, therefore, that the Tasaday should call the bolo *fais* and their supposed stone axes, *batu fais.*

The Tasaday *knew* the bolo or *fais*—and how to use it. The famous stone "heirloom tool" shown in Lynch and Llamzon (1971) and in Fernandez and

Lynch (1972, figure 10 and plate 2) is handled like a bolo by a Tasaday—i.e., held between the thumb and the forefinger for "scraping" in an outward movement from the body, as when any normal Filipino prepares rattan or bamboo. That the bolo was used *before Dafal* is implicit in the speculation by Fernandez and Lynch that

> the use of rattan for hafting may have followed the introduction of the bolo: cutting this plant would be a difficult task for the stone axe, *"because* the stone tool 'heirlooms' which the Tasaday say they have had for generations" (i.e., certainly before the reported advent of Dafal) are also hafted through the use of rattan. As a matter of fact, they are not only better worked but also better hafted with much more cleanly shaved rattan than the ones made for the curious visitors of the Tasaday forest. [Salazar 1973:104–105]

These demonstration tools seem to have been hafted in fact through the use of the bolo. Of the nine hafted "Tasaday tools" found in the ethnological museum at Nayong Pilipino (in Manila), at least three are hafted with bamboo and rattan worked with the help of a bolo. The others are hafted with twigs and vines that were also cut with a bolo. One tool, made of ignimbrite (adobe), can only be used once, because the stone material is extremely brittle. In any case, none of the tools could possibly be used to cut rattan or bamboo—nor wood, for that matter.

In Philippine (and world) prehistory, metal came much later than agriculture. In the case of the Tasaday, however, the *fais* does not have to presuppose knowledge of agriculture. This is implicit elsewhere. The Tasaday have terms for 'grain' *(bolak)*, 'grind' *(giling)*, 'mortar' *(lesung)*, 'pestle' *(sinong)*. They likewise have the word *mulen,* which Fernandez and Lynch translate as 'bury the vine carefully once more in soil' (1972:304), whereas Nance (1975:401) understands it not as 'to plant', as one Tasaday used it, but rather as 'to put something on the ground'. Molony with Tuan (1976:79) has *femula* with the meanings 'to plant, for example the tomato plants of outsiders' and 'yams'. The term is of course cognate with Western Bukidnon Manobo *pemula,* 'to plant something,' *pinemula* being in the same language 'a plant'. Fox in fact observed "incipient agriculture" at the very outset among the Tasaday (Salazar 1971:37). Subsequently, Fernandez and Lynch (1972:306) described this as "a system of monitoring and fussing over the wild yam's growth, marking it for future harvest, and removing tubers in such a way as not to kill the plant," but they limit it to the species of yam called *biking,* all the other species having been introduced by Dafal, who even taught them how to leach a poisonous species. This means that this "trapper of wild pig" and "collector of coconut pith" is also an expert

> on wild yams and on the preparation of at least one poisonous species. He must have also introduced their names *(kalut, bugsu, lafad, malafakid, banag, fugwa)* into the Tasaday vocabulary, after having found them in the forest zone II and taught their use to the Tasaday who are presumed to have lived in that same environment for a thousand years or even two without discovering other yam sorts than their very own *biking* before Dafal! [Salazar 1973:106]

Indeed, despite their apparent genius in learning all that Dafal could (and also probably could not) teach, the Tasaday were too slow-witted during all the pre-

vious centuries to take advantage of the very environment that Yen's ethnobotanical research shows them to know very well! With such contradictory gifts, they
thus deserve their prehistoric fate as well as their persistently preagricultural ethnographers.

But at least two of these ethnographers, Baradas and Yen, noticed that rice
was being smuggled into the caves. For, after their initial disgust at such food,
the Tasaday had apparently taken to rice and kept hankering for it—as well as for
salted fish ("Momo Dakel's tadpoles," as they called it). It might be of interest
to note that the Mentawaians of Sumatra, traditional yam eaters and for some generations now rice cultivators, still prefer to sell their rice and enjoy their yams.
As for the "preagricultural Tasaday," in less than a year—in fact almost immediately (Headland 1989b, and this volume)—they acquired a taste for rice, which
Cebuanos would not quite fully understand.

But what about their isolation? A number of terms again contradicts this sup-
position, even if it is granted that glottochronologically determined separation of
languages implies the actual physical separation of their speakers. The word *muna*
(Tagalog "before") is found, strangely enough, in Tasaday speech. And so is *efe*
("chief," "owner"), a word originally borrowed from Spanish *jefe,* and found
today in many Philippine languages. The most telling word is *diwata.* Whatever
meaning the Panamin scientists and linguists might give to it, the term is Sanskrit
and

> is associated not only with the Austronesian cognate *hantu,* but also with *djin,*
> *setan* and other terms related to Islam. This suggests an Islam-borne conglom-
> erate of folk-religious ideas which may have started from the original homeland
> of the Malays, Sumatra, since it is here that the connection *hantu/diwata* appears
> to be strongest. In this context, the *diwata* concept could not have reached the
> Tasaday earlier than the accelerated expansion of Islam in Indonesia in the 14th
> century. In the Philippines, Islamic influences of Sumatran flavor penetrated the
> Sulu region during the end of the 14th century and did not reach the Cotabato
> basin till the 15th century. In that case, how long did it take for the term to reach
> and then be adopted by the Tasaday or the "ancestral group" to which the Tas-
> aday may have belonged? It is quite futile to speculate. [Salazar 1973:99]

In any case, the presence of *diwata* in the Tasaday speech implies

> that *either* they already had the term before separating from the Blit [Manobo]
> (or with the Blit from the common indigenous Mindanao stock) and therefore
> had contact like all the other related groups with cultural influences from the
> coast, *or* they had contact with their relations and other advanced or advancing
> coastal groups after their supposed separation. In either case, the theory of "ef-
> fective isolation" becomes untenable, because the contact must have been long
> and intense enough for a culture-heavy concept like *diwata* to penetrate, replace,
> or coexist with other religious ideas. [ibid:98–99]

Another argument against isolation is that of Christian Adler (1986). According to him, a foraging group needs 2.5 square kilometers per member or, in
the case of the Tasaday, a total of 62.5 square kilometers. A hunting/gathering
area of that size around the Tasaday cave site would encompass a great number
of villages of the Ubo, Manobo, Tboli and other ethnic groups. Aside from this,

a group like the Tasaday could not possibly survive for a long period genetically without being part of a broader breeding population of some 500 tribal members. In both cases, isolation is impossible.

The Tasaday do not appear to be a cave-dwelling people either. When first observed at the caves in 1972, the Tasaday women had to pass their babies to the men in order to reach the supposedly inhabited upper cave, because no steps had obviously been made during all the supposed centuries the Tasaday had lived here. Later on, the upper cave was abandoned for the more congenial lower cave which, nonetheless, was furnished shortly thereafter with sleeping platforms and racks for drying wool. It was clear that the Tasaday were not used to sleeping on the humid rock floor.

The latticed sleeping platforms were certainly reminiscent of house floors for the Tasaday. They were also uncomfortably untroglodytic with "a split-bamboo broom." With it, Cave III was regularly kept clean by them. This urge to sweep

> would have to be explained. . . . Would it be too simple to admit that, after all, the Tasaday probably knew and had houses? They now still have sheds or temporary shelters "fashioned out of wood and palm leaves" called *lawi* which, quite distinct from the "roof" or *tifang* (cf. Bikol *atop*, Tagalog *atip*, Ivatan *atep*) a simple "lean-to" would not possess, should be related to Tagalog *bahay*, Malayan, Bikol, Bisayan, and Ilokano *balay* and Ivatan *vahay* through Maranaw *oalai* and Magindanaw *walay* [all meaning "house"] by metathesis. Even the term gathered by Fox—*dungdung*—recalls Tagalog and Kapangpangan *dalung-dung* "forest," "grass cabin," "hut" or "cottage" . . . It may be mentioned that, among the related Manobo of the interior of Southwestern Cotabato, the houses are "temporary in nature" and made of bamboo, cogon grass [Imperata sp.], tree trunks and tree barks. [Salazar 1973:108–109]

Finally, the Tasaday distinguish three types of props. *Bugsod* and *musag* refer to crossed sticks holding the trough above the fire (as in making palm starch), whereas *tukud, tukuran* may also refer to house props, as in most other Philippine languages.

One sees that the Panamin set of data can be used precisely to deny and contradict the thesis that the so-called Tasaday constitute an isolated cave-dwelling, stone tool–using, and foraging group of people. Furthermore, the discrepancies in the reports as well as the quite unusual persistence of the Panamin scientists and reporters to present the Tasaday as a "prehistoric" people in spite of the evidence would point if not to some manipulation at least to some kind of bias. A hoax could only be surmised. It is the second set of data that would prove it.

The Second Set of Data

Both Iten's and ABC's interviews with the Tasaday are now well known. The more recent BBC report (Lerner 1989) was shown on British television in 1989. But all three have in common the fact that the Tasaday themselves are made to speak about their involvement in what a reporter has called "a masquerade." The main protagonists are the Tasaday Bilangan and his sons (particularly Lobo), as well as Datu Galang and, in the case of Iten's reporting, even Fafalo, Datu Dudim's son who occasionally manned the transmitter for Elizalde "and had to transport rice and other foodstuffs to the Tasaday." What they told their interviewers was largely corroborated by Bidula (otherwise known as Dula in Tasaday), when she testified before a congressional committee at Lake Sebu in 1988. The core of the testimony is that Elizalde, through both Dafal and Mai Tuan, recruited from among the Blit and the Tboli in order to form a "stone-age group." This is equally the gist of the story told by Elizir Bon to the delegates of the International Conference on the Tasaday Controversy in 1986. At the same time, Elizir showed how he was related to some of the so-called Tasaday. Blessen and Joel Bon did likewise.

Both Blessen and Joel have since been persuaded by close associates of the former Panamin secretary to "retract," although it is not quite clear what, since both did nothing at the Conference but authenticate their relationship to some of the so-called Tasaday. This relationship they will not be able to deny. In any case, it was Elizir Bon who made all of the revelations about the setting-up of the Tasaday group. These are documented in the forthcoming proceedings of the Conference. Elizir, of course, cannot recant, even if he wanted to, since he was killed a few months after the Conference.

There have been other retractions. One was that of George Tanedo, the leader of the group of relatives who came to testify at the Conference. George is the adoptive brother of Igna, the woman from Blit who was the early "interpreter" of the Tasaday. George confessed that he was doing the whole thing to get a share in the lands reserved for the Tasaday, although he himself had posed as a Tasaday (for President Ford) and is therefore presumably qualified to get a share in the reservation. Bidula also recanted, saying that she was not really a Tboli who had allowed herself to be recruited as a naked Tasaday but that she was in fact and reality a Tasaday. For this deposition, she was brought to Manila by Mai Tuan and company. Her testimony was recorded. A copy of it was procured and replayed to some Manobo, who identified the language in which she spoke (which was supposedly Tasaday) as "Southern Manobo" spoken very rapidly.

The question as to whether Tasaday speech is an "independent language" may soon be settled, as Dr. Ernesto Constantino is trying his best to have Bidula's testimony transcribed by somebody from the area and then analyzed more properly.[2] An educated guess is that her idiolect, at best, will turn out to be a dialect of Blit Manobo, if not downright Blit Manobo. In any case, by their own admission and in the transcription and translation by Constantino's research team of the interviews by the London-based television company, the Tasaday are multilingual, like most of the people of the area.

Datu Galang has also retracted. He did it for Iten and for ABC in consideration of monetary and material rewards. He came especially to Manila to ask forgiveness from his congressman (Chiongbian) for telling a lie. How could he have been offered by Elizalde to pose as a Tasaday when he had never met the man?

All this retracting proves precisely the truth of what is being denied. They are overdoing it. All this I have seen for myself in my own case. For the Congressional investigation they made a television clip of both Blessen and Joel Bon telling an interviewer that I had financed their coming to Manila and instructed them what to say at the Conference. I know for a fact, however, that I had interviewed them in my own house upon their arrival in order to fill out a genealogical chart of their relationship to the so-called Tasaday. I also had nothing to do with their transport to Manila. After the interview, they left my house. We only met again at the Conference session.

It is clear that the Panamin people are ready (and able) to distort everything. The brief history of the congressional investigation of the Tasaday controversy is a case in point. But it is best I leave discussion of that at this point to others.

Tracing the Tasaday Genealogies

I would like to end this chapter with Bilangan and his family. One reason I address this here is that they have not retracted, so far, in the face of probable pressures. Another reason is that his genealogy, and the genealogy of his wife, Etet, show how intertwined the Tasaday phenomenon is with the local family structure.

The genealogies, here grossly simplified, were obtained by George Tanedo from Datu Montang Tuan and Datu Magatal Bilagan, and corroborate the ones I elicited from Elizir, Blessen, and Joel Bon for the International Conference in Quezon City. Figure 1 shows Bilangan (whose real name is Tinda) and his rela-

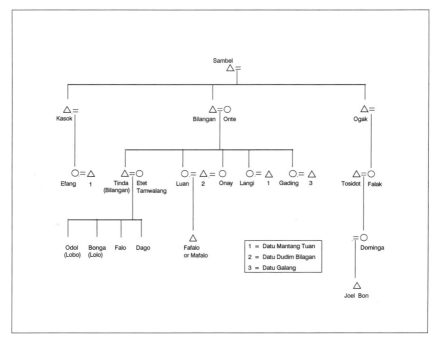

FIGURE 1

Tinda (Bilangan) and his relatives (according to Datu Mantang Tuan and Datu Magatal Bilagan)

tives, both consanguinal and affinal. Bilangan is twice the brother-in-law of Datu Dudim Bilagan through his (D.D.'s) second and third wives, Luan and Onay, respectively, who are Bilangan's younger sisters. He is likewise the brother-in-law of Datu Montang Tuan, which ensures the correctness of the genealogy. Another brother-in-law of Bilangan is Datu Galang! Datu Galang cannot therefore maintain that he had never before set eyes on Elizalde nor that he had never been offered by him to pose as a Tasaday. The sociofamilial context would tend to show that Datu Galang might be lying with regard to his retraction.

Fafalo (or Mafalo), Datu Dudim's son, is likewise a nephew of Bilangan and thus a cousin of Lobo, whose real name is Odol. It is no wonder, therefore, that Fafalo was there for the conclave with Iten! Finally, the other "retractor" Joel Bon is actually related to Bilangan through his great grandfather Ogak, Bilangan's uncle. It is improbable, therefore, that Joel did not know anything about the constitution of the Tasaday group.

In the testimony of Elizir Bon, it was Datu Dudim who acquiesced to the plans of Elizalde. It was also he who persuaded Tinda to become Bilangan, carrying with him his wife Etet and their children. As shown in Figure 2, Etet herself is related to Datu Dudim through her grandfather Landong, eldest brother of Bilagan, the father of Datu Dudim. This probably reinforces Bilangan's hand in relation to Datu Dudim, Bilangan being the eldest brother of the latter's two wives.

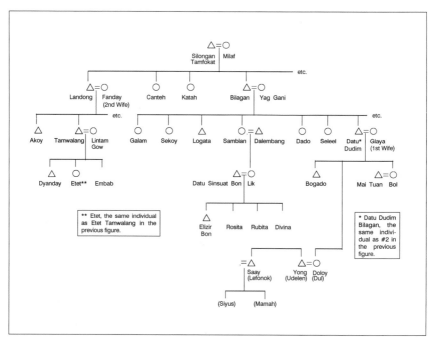

FIGURE 2

Etet, wife of Bilangan, and her relatives (according to Datu Mantang Tuan and Datu Magatal Bilagan)

That should explain why, until now, Bilangan has not succumbed to any pressure to retract!

Datu Dudim himself is close to a source of such pressures, namely Mai Tuan, the former Panamin man and now the mayor of Tboli town. Mai is said to be the common-law husband of Bol, Datu Dudim's daughter with his first wife Glaya. Another daughter, Doloy, is actually the imperious Dul of the Tasaday. Finally, Elizir Bon is also of the family. He is a descendant of Samblan, elder sister of Datu Dudim. Elizir was thus very close to the center of the events and decisions which led to the constitution of the Tasaday. He was certainly much closer than either Blessen or Joel, or even George Tanedo, Igna's adopted brother. And Elizir showed it too in his testimony. And probably paid dearly for it.

Conclusion

All this contextualizes, on the level of the actors (and victims), the making of a hoax. On that genealogical, familial level, there can be no denying of connections and even responsibilities. But how restricted indeed these are, compared to the vaster context of liabilities and conflicting agendas.

This others will probably have to tackle.

Notes

1. This book manuscript, promised several times by Fernandez, but never produced, was first mentioned in print as "forthcoming" in Panamin's first research publication 18 years ago (Fernandez and Lynch 1972:330).
2. *Editor's note:* Salazar wrote this statement before the Tasaday symposium in Washington, DC, in 1989, where the papers by the four linguists on that panel did, indeed, settle this linguistic question. Those four papers are published in this volume (see chapters by Elkins, Johnston, Molony, and Reid)—TNH.

PART II

Supporters of the Early Reports on the Tasaday

● *chapter six*

The Genealogical Evidence

AMELIA ROGEL-RARA AND EMMANUEL S. NABAYRA

n the 15 years between the discovery of the Tasaday in 1971 and a resurgence
of interest in the group in 1986, a number of respected scientists have made
contacts with them, notably anthropologists Robert Fox, Frank Lynch, Carlos
Fernandez, and Jesus Peralta; linguists Teodoro Llamzon, Richard Elkins, and
Carol Molony; ethnobotanists Douglas Yen and Hermes Gutierrez; and ethologist
Irenaus Eibl-Eibesfeldt.[1]

Data collected during these contacts included genealogical inputs which, although differing in some minor points, are basically in agreement and are easily
reconcilable with each other (Elizalde with Fox 1971a, 1971b; Fernandez 1977;
Lynch et al. 1973; Molony with Tuan 1976; Nance 1975; Peralta 1971b; Rogel
1972 [cf. Nance 1975:182–183, 209, 222]; and Yen and Nance 1976).

However, in 1986 journalist Oswald Iten, after only two days in the Tasaday
vicinity, of which only about an hour was spent at the Tasaday caves, published
a sensational report claiming that the Tasaday tribe was all a hoax: that it was
merely a group of Tboli and Manobo farmers posing as cave people (ABC-TV
1986; Benedicto 1987; Bower 1989b; Central Independent Television 1987; Iten
1986a, 1986b; Iten and Lozano 1986; Jones 1989; Lerner 1989; Lopez 1986).

Later that year, during an international conference convened in Manila, Zeus
Salazar of the University of the Philippines echoed Iten's claim that the Tasaday
were only Tboli and Manobo imposters. Salazar presented three genealogical
charts he had drawn up a few hours before his lecture, in which he endeavored to
show the supposed Tboli/Manobo identities of some Tasaday (Benedicto 1987;
Lerner 1989; Salazar 1986). In the same conference, Salazar introduced a number
of Tboli who claimed to be relatives of certain Tasaday individuals (Lopez
1986:8–9; Salazar 1986, 1988). On this basis, Salazar proclaimed the Tasaday "a
hoax" (Azurin 1988 [cf. Lopez 1986]; Bailen 1986:109; Lerner 1989; Salazar
1986).

Salazar reiterated his claims at the 1988 International Conference of Anthropological and Ethnological Sciences (ICAES) in Zagreb, Yugoslavia, where he
showed eight amended versions of his 1986 "genealogical charts" (Salazar
1988).[2] The issues raised, however, were not resolved.

In August 1988, similar views on the Tasaday were presented by David
Hyndman and Levita Duhaylungsod in a joint paper on the Tasaday at the Fifth

International Conference on Hunting and Gathering Societies, in Darwin, Australia (Hyndman and Duhaylungsod 1990). Again, however, the issues remained unresolved (Headland 1989c; Olofson 1989).

It was against this background that we conducted studies to provide definitive answers by delving in depth into the genealogy not only of the Tasaday but also of their closest neighbors. The highlights of our genealogical studies are presented in this chapter.[3]

The Central Questions

Among many questions raised, the broadest and most significant to us were: (1) Which genealogy, if any, was correct? (2) Why was there such a vast difference between the data and conclusions of the original ethnographers and those of Professor Salazar? (3) What about the human subjects of this debate? Who were they and how had they fared?

Research Methodology

Standard ethnographic procedures were used for gathering, recording, analyzing, and presenting data. In this connection, we acknowledge the help of anthropologist Carlos Fernandez, who contributed 12 pages of handwritten questions and suggestions which greatly aided our research.

For purposes of this research and to avoid confusion, we have coined the term ''Real Tasaday'' to refer to the community identified in the seven genealogical charts and related kinship data prepared in the 1970s by field researchers on the basis of primary data (see Rogel-Rara and Nabayra 1988a, 1988b, 1988c, 1989). For the personalities shown in Salazar's charts, we have used the term ''Tasaday Poseurs.''

We collected exhaustive pedigrees at the Tasaday caves on 20 full-blooded ''Real Tasaday'' adults and on 20 non-Tasaday adults living at the caves as spouses of Tasaday (see Appendix). Also included within the scope of this study were two full-blooded Real Tasaday females who were then married to non-Tasaday males from outside the forest, and these two men themselves (see Rogel-Rara and Nabayra 1988a, 1988b, 1988c, 1989, and especially the charts there showing the genealogies of Dula, Mahayag, Biking, and Si-el/Dina).

Salazar listed 17 persons in his genealogical charts (1986, 1988) showing, he claimed, both their ''original'' names and their ''Tasaday Poseur'' aliases.[4] We were able to locate and interview 14 of these 17. Two others were reported by relatives to have died (Ebak in April 1973 and Kultow before World War II); and one (Etet Tamwalang) appears to be nonexistent.[5] Our main argument in this chapter is that only two of these 17 individuals (Dula and Si-el) are Tasaday, and none of the other 15 were members of the Tasaday community of 26 people in 1971–72, as Salazar alleges.[6]

We interviewed the 14 remaining Tasaday Poseurs in four mixed communities of Manobo and Tboli-Ubo near the Tasaday-Manobo Preserve. They are swidden cultivators who also hunt. All 14 were interviewed with their relatives. Seven of the Poseurs resided in the village of S'lung and one (Doloy) in the village of An-twal, both villages located on the southwestern edge of the Preserve, about 50 km inland from the Celebes Sea at Maitum and a one-day walk from the Real Tasaday home site (see Figure 1). Two others (Udol and Tinda) lived in Takboh, about 12 km northwest of Lake Sebu; one (Agen) lived in Lumoyon, at the northeastern edge of the Preserve; one (Bonga) at Blit, and one (Itut Longkul) at Talahek (see Appendix). This latter individual is the only one of the three "Etuts" (aside from Real Tasaday Etut) in the area. The other two women named Etut lived too far outside our area of inquiry.

All in all, then, extensive data were compiled on the original 26 Real Tasaday personalities reported in the 1971–72 studies, on 22 non-Tasaday persons who have since married Real Tasaday, on the 15 non-Tasaday "Poseurs," and on cer-tain non-Tasaday individuals who have since acquired affinal ties with the Real Tasaday (namely, Datu Dudim, Mai Tuan, Dafal, and Datu Galang Tikaw) and who were said to be recruiters of Tboli and Manobo farmers to become Tasaday Poseurs.[7] By checking for redundancy and overlapping kinship networks of 156 individuals of questionable identity, we correlated the pedigrees of 111 individ-uals. Forty-five were determined to be nonexistent. As a further precaution against erroneous enumeration resulting from the widespread use of nicknames and aliases and from the customary name changing practiced by the Tboli and neighboring tribes, we conducted face-to-face field interviews with each living ego personality (see Appendix).

To verify the identity of subjects other than by name, we collected data on invariant demographic, physical, and personality characteristics and on demo-graphic variables, such as subjects' place of origin, sex, year of birth or relative age, birth order, place or places of residence, family and/or genealogical position within a given kinship matrix (lineal, collateral, and generational), physical fea-tures (as seen in photographs), and other attributes unique to the subjects whose identity was being certified. We also obtained the official census listing of all in-habitants in all the villages within a radius of 30 km of the Tasaday home site. This greatly facilitated location and identification of the specific subjects of our field research.

Although our review of previously published data actually began in 1987, the gathering and recording of field data began in August 1988 and was completed May 1989. The interviews were conducted at 21 locations, including the Tasa-day's *Ilib Fusaka* ("original cave") (see Appendix and Figure 1.)

The "Real Tasaday" Population

The *Ilib Fusaka* habitation site population totaled 70 individuals, as follows:

26 full-blooded "Real Tasaday" consisting of 14 adult males (13 married), 5 male children, 5 adult females (3 married, 1 widowed), and 2 female children;

22 half-blooded Tasaday consisting of 11 males and 11 females, all children ranging in age from less than 1 to 10 years;

22 persons with no Tasaday blood but considered by the community as "Tasa-day" by marriage or adoption and residence.

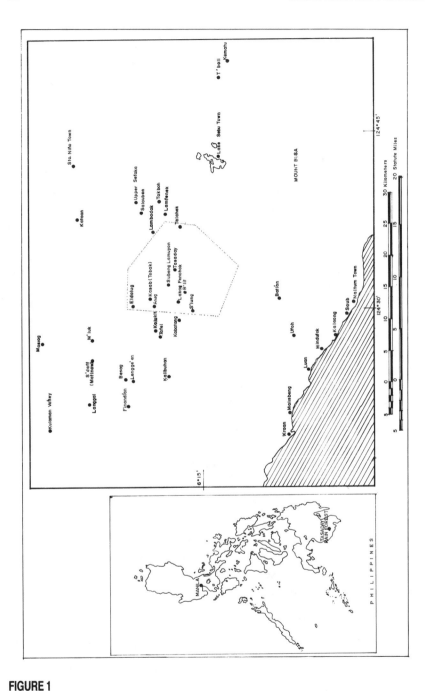

FIGURE 1

Location map of the Tasaday preserve (inside dotted line) and neighboring settlements, South Cotabato, Philippines (*Sources:* Office of the President 1972; Bureau of Coast and Geodetic Survey 1956; NAMIRA 1981; Department of Agriculture and Natural Resources 1972; Rogel-Rara and Nabayra 1988–89.)

The full-blooded Tasaday ranged in age (estimated for most) from infancy to age 80. Fakel, a male, was born to Dul on May 5, 1989; Sikey, a female, was about 80—her husband, Kuletaw, also about 80, died in March 1989. The others were Bilangan, about 60; his wife Etut, 50; Lefonok and Udelen, both near 60; Mahayag, male, and Dul, female, mid 40s; Balayem, male, 40 plus; Lolo, Gintuy, and Adug, males, 30 to 35; Lobo and Odoq, males, near 30; Kalis, female, and Biking, Natek, and Si-us, males, mid 20s; Maman, male, 20; Okon, female, 16; Degu, male, 13; Diha, female, 11; Sungo, male, 9; Talihin, male, 7; Bihug, female, 5; and Klohonon, male, 3. (Dula and Si-el, both females, were interviewed in their homes outside the forest.) The half-blooded children ranged in age from 10 years to less than 1 year.

Those with no Tasaday blood were the 20 in-married spouses and 2 adopted children: Lin, about 10 years old, daughter of Gintuy's wife, Suwal, by her former husband Tobak, a Tboli-Ubo; and Sem, also about 10 years old, son of Bilangan's second wife, Kumbong, by her former husband Igot (deceased), a Blit Manobo.

Of the non-Tasaday in-married spouses (19 female and 1 male), the oldest was Sindi, a twice-widowed Blit Manobo female who, in 1972, became the first outsider known to have married into the group. In 1989 she appeared to be in her late 40s. Kumbong, a Blit Manobo widow who married Bilangan about 1986, appeared that year to be in her late 30s; Linsu, mid-30s; and the rest (in 1989) to be in the mid-20s to early teens. Two daughters of Kumbong from her first marriage are both married to Tasaday men, Sabi to Si-us, and Kading to Natek. Salim, the only non-Tasaday male to have married in, is about age 25 (in 1989).

The Poseurs Today

Seven of the 17 Poseurs live in the village of S'lung, just outside of the southwestern edge of the Tasaday Preserve (see Figure 1 and Table 1). Two of the more prominent personalities in the area are Datu Mantang Tuan of S'lung and Datu To'Sina of Kabatang. Datu Mantang Tuan and his cousin, Datu Magatal, had been mentioned by Salazar as sources for his "genealogical charts" of the Tasaday, while Datu To'Sina is identified in one of Salazar's charts as the father of the Poseur "Bedula [Dula]" (see Salazar 1988).

Datu Mantang, in an interview, denied that he had ever given any genealogical information to Salazar or to Salazar's acknowledged informant, George Tanedo, Mantang's relative. Mantang also said it was impossible for his cousin Magatal to have given any information to Salazar in 1986 because Magatal died more than 20 years before that time. Mantang is also the father of Bonga Mantang, who is identified by Salazar as Poseur Lolo (Figure 2). Mantang introduced us to his son, Bonga, who denied that he had ever been a Tasaday Poseur. Bonga is better known in the area as "Kumander Machinegun," formerly of the Moro National Liberation Front (MNLF).

On the other hand, Bonga's brother-in-law, Kafal Ayunan, is identified in Salazar's chart as Mahayag (Figure 3). Kafal, a farmer who lives in S'lung, is married to Mantang's daughter Di-ok. Kafal said that he was offered incentives by George Tanedo to impersonate Tasaday Mahayag. Two of his neighbors, the half-brothers Fidlo Swing and Yabis Baham, are also identified in the Poseur charts as "Gintuy" and "Adug" respectively (see Figures 4 and 5). Yabis said that Fidlo accepted George Tanedo's offer of land in Tasaday in return for Fidlo's impersonating Gintuy. Then Fidlo persuaded Yabis to impersonate Adug.

Other S'lung residents are Saay Baleg and Yong Balungay, cousins who are supposed to be Poseurs Lefonok and Udelen, respectively (see Figures 6 and 7). They both confirmed being offered land for posing as Tasaday. Virtually the same stories were told by Bulaha Antew ("Natek") (see Figure 8) and Luding Otam ("Biking") (see Figure 9), also S'lung farmers. Tinda Dayaw and Udol Lambayen, father-in-law and son-in-law, both farmers living just above Lake Sebu, told a somewhat different story. They said they were approached by Lobong Badang, a Tboli security guard from a Maitum logging firm, who offered both of them permanent jobs as forest guards in return for playing "Lobo" and "Bilangan" (see Figures 10 and 11). Lobong Badang is a son-in-law of Datu To'Sina. He admitted having approached Tinda and Udol on the instruction of George Tanedo. Agen Magintey, a Tboli farmer living in Lumoyon, said he was also approached by Lobong Badang to impersonate Lolo (see Figure 12). Agen said he declined because he did not want to offend his sister Funding, wife of Tasaday Lobo, and his brother Salim, husband of Tasaday Kalis. Doloy Bodul confirmed that he was supposed to impersonate Tasaday Dul (see Figure 13). Doloy, married, a rattan trader in Betian, not far from S'lung, was well known in the area to be fond of impersonating women. He claimed that he was approached by Lobong Badang and George Tanedo to impersonate Dul because, according to Lobong, they could not find a Tboli woman willing to do the job.

Blessen Boone Tunggay-Tanedo and Joel (Junwel) Boone, two of the "witnesses" presented by Salazar in the 1986 conference, when interviewed in Zion, Maitum, revealed their true genealogical data, which is quite different from the data contained in Salazar's "Blessen" and "Joel" charts. The third "witness," Elizir Boone, had died, shot by a police posse serving a warrant of arrest from the Maitum court for the kidnap-rape of a minor (see relevant police reports: Police of Kiamba 1987; Police of Maitum 1987; and Provincial Inspectorate 1987).

Genealogy of the "Real Tasaday"

A composite genealogical chart based on the new data shows kinship connections and descent lines of seven generations of Real Tasaday (Rogel-Rara and Nabayra 1989). Earlier studies showed only four generations (Elizalde with Fox 1971a, 1971b; Fernandez and Lynch 1972; Peralta 1971b; Rogel 1972; [cf. Nance 1975]).

The earliest progenitors (G-0) recalled by the elder Tasaday were Lubas (male), who lived in Tasaday, and Layas (female), who came from the Tasafang, one of two interior forest groups with whom the Tasaday socially interacted in the past.[8]

Lubas and Layas had an only son, Fangul (in G-1), who was born in Tasaday and lived there. (Early researchers thought Fangul was a mythical ancestor of the Tasaday.) Fangul married the Tasafang woman Tukol (or Tukiyel), with whom he had five children (G-2), all born in Tasaday: four males—Ligbalug, Kasay, Linggaw, and Sambel—and one female. One of the male offspring, Kasay, was believed to have died in his preteens when he failed to return from gathering food in the forest. The name of the female sibling can no longer be recalled, even by her nephew Bilangan—the oldest living male in Tasaday. She apparently left Tasaday as a child bride for a man from Tasafang and never returned.

After Tukol died, Fangul married Tukol's younger sister Biq and they had one offspring, Salibuko (male). (Tukol and Biq were the daughters of Dakula, a Tasafang male, and Gansingan, a Tasaday female who married in Tasafang and stayed there. Tukol and Biq grew up in their parents' home in Tasafang.)

The members of the G-2 generation were the immediate predecessors of tribal members contacted by Manuel Elizalde, Jr., in 1971. Ligbalug was the father of Tikaf; Linggaw, the father of Kuletaw; Sambel, the father of Bilangan; and Salibuko, the father of Balayem.

The surviving members of the G-3 generation were the community elders when the Real Tasaday were contacted by Elizalde (Elizalde 1971a, 1971b; Elizalde with Fox 1971a, 1971b [cf. Nance 1975; Terry 1971]). These were: Tikaf, Kuletaw, Bilangan, and Balayem. A fifth member of this generation, Basiw, brother of Kuletaw and father of Lefonok and Udelen, died prior to contact.

Lobo and his brothers, Lolo, Natek, and Degu, belong to the G-4 generation, along with Mahayag, Adug, Gintuy, Lefonok, Udelen, and Balayem's children with Sule, the male child Yuf and the female child Med/Jowe.

The most numerous generation at present in Tasaday is the G-5 generation, which consists of 26 members. Of these, 13 are full-blooded Tasaday: Lefonok's children, Odoq (male) and Kalis (female); Udelen and Dul's children, Si-us (male), Maman (male), Okon (female), Diha (female), Sungo (male), Talihin (male), Bihug (female), Klohonon (male), and Fakel (male); and Mahayag's Biking (male) and Si-el/Dina (female).

The half-blooded members of the G-5 generation (13 individuals) are: Gintuy's Lawingan and Sayo (males) and Bilin, Linda, and Memek (females); Lolo's Nani (male) and Bitsi, Binit, and Malya (females); Lobo's Luy and Nerma (females) and their still unnamed baby brother; and Natek's Bagting (male).

As of May 1989, the nine members of the G-6 generation (six males and three females) were all half-blooded Tasaday. These were: Odoq's daughter Ilia and his sons Moses, Bula, and the still unnamed youngest; Kalis's two sons, Yuni and Tufi, Biking's daughter Dawing; and Si-el/Dina's son, Fleno.

The Manobo of Blit

The Manobo community named Blit is important in the Tasaday story because of its new role as the source of Tasaday spouses and because its recent proximity to the Tasaday caves has led to speculation that the Tasaday may have traded with

Blit for cultivated food before the 1971 time of contact (Headland 1989a, 1989c, and this volume).

Detailed interviews with Datu Dudim, his brother Datu Magafid, Dudim's son Mafalo, Unggo Lugata (son of Dudim's deceased brother Datu Lugata), Datu Lasang (son of Dudim's father's deceased brother Datu Lendung), and many other Blit residents enabled us to elicit approximate dates in this Manobo group's history by correlating known dates with age estimates and conventional assumptions, such as generational time span.

The Blit Manobo trace their ancestry to the Manobo of Kulaman Valley, ten days' walk to the northwest, where their ancestors lived about two centuries ago (see Figure 1).[9] From there, they moved gradually southeastward in several stages: from Kulaman to Finandi'an and Besag (about four-and-a-half days' walk northwest from Blit), and from there to Kolukit (one-and-a-half days northwestward from Blit), where they stayed for three generations, before moving to Tafel (birthplace of two generations, including Datu Dudim's generation). From Tafel, the group moved eastward to Afag (birthplace of Mafalo Dudim and siblings), before moving south toward Blit. They arrived in Blit not long before the Tasaday were discovered (cf. Mabandos 1989).

Blit social and trade intercourse was oriented to the north, where the Blit Manobo had consanguineal and affinal relatives. Blit relations with the Tasaday began in 1972, with the marriage of Sindi, Datu Dudim's daughter, to the Tasaday Balayem. Before that time, there was no social or trade intercourse between Blit and the Tasaday.[10]

Analysis

The present research supports the genealogical data accumulated by other field researchers in the early 1970s. The addition of three generations of Real Tasaday to the four earlier reported has effectively extended the time horizon to 175 years (assuming that each generation is 25 years).

The seven Real Tasaday charts produced by the earlier researchers show high convergence in all key respects. There are minor variations in names between charts in terms of orthography and phonetics but on the whole there is strong agreement. Variances are also noted in respondents' birthplaces; and one individual (Ukan) who died in late 1971 or early 1972 was not included in the first two charts but was included in later charts after relatives identified him when shown photographs. Earlier charts showed unnamed young children whose names were placed on later charts, in accordance with the claimed practice of naming a child only after it "begins to smile in response to another person's smile."

In contrast, the Tasaday Poseur charts almost completely contradict the Real Tasaday charts in all key aspects. Furthermore, the Poseur charts do not indicate whether the individuals shown are living or dead, do not specify the gender of nine individuals, and erroneously identify a Tboli male, Doloy (Figure 13), as a Tasaday female, Dul. In addition, there are irreconcilable deviations within the set of Poseur charts itself. For example, the female Dul is shown in one chart as

"Tasaday Poseur" Bonga
Mantang or Kumander
Machinegun (incorrectly
identified as Tasaday Lolo)
(photo by Jun Casquejo 1988)

FIGURE 2

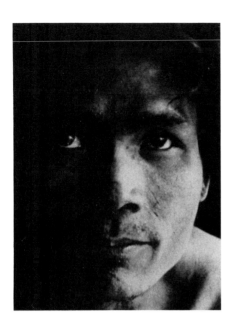

"Real Tasaday" Mahayag, son of
Kuletaw and Sikey (photo by
John Nance 1972)

"Tasaday Poseur" Kafal Ayunan
(incorrectly identified as Tasaday
Mahayag) (photo by John Nance
1972)

FIGURE 3

"Real Tasaday" Adug, son of
Kuletaw and Sikey (photo by
John Nance 1972)

"Tasaday Poseur" Yabis Baham
(incorrectly identified as Tasaday
Adug) (photo by Jun Casquejo
1988)

FIGURE 4

"Real Tasaday" Gintuy, son of
Kuletaw and Sikey (photo by
John Nance 1972)

"Tasaday Poseur" Fidlo Swing
(incorrectly identified as Tasaday
Gintuy) (photo by Jun Casquejo
1988)

FIGURE 5

"Real Tasaday" Lefonok, son of
Basiw (photo by John Nance
1972)

"Tasaday Poseur" Saay Baleg
(incorrectly identified as Tasaday
Lefonok) (photo by Jun Casquejo
1988)

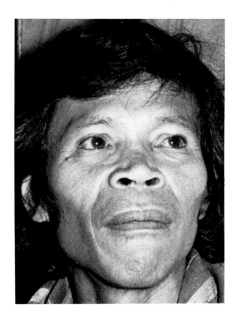

FIGURE 6

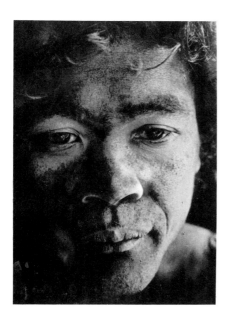

"Real Tasaday" Udelen, son of
Basiw (photo by John Nance
1972)

"Tasaday Poseur" Yong
Balungay (incorrectly identified
as Tasaday Udelen) (photo by
Jun Casquejo 1988)

FIGURE 7

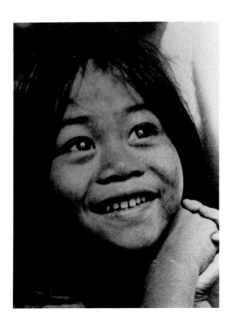

"Real Tasaday" Natek, son of
Bilangan and Etut (photo by John
Nance 1972)

"Tasaday Poseur" Bulaha Antew
(incorrectly identified as Tasaday
Natek) (photo by Jun Casquejo
1988)

FIGURE 8

"Real Tasaday" Biking, son of Mahayag and Dula (photo by Robert B. Fox 1971)

"Tasaday Poseur" Luding Otam (incorrectly identified as Tasaday Biking) (photo by Jun Casquejo 1988)

FIGURE 9

"Real Tasaday" Lobo, son of
Bilangan and Etut (photo by
Robert B. Fox 1971)

"Tasaday Poseur" Datu Udol
Lambayen (incorrectly identified
as Tasaday Lobo) (photo by Jun
Casquejo 1988)

FIGURE 10

"Real Tasaday" Bilangan, son of
Sambel and Ti' (photo by John
Nance 1972)

"Tasaday Poseur" Tinda Dayaw
(incorrectly identified as Tasaday
Bilangan) (photo by Jun
Casquejo 1988)

FIGURE 11

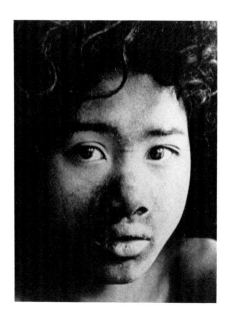

"Real Tasaday" Lolo, son of
Bilangan and Etut (photo by John
Nance 1972)

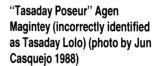

"Tasaday Poseur" Agen
Magintey (incorrectly identified
as Tasaday Lolo) (photo by Jun
Casquejo 1988)

FIGURE 12

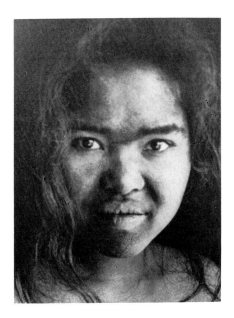

"Real Tasaday" Dul, daughter of
Kaong and Ulan (photo by John
Nance 1972)

"Tasaday Poseur" Doloy Bodul, a
male (incorrectly identified as
female Tasaday Dul) (photo by
Jun Casquejo 1988)

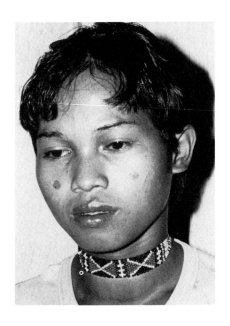

FIGURE 13

the daughter of a female by the name of Glaya (Salazar 1986) and in another chart as the daughter of a different female by the name of Luan (Salazar 1988); and the siblings Si-us and Maman are given two different biological parents—"Saay" (Lefonok) in 1986, and "Doloy" (Dul) and "Yong" (Udelen) in 1988 (see Tables 1 and 2).

The Poseur charts (Salazar 1986, 1988) show two sets of names for each person (see Table 1). One set (shown in column 2 of Table 1) is identical with the names of Real Tasaday; Salazar labeled this set "fictive." The names in the other set are claimed by Salazar to be the "original" names of Tboli and Manobo individuals who posed as Tasaday (column 1). Our research showed (see Table 2) that the Tboli-Ubo Poseurs are separate individuals from the Real Tasaday per-

TABLE 1
List of the 17 "Tasaday Poseurs"

Original Tboli/Manobo Names[a] (in alphabetical order)	Fictive Tasaday Names
1. Agen [Magintey] (in 1986) (M)	Lolo
Bonga [Mantang] (in 1988) (M)	Lolo
2. Bedula Tusina [To'Sina] (F)	Dula
3. Bulaha [Antew] (M)	Natek
4. Doloy [Bodul] (F)	Dul
5. Ebak (M)	Blayem/Bayem [Balayem]
6. Etet Tamwalang (F)	Etut
7. Fedlo [Fidlo Swing] (M)	Gintui [Gintuy]
8. Gina [Dina] (F)	Siyel [Si-el]
9. Kafal [Ayunan] (M)	Mahayag
10. Kultow/Kwitow (M)	Kuletaw
11. Luding [Otam] (M)	Biking
12. Saay [Baleg] (M)	Lefonok
13. Sikdi/Sikul (sex not given)	Sikey
14. Tinda [Dayaw] (M)	Bilangan
15. Udol/Odol [Lambayan] (M)	Lobo
16. Yabes [Yabis] [Baham] (M)	Adug
17. Yong [Balungay] (M)	Udelen
18. no name entry (F)	Kalis
19. no name entry (M)	Udo
20. no name entry (M)	Ukan
21. no name entry (M)	Sasa
22. no name entry (M)	Siyus [Si-us]
23. no name entry (M)	Mamman [Maman]
24. no name entry (M)	Tekaf
25. no name entry (M)	Ginun
26. no name entry (M)	Ilib

[a]Based on Salazar 1986 and 1988. Where our spelling differs from Salazar's, we have put our spelling in brackets; likewise, last names of individuals in the left column supplied by us, and not provided by Salazar, also are in brackets; symbols indicating sex (M/F) are Salazar's.

TABLE 2

Real Tasaday and Tasaday Poseurs

Names of the 26 Real Tasaday individuals in 1971–72 (listed in alphabetical order)[a]	Real names of Poseurs incorrectly identified as the Tasaday person in the left column
1. Adug (M)	Yabis Baham (M)
2. Balayem (M)	Ibek Kote (died 1970s)
3. Biking (M)	Luding Otam (M)
4. Bilangan (M)	Tinda Dayaw (M)
5. Dul (F)	Doloy Bodul (M)
6. Dula (F)[b]	Dula (F) (same person)
7. Etut (F)	Etet Tamwalang (nonexistent)
8. Gintuy (M)	Fidlo Swing (M)
9. Ginun (dead) (M)	no poseur named
10. Ilib (died 1979) (M)	no poseur named
11. Kalis (F)	no poseur named
12. Kuletaw (died March 1988) (M)	Kultow (M), son of Datu Dalembang Bon (died post-WW2)
13. Lefonok (M)	Saay Baleg (M)
14. Lobo (M)	Udol Lambayen (M)
15. Lolo (M)	Agen Magintey (M) also Bonga Mantang (M) (alias Kum. Machinegun)
16. Mahayag (M)	Kafal Ayunan (M)
17. Maman (M)	no poseur named
18. Natek (M)	Bulaha Antew (M)
19. Odoq (M)	no poseur named
20. Sasa (died 1979) (M)	no poseur named
21. Sikey (F)	no poseur named
22. Si-el/Siyel-Dina (F)[c]	Dina (F) (same person)
23. Si-us/Siyus (M)	no poseur named
24. Tikaf (dead) (M)	no poseur named
25. Udelen (M)	Yong Balungay (M)
26. Ukan (died 1972) (M)	no poseur named

[a]Data based on Rogel-Rara and Nabayra (1988–89).

[b]Dula, the Real Tasaday, and Dula the "Poseur" are one and the same person. Her original name was Dula (when she was the wife of Mahayag); later, when she was the wife of Banas Dayong in Lemfenek, she was called "Bedula."

[c]Si-el was later named "Dina" by her parents (Mahayag and Dula) to honor Tboli Fludi Tuan, who has a daughter named Dina.

sonalities they were supposed to be. In Table 2, the Real Tasaday identities are shown in column 1 and the real identities of Poseurs are shown in column 2.

It was noted that the Poseur charts fail to account for 6 persons who appear in the Real Tasaday charts. Another curious discrepancy is the giving of the same Real Tasaday name (Lolo) to 2 Poseurs (Agen and Bonga, shown in Figures 12 and 2) in two charts of Salazar's set.

In terms of family units and genealogical connections, Salazar shows the Tasaday Poseurs as part of six different extended family units, each with different sets of ancestors linked to each other through marriage with Manobo and Tboli families residing outside the forest. In contrast, the ethnographers' charts of the Real Tasaday show all family units tracing lineage back to a common male ancestor in the forest and that all of the Real Tasaday were born in that habitat. The Poseurs, according to Salazar, were all farmers residing outside the forest, although his charts fail to cite places of residence.

Our own investigation of the Tasaday Poseurs indicates that they are, indeed, Tboli and Tboli-Ubo farmers, most of them residing in the agricultural village of S'lung, just inside of the southwestern border of the Tasaday Preserve, and that they began laying claim to Tasaday identities only very recently, around 1986. They admitted that they had been offered incentives of land within Tasaday and/ or cash in order to impersonate specific Tasaday individuals.

Our attempt to confirm Salazar's Tasaday Poseur charts of 1986 and 1988 led us to realize that, although some portions of these charts are correct, one chart ("Elizir Boone's Relationship with the Tasaday") appears to be a composite of several charts, with some connecting entries that are erroneous or fabricated. For example, the portion showing Elizir Boone's ascendants all the way to Datu Belagen starts off as accurate and factual; the supposed connection between Datu Dudim's wife Luan and "Tinda (Bilangan)" is a total fabrication; Datu Dudim and Luan have only one offspring, Mafalo, not "Doloy (Dul)"; and the portion on "Kafal (Mahayag)" and "Bedula (Dula)" has been totally denied by the persons concerned.

Two charts, "Blayem [Balayem]" and "Bedula Tusina [To'Sina]," start off accurate, but are flawed by the insertion of a personality who does not belong to the family.[11] The first of these, the "Blayem" chart, shows the parents and siblings of Igna Kilam (former wife of Mafalo Dudim). "Ebak (Bayem)," however, is an artificial insertion. The only "Ebak" known in the area (whose name is actually Ibek Kote) was only distantly related to Igna and he—Ibek—died in April 1973. There was nobody called "Bayem" in the area. The second chart, the "Bedula Tusina" chart, resembles the true genealogical chart of Datu To'Sina's family, except that, again, an imposter has been inserted, in this case "Bedula." In actual fact, To'Sina has only one daughter, Kloguy, wife of Lobong Badang. His other children are males: Bongut (also known as Fidlo), Wel, Ambut, and Ugot. There is no "Bedula" in To'Sina's family; however, To'Sina's distant nephew, Banas Dayong, is the husband of Tasaday Dula, who was formerly the wife of Tasaday Mahayag.

Our own composite chart of the Tasaday Poseurs (Rogel-Rara and Nabayra 1988a, 1988b, 1988c, 1989), which goes back several generations, was constructed from information provided by the Poseurs themselves in field interviews conducted at their respective homes in the presence of their families. This was principally from August 1988 to May 1989, and confirmed by knowledgeable parties in the area.

An interesting fact that came to light in the course of these interviews is that, as the Tasaday married into the larger tribal marital system, some Poseurs became their relatives by affinity. Poseur Agen Magintey probably has the most in-laws among the Tasaday. With the marriage of his sister Funding to Lobo, he now has affinal ties with Bilangan, Etut, Lobo, and Lobo's brothers, Lolo, Natek, and Degu. Through his brother Salim, who married Lefonok's daughter Kalis, Agen now has affinal ties with Lefonok and his son Odoq.

The more interesting aspects of the new genealogical information appear to be the following:

1. Even before the time of the earliest remembered progenitors of the Real Tasaday—Lubas and Layas—they were already living in their *Ilib Fusaka* ("ancestral cave").

2. On the other hand, it turns out that the Blit Manobo are relative newcomers to the area. The progenitors of the present Blit population were inhabitants of places many days' walk away from the present Blit. Datu Dudim's ancestors were inhabitants of Kulaman Valley, ten days' walk northwest from Blit. Their descendants gradually found their way to Kolukit, one-and-a-half day's walk northwest from Blit, and only after several generations did they reach Blit. Datu Dudim, one of the earliest settlers in Blit, was born in Tafel, one day's walk to the northwest from Blit. Dudim and family first moved eastward to Afag, and from Afag, one day's walk due north from Blit, moved to Blit only recently. (Dudim's father, Datu Belagen, is buried in a place between Tafel and Afag, although he visited Blit during his lifetime. Mafalo, Datu Dudim's 45-year-old son, was born in Afag and came to Blit as a young man.) Blit itself has moved several times within the locality and, since 1971, has moved several kilometers closer to the Tasaday home site.

3. Although sporadic contacts were made by the Tasaday with the Tboli-Ubo hunter Dafal prior to 1971, these cor.'acts did not give rise to regular intercourse between the Tasaday and the Tboli-Ubo or Blit Manobo. The normal direction of Blit social and economic intercourse was oriented to the north, where they had many relatives, consanguineal and affinal, and of whose socioeconomic system they were a part.

The data show that all Tasaday marriages before 1972 were with members of other forest bands, primarily with the Tasafang. Etut, who is reported to be from Sanduka, said she was born in Tasafang to Sindan (her father) and Bengen (her mother), but when Bilangan's parents met with them to arrange her marriage to Bilangan, they met in Sanduka.

Etut said there was only one main cave in Tasafang, although it was comfortable and could accommodate many people. Dul, Dula, and Balayem recalled that this cave had sheltered more residents than were in Tasaday in the early 1970s. Dula, however, was the last bride from Tasafang. Her mother, Okot, was a sister of Dul's mother, Ulan. Because Dula grew up in Tasafang, it was not realized that her bridegroom, Mahayag, was actually her first cousin on her mother's side. Sikey, the mother of Mahayag, is the surviving sister of Okot and Ulan.

For still not fully determined reasons, contact between Tasaday and Tasafang was cut off some time after the marriage of Mahayag and Dula. Some Tasaday say there were violent weather disturbances accompanied by landslides and that when some Tasaday finally reached Tasafang, there was no one there. Elderly residents of Maitum recall that in the past there was a period of extraordinarily severe weather disturbances that brought heavy floods. Mafalo recalls that, as a young man, he was almost washed away by flood waters in Blit. Other Manobo report that an earthquake once created a deep fissure in Kulaman Valley. And Tboli elders recall a period of violent eruptions of Mt. Matutum. Aside from these geophysical calamities, the recurrence of epidemic outbreaks should also be considered as a possible cause of the depopulation of Tasafang. Historical records show that smallpox epidemics decimated entire villages in Cotabato during the Spanish regime (Forrest 1780) and continued into the early years of American rule in the Philippines. Other epidemics killed many people during and after World War II. This subject could very well become the focus of future research.

From all indications, the loss of Tasafang made the problem of finding spouses more critical to the Tasaday in 1971 than had been generally understood. Left on their own, the only option then open to the Tasaday would have been incestuous unions—which they considered unthinkable, even though, unknowingly, some first-cousin marriage had already occurred. On the basis of the new genealogical data, it appears that, even if Tasafang had continued to exist as a source of spouses, it would not have provided a lasting solution because of genetic factors.

Sindi was the first non-Tasaday to marry into the group. Her marriage to Balayem, even if childless, marked the end of an era when Tasafeng was the *tufasan meliton*, "source of [Tasaday] spouses," and the opening of a new era in which Tasafeng was replaced by Blit and neighboring areas outside the forest as the new *tufasan meliton* or, in the contemporary term, the *tanaq bayi* (which is *tufasan meliton* translated into Blit Manobo).

Sindi was not an outcast from Blit. She is the daughter of Datu Dudim, acknowledged leader of the Blit Manobo; and her brother Mafalo is a recognized leader in his own right. Sindi and Mafalo were responsible for most of the 22 marriages that have taken place between the Tasaday and spouses from Blit and environs.

The Tasaday's entry into the much larger tribal social system has put many of the Tasaday's old values to the test. The divorce of Dula and Mahayag was one such occasion. This couple appeared to have had a long-held misunderstanding which could not be resolved under their old set of values, which stressed, among other things, the permanence of marriage ("till our hair turns gray"), monogamy, and unity and friendship within the group. It got to the point, however, when Dula asked Sindi for help. Sindi took Dula to Blit and asked her brother Mafalo to help. The details are not very clear on how Mafalo handled it, but the net effect was that Dula and Mahayag, with the help of Mafalo and Datu Dudim, agreed to part ways. Dula subsequently married a Tboli, Banas, and Mahayag got two new wives in place of the one he lost. Mahayag's multiple marriage also marked the end of an era when the Tasaday norm was monogamy and opened a new chapter

in Tasaday history where polygyny, as practiced in the tribal world outside the
forest, became an accepted fact of life in Tasaday.

As of May 1989, only Dul and Udelen among the elder Tasaday were un-
touched by the new departure in marriage customs. Bilangan, father of Lobo and
Lolo, had taken a second wife from Blit; Adug and Gintuy had two wives each;
Si-us also had two wives; Lobo, with three wives, had the most; and Balayem, as
earlier mentioned, now has two wives.

From the time of Sindi's entrance in 1972, all subsequent Tasaday marriages
have been with Blit Manobo or Tboli-Ubo. Consequently, in the G-5 generation
fully 50% are half-blooded Tasaday and only one-half are full-blooded Tasaday.
Since the only immediate source of spouses is Blit and its neighbors outside the
forest, the next generation will all be half-blooded Tasaday. No more pure Tasaday will be born.

Conclusion

The evidence that we have gathered makes it quite clear that Salazar's Poseur
charts are fatally flawed and that the "Real Tasaday" charts are valid and factual.
We have not only substantiated and confirmed the essentials of the earlier ethnographers' reports but we have also gone further and established the presence of at
least three earlier generations domiciled in the Tasaday cave habitat.

As to the reasons for the vast difference between the data and conclusions of
the original ethnographers and those of Professor Salazar, there are two possible
explanations:

1. The early ethnographers obtained their data from the Tasaday people
   themselves, whereas Salazar obtained his data from George Tanedo, in
   Manila, without ever going to the field. The early ethnographers spent
   many days in the field. Salazar, as he acknowledges in his "Third and
   Final Footnote on the Tasaday" (1988), obtained his data from Tanedo
   and companions on the night immediately before his morning lecture at
   the 1986 international conference at the University of the Philippines.

2. In effect the early ethnographers and Salazar were each describing *two
   entirely separate sets of people,* although Salazar may have been misled
   into believing that the Poseurs and the Real Tasaday were identical to
   each other.

In the course of our fieldwork, we located and interviewed all possible informants—Real Tasaday and Poseurs—and all other living informants in their
areas of habitat. We missed only the dead and the nonexistent.

On these bases, we can safely say that the Tasaday exist, that they are making
a successful adaptation to the 20th century, and that they are thriving and increasing in number in the Tasaday Preserve, the last climax forest of Mindanao, which
owes its survival to the Tasaday.

Notes

1. Important reports on the discovery of the Tasaday are Elizalde 1971a, 1971b; Elizalde
   with Fox 1971a, 1971b; Lynch and Llamzon 1971; Lynch et al. 1973; MacLeish 1972;

Nance 1975; National Geographic Society 1972; NBC-TV 1971; NDR-TV 1972; Panamin 1972; and Terry 1971. The important reports after 1985 are ABC-TV 1986; *Asiaweek* 1986; Adler 1986; Bailen 1986; Central Independent Television 1987; Committee on National Cultural Communities 1988; Dandan 1989; Hidalgo and Hidalgo
1989; Iten 1986a, 1986b, 1988; Iten and Lozano 1986; M. Lopez 1986; Malayang
1986; NBC-TV 1986; Peralta 1987; Salazar 1986; and Tan 1986. An unbiased up-to-
date review of the recent controversy appears in Grumet 1990.

2. Salazar presented three genealogical charts in 1986; he did not present a paper. Genealogical charts appended to Salazar's 1988 paper included: (1) "Genealogy based
from [sic] the book Discovery of the Tasaday . . . Nance, 1981"; (2) "Blessen Tong-
kay's [sic, Tunggay] relationship with the 'Tasaday' "; (3) "Elizir Boone's relationship with the 'Tasaday' "; (4) "Blayem's genealogy [Balayem is the brother of
Igna]"; (5) "Joel Boone's Relationship with the 'Tasaday' "; (6) "Bedula Tusina's
relationship with the 'Tasaday' "; (7) "Chart I [of] Tinda (Bilangan) and his relatives"; and (8) "Chart II [of] Etut (wife of Bilangan) and her relatives."

3. Only the bare outline of our study can be presented in this short chapter. The complete
study is in process of publication (Rogel-Rara and Nabayra 1988a, 1988b, 1988c,
1989). Scholars may place reservations for copies with the Tasaday Community Care
Foundation (P.O. Box M367 Makati Central Post Office, Metro Manila, Philippines).
Our studies are based partly on a series of 24 genealogical charts, too lengthy to be
reproduced herein. Microfiche copies of those 24 charts, with facial photographs of
the subjects, may also be ordered from the Foundation.

4. These are the first 17 names listed in Table 1 of this chapter.

5. We did trace down 3 individuals with the name Etet in the area, but none was connected to the Tamwalang family, and members of that family said they had no relative
by that name (Rogel-Rara and Nabayra 1988a, 1988b, 1988c, 1989).

6. Dula testified in a formal congressional inquiry that she had been forced by George
Tanedo to say falsely that she was only a Tboli named Bedula and that she only posed
as a Tasaday named Dula (Committee on National Cultural Communities 1988).

7. Cf. the genealogical charts and related kinship data of Elizalde with Fox 1971b; Fernandez and Lynch 1972; Rogel 1972; Yen and Nance 1976; Peralta 1971b; photographs in Nance 1975; Rogel-Rara and Nabayra 1988a, 1988b, 1988c, 1989; Adler
1986; Salazar 1986, 1988; Hyndman and Duhaylungsod 1990; Iten 1986a, 1986b,
1988, 1989; ABC-TV 1986; Central Independent Television 1987; Lerner 1989.

8. In this essay, "G-0" represents the earliest known generation, "Generation zero,"
"G-1" represents the first descending generation, "G-2" the second generation, etc.

9. The Kulaman Valley is situated at 6° 27′ N lat. and 124° 19′ E long, at an elevation
of 664 m above sea level. It is 32 km on a straight line from the Tasaday's cave site.

10. Due to space constraints, the complete history of Blit cannot be discussed in this essay.
It will either be published separately or incorporated in a forthcoming publication of
the Rogel-Rara and Nabayra report on Tasaday genealogy.

11. Salazar spells Balayem's name alternately as Blayem and Bayem.

Appendix
List of Respondents Interviewed, by Place of Residence

Note: The distances referred to below in kilometers refer to straight-line kilometers; distances would be greater when traveled on foot (see Figure 1)

I. Inside the Tasaday rain forest (the area marked with dotted lines in Figure 1)

1. Bilangan	14. Okon	27. Kumbong Kebet
2. Lefonok	15. Odoq	28. Sabi Igot
3. Udelen	16. Kalis	29. Kading Igot
4. Balayem	17. Adug	30. Bining Talusan
5. Mahayag	18. Gintuy	31. Memit Mufak
6. Dul	19. Biking	32. Sin'ay Mufak
7. Etut	20. Sindi Dudim	33. Gili Gun
8. Lolo	21. Sule Dudim	34. Sita Gun
9. Lobo	22. Salim Magintey	35. Linsu Ulet
10. Natek	23. Funding Magintey	36. Suwal Tekay
11. Degu	24. Ning Inangkol	37. Saduwen Mindal
12. Si-us	25. Lufin Tikaw	38. Lu'ing Lagasi
13. Maman	26. Lewin Fayon	39. Fandey Gun

II. Talahek, a Tboli-Ubo settlement along the Fenek River, just inside the eastern border of the Reserve and 7 km east of the Tasaday caves:

1. Banas Dayong	3. Insik Kafal
2. Dula, daughter of Ba'wel (Bauwe) Fasan	4. Itet Lungkol

III. Lemfenek, a Tboli-Ubo settlement near Talahek and 1 km east of the Reserve:

1. M'ning Wali	2. Si-el/Dina, daughter of Mahayag

IV. Takboh, a Tboli-Ubo settlement at the junction of Kanan Creek and Sefaka River, north of Datal Tabayong and 4 km east of the Reserve:

1. Datu Dafal Mindal	2. Kadling Dafal	3. Tinda Dayaw

V. Upper Sefaka, a Tboli-Ubo settlement along the Sefaka River, north of Takboh and 7 km northeast of the Reserve:

1. Datu Udol Lambayen

VI. Kasab/Tobak area, a Tboli-Ubo-Manobo settlement located within the northeastern borders of the Reserve:

1. Datu Galang Tikaw

VII. Subeng Lamuyon, a Tboli-Ubo-Manobo settlement located at the junction of the Lamuyon Creek and the Lawa River, inside the Reserve and 3 km northwest of the Tasaday caves:

1. Agen Magintey

VIII. Blit, a Tboli-Ubo-Manobo settlement located at the junction of the Blit Creek and the Lawa River, inside the Reserve and 4 km southwest of the Tasaday caves:

1. Datu Dudim	5. Dion Boone	9. Abilin Talawud
2. Datu Magafid	6. Bol Dudim	10. Abilin Gun
3. Mafalo Dudim	7. Unggo Lugata	11. Luan To'bong
4. Totoq Dudim	8. Bonga Mantang/ Kumander Machinegun	12. Klaya (Glaya)

IX. Lakag Fenohok, a Tboli-Ubo and Manobo settlement inside the Reserve and located near Blit Creek, north of the Blit settlement and 5 km west of the Tasaday caves:

1. Datu Sulaw and his family

X. Eldolug, a Tboli-Ubo-Manobo settlement located just inside the northwestern corner of the Reserve:

1. Datu Lasang   2. To' Ani

XI. Kabatang, a Tboli-Ubo-Manobo settlement located along Kabatang Creek (a tributary of the Sungen River), and 1 km west of the Reserve:

1. Datu To'Sina   2. Datu Kitab Sina

XII. S'lung, a Tboli-Ubo and Manobo settlement located just inside the western boundary of the Reserve:

1. Datu Mantang Tuan	5. Kafal Ayunan	9. Yong Balungay
2. Tafiduh Mantang	6. Bulaha Antew	10. Luding Otam
3. Kumander Indab Labyan	7. Saay Baleg	11. Lobong Badang
4. Kafelya Labyan	8. Doloy Bodul	12. Yabis Baham

XIII. Tafel, a Tboli-Ubo and Manobo settlement located at the junction of the Tafel Creek and the Sungen River, and 4 km west of the Reserve:

1. Noli (Kalan) Sakong   2. Ben Sakong

XIV. Ufoh, a Tboli settlement along the Ufoh creek (a tributary of the Kalaong River), located halfway between the southern boundary of the Reserve and the seacoast:

1. Perido Kusin

XV. S'daff (or Matinaw), a Manobo settlement at the junction of the Sungen River and the Balwen River, 16 km northwest of the Reserve:

1. Tanggal Mayo	3. Igna Kilam	5. Mugal Kilam
2. Eddie (Ugtot) Mayo	4. Takil Kilam	

XVI. M'luk, a Manobo settlement along the Balwen River, just across from S'daff and 8 km northwest of the Reserve:

1. Fengeq Ibek

XVII. Besag, a Manobo settlement along the Balwen River about a day's hike south of S'daff and 12 km west of the Reserve:

1. Datu Ampak and his family

XVIII. Lengge'en, a Manobo settlement 1 km south from Besag and 12 km west of the Reserve:

1. Datu Teves and his family

XIX. Kalibuhan, a Manobo settlement located at the headwaters of the Kraan River, about 3 hours' hike south of Besag and 15 km west of the Reserve:

1. Kumander Mamalu

XX. Maitum town, formerly a Tboli settlement and now a residence of Ilokano and Bisayan settlers as well as Tboli, located along the Celebes Sea, south of the Daguma Mountain Range, about 20 km. south of the Reserve:

1. Sanyat (Pilar) Boone-Tanedo	4. Franklin Tanedo
2. Famfayan Tasig-Boone	5. Blessen Boone Tunggay-Tanedo
3. John Boone	6. Joel or Junwel Boone

XXI. Kemato or Tboli town, a Tboli settlement at the headwaters of the Allah River, about 28 km east of the Reserve.

1. Mayor Mai Tuan
2. Fludi Tuan
3. Dad Tuan

● *chapter seven*

The Tasaday Language: Evidence for Authenticity?

Carol H. Molony

T he crux of the view that the Tasaday are a hoax, in my opinion, is as follows: Several adults and children from tribal groups in South Cotabato, speaking as their first language more than one language, were coaxed to masquerade, from time to time, as monolingual speakers of a heretofore unknown language, and to live in caves, to use stone tools, to wear orchid-leaf clothing, and to deny knowledge of domestication of plants or animals or of people and the world outside of their forest.

Contrast this with the editor's statement in the introduction to this volume: "A small band of people known as Tasaday lived in caves in the southern Philippines following a stone tool–using foraging mode of subsistence, without iron, eating only wild foods, and having no contact with agricultural peoples until the 1960s."[1]

The hoax theory continues as follows: Whenever investigators were to arrive (and their pending arrival was supposedly announced in advance), then these people left their villages and fields to enter the forest and the caves; they appeared as "Stone Age survivors"; and after the investigators left, they returned to their villages and fields outside of the forest.

What kinds of evidence could possibly be used to settle this controversy? Unlike the "Piltdown Man" hoax, we cannot use a new chemical technique to shed new light on old data. On the one hand, we have much better evidence: the people in question are still alive and talking. On the other hand, important evidence can no longer be gathered; due to extensive contact with neighboring peoples since 1971–72, the Tasaday have had ample opportunity to learn new languages and technologies. Most important, however, I believe that some of the preliminary research, done in 1971 and 1972, gives ample evidence of who these people really are and of their heritage.

I collected linguistic and social anthropological data in two visits to the Tasaday totaling two weeks in 1972. During both visits I tape-recorded conversations of these people, which I transcribed and analyzed between my two trips and after them. The data I collected, my analyses, the agreement of my data with those of the two linguists who had visited them earlier (for even shorter periods of time), and the agreement with the other kinds of data gathered by myself and the other scientists, show that it is highly unlikely that the people called the Tasaday were recruited from neighboring tribes to be part of a hoax. The linguistic data offer the strongest arguments that these people were authentically separated from their "more modern" neighbors (that is, those with agriculture and other advancements), at least in recent times.

How Linguistic Research Can Shed Light on the History of a Speech Group

Language has proven to be an effective though indirect source of evidence of a people's history and intensity of contact with speakers of other languages. There are three immediate reasons for this. First, language is conservative; that is, language forms remain long after they (and their object) become obsolete. Second, language use is shared regularly among its speakers. Third, language regularly reflects other aspects of the social behavior and material culture of its speakers, including innovations, whether created or borrowed.

In making judgments about a people's past history, linguists look for the corroboration of other kinds of data when available, for example: (1) historical records, whether written or oral; (2) physical characteristics of people (ranging from the broad category of racial characteristics to the more specific such as blood type or blood indications of previous contact with communicable diseases—measles, chicken pox, etc., known to be introduced to Southeast Asia only in the last few hundred years); (3) material culture, both current and past as determined by archaeological investigation; and (4) social and cultural characteristics, such as kinship structure, religion, and subsistence type(s).

My Introduction to the Tasaday

When I heard the reports in 1986 of the hoax claim, I reflected on how I was first asked to visit the Tasaday back in 1972. I had wondered why the invitation came to me. Filipino linguists could have learned a new Philippine language faster than I, and American linguists of the Summer Institute of Linguistics (SIL) had worked for years with Manobo languages, the group of which the Tasaday language had already been clearly shown to be a member. Nevertheless, on a short business trip to Manila from Ternate, Cavite Province, Philippines (where I was two years into a three-year study of changes since the 17th century of Philippine Creole Spanish and its speakers), I received a call from the ethnobotanist Douglas Yen asking me to come down to Mindanao for even a short time to do a pilot sociolinguistic study; he needed a linguist to help him in the elicitation of useful plants and their names. Richard Elkins, the SIL linguist who had first accompanied Yen (and whom I had recommended to Yen), had just fallen ill and had to leave the field. Yen knew that I was experienced in doing historical reconstructions of Philippine languages and the cultures of their speakers. I was too curious not to go see these people and their rain forest for myself.

I had been as skeptical in 1972 as other social scientists with whom I had talked, and had tried to find an explanation for the surprising reports. One explanation for the reports was exaggeration, by far the most likely one, in my estimation. Another possibility was that it was a plain hoax, and a third was that some children had somehow been left in the forest (perhaps to escape warfare or disease) and had grown to adulthood there alone, growing up without learning much of their parents' culture. Yet another explanation was that the Tasaday were genuine foragers living in the forest for centuries until the rapid decline of Mindanao's forest in the 20th century brought them into contact with agriculturalists. In retrospect, this last explanation, of rapid deforestation, received far too little attention back then.

Field Conditions

My 1972 field research with the Tasaday was short—just 14 days total—because I was taking time away from my ongoing research in Luzon to the north. Some of what I saw while I was with them continued to feed my suspicion about them. I noticed that they had a few bits of cotton cloth and baskets in the back of their cave, and when I inquired about this, John Nance told me that Elizalde had asked them to put these things away. Also, I saw about ten words on my lists which were different from those on the several lists gathered by earlier researchers. The importance of their speech in containing clues to their past became ever more evident.

At the beginning of my short visits to the Tasaday I used a multilingual research assistant (a term more appropriate for his role than "translator"). As my competence increased, I moved toward monolingual interaction with the Tasaday, so that about 40% of the 800 word vocabulary and half of the 45 pages of texts I subsequently published (Molony with Tuan 1976) were gathered without the help of a translator. In order to accomplish monolingual interaction, I used accepted linguistic elicitation techniques. For example, the first utterances I learned in Tasaday were "How do you say X?" and "What do you call X (pointing to something) in Tasaday?" Table 1 shows the distribution of these 800 vocabulary items.

I expected to find in Tasaday speech, as in every other Philippine language, words borrowed from Sanskrit, Chinese, and Spanish. I carried to South Cotabato volumes on vocabulary from these sources in Philippine languages. The historical dates of the first Philippine contacts with speakers of these source languages are known; therefore, presence or absence of borrowed words would give clues to times of contact. Because the 1971 reports had indicated the absence of agriculture among the Tasaday, and because an ethnobotanist was in the field to investigate this claim, I especially wanted to search for terms associated with agriculture in Tasaday speech as evidence of recent knowledge of agriculture. To that end I carried with me Harold Conklin's (1957) publication, which included a list of some 200 words commonly associated with agriculture in Philippine languages.

In gathering Tasaday vocabulary I had the opportunity to use the lists of the earlier researchers, particularly Teodoro Llamzon (1971b) and Richard Elkins (1971, 1972). I checked these lists and built from them. Using the lists of Sanskrit

TABLE 1

Types of Words in 800-Word Vocabulary

Total Number:
  136 Adjectives:
            81, plus
                    4 color terms
                    18 terms of number, quantity
                    12 demonstratives
                    12 time terms
                    9 direction terms
  400 Nouns:
            28, plus
                    31 environment (e.g., rainbow, cloud, forest)
                    10 cultural, plus:
                        6 betel chew, etc.
                        5 people
                        8 clothes and adornment
                        9 material goods: fire drill, etc.
                        12 re making palm starch
                        22 re hunting
                        10 medicine, disease, accidents
                        17 pronouns
                        17 kin terms
                        10 status (e.g., widow)
                    106 human and animal body parts, exudations
                    66 animals
                    43 re plants, plant parts, stages of growth
  219 Verbs (mostly action: to move, to cut, to run, etc.)
  34 Grammatical markers: 25, plus 9 emphatics
  11 Exclamations, interjections

  800 Total

and Chinese loan words into Philippine languages compiled by the Filipino linguists Arsenio Manuel (1948) and Juan Francisco (1964), and my knowledge of Spanish and English loan words in Philippine languages, I searched for evidence of contact with speakers of those languages and with neighbors who had borrowed from them.

Results of My Linguistic Analysis

No Spanish loan words were to be found in the Tasaday speech, especially those commonly borrowed into Philippine languages, with the possible exception of *tata* (father), a word found in many places in the world. Isidore Dyen (personal communication, 1974) points out that the etymology of this word is enigmatic, and it can hardly be used by itself for interpretation of late contact. That probably no Spanish and certainly no English words were borrowed is one of indirect evidence for relative isolation. That Tasaday readily learned to use many English words during 1971–72 indicates that they were not indisposed to borrowing words.

Admittedly, *absence* of forms is a weaker argument than presence of forms. What loans could one expect to find in Tasaday? One response might be to look at loan words borrowed into neighboring and related languages. I looked into a published vocabulary of another Manobo language, that of Central Mindanao Manobo done by the Elkinses (Elkins and Elkins 1954). Their 1,000-word vocabulary shows some 42 loans from Spanish and four from English. The majority of these are words for introduced tangible items, such as the Spanish *ahus* (garlic), *asuka* (sugar), and *baka* (cow), and from English *abukadu* (avocado). Other loans are for reckoning time: *birnis* (Friday) and *wibis* (Thursday) from Spanish. These words would not be expected without the associated artifact or concept. A few loan words that one might expect to find in Tasaday because of their presence in neighboring languages are *abri* (open), *kanta* (song), *diskursu* (speech), *piru* (but). I was not successful in eliciting these words from the Tasaday people.

It may be relevant to mention here that Tasaday has words not shared by its neighbors, for example, 'sun/day' *(fəglo'on)*, 'moon' *(sebang)*, and 'star' *(tub-ali)*. 'Sun,' 'moon,' and 'star' are considered among the most basic words in any language. Cognates with other Philippine languages do appear, however, for 'sun' *(adaw)* and 'moon' *(bulan)*, hidden among Tasaday plant names: *bulan kay* (moon tree) and *lawingan adaw* (day vine). It is difficult to make a case for the antiquity of the Tasaday on the basis of these words, but they are tentative evidence for lack of extensive contact between the Tasaday and other related language groups. That we find no lexical relics of the "more advanced" subsistence and social systems of neighbors of the Tasaday is another indirect indication of a long period of isolation.

Many words have been borrowed from neighboring non-Manobo languages, including Tboli and Tiruray. These could have been borrowed by Proto-Manobo speakers, or later, for example, after Tasaday became separated from other Manobo speakers. Analysis of sound shifts of cognates between these languages would reveal clues to migrations and contacts between these peoples. (Charles Frake, then of Stanford University and now of SUNY, Buffalo, in a personal communication, May 23, 1974, cited Tasaday '*ə fəl,* 'brother-in-law,' which would be *'əfəg* if inherited from Proto-Central-Philippine.)

The Tasaday said back in 1971–72 that they knew of no people outside their forest until they met the trader Dafal, a Blit Manobo. Beginning sometime around 1960, Dafal had come to see them many times, staying for long periods of time, and teaching them to use many advanced techniques and tools. Yen said in his 1976 publication on the ethnobotany of the Tasaday (Yen and Nance 1976) that the best historical control we have on technical lexical inventory with the Tasaday is that associated with the making of caryota palm starch, *natək,* since Dafal is said to have taught the process only about 12 years before our 1972 period of fieldwork. Of the eight words Yen lists associated with *natək* making, five are cognates with Blit Manobo while three are not. This count suggests that Tasaday may use some words for *natək* that were already in their linguistic inventory before they were taught the process by Dafal. Trapping also may be associated with words already existing in the Tasaday language. In summary, the lexical inventory in these domains tends to corroborate the thesis that the Tasaday had little or no contact, until Dafal's appearance, with their neighbors after those neighbors developed their present technical skills and culture.

There is one possible piece of contradictory evidence to the thesis that the Tasaday's closest affiliation is with Manobo from which it has been separated for many generations, namely, that Tasaday plant names and terms for plant forms and parts, according to Yen's data collection, are skewed toward the Tboli language. That is, Tboli seems to have had a real influence on this specialized vocabulary. This may be a very weak indication of relatively recent contact. (My surmise is, of course, necessarily tentative.)

Back in 1972, the researchers were especially interested in the lack of agriculture. Seeking to answer which was the more plausible, whether Tasaday lost the knowledge of agriculture or whether they never knew it in the first place, the 1971–72 publications tended toward the latter viewpoint. Tasaday, however, is clearly a Central Philippine language, and it is widely agreed that Proto-Central-Philippine speakers had agriculture. This, then, argues for the viewpoint that the Tasaday were an agricultural people who for some reason dropped that subsistence pattern and all its trappings when they undertook a forest-gathering subsistence, even though such a shift overwhelmingly contradicts current knowledge about changing subsistence patterns. There are many cases of hunter-gatherers who later became agriculturalists; that this direction could be reversed is less plausible but not impossible. Robert Blust, then at the University of Leiden in Holland and now at the University of Hawaii (personal communication, 1974), reports that the Punan, or Penan, of Borneo have completely dropped agriculture to take up hunting and gathering. (This same argument for the Punan has been more recently taken up by Carl Hoffman [1984, 1986].) similarly, local inhabitants on Halmahera, Eastern Moluccas, Indonesia, reported to me in 1974 that some Tobelo speakers had left their agricultural home on the coast to escape taxes imposed by regional kings and Europeans and had become hunters and gatherers in the inland forests. Thus, the hypothesis of the Tasaday undergoing the cultural loss of agriculture appears to have parallels in other Southeast Asian contexts.

One possible language test for the presence of agriculture in the past is this: we already know Tasaday is a Central Philippine language. One of its features as a Central Philippine language is regular sound shifts corresponding with those of other Central Philippine languages from Proto-Austronesian. These can be demonstrated through a series of changes from Proto-Austronesian to Proto-Philippine to Central Philippine to Proto-Manobo to Tasaday. Now, the best evidence we have so far, though tentative, indicates that agriculture was widespread among Central Philippine language speakers. Robert Fox (personal communication, 1974) presented evidence that Tabon cave dwellers in Palawan had agriculture at least 4,000 years ago. Widespread use of pottery along with other finds such as shell knives for harvesting in other parts of the Philippines, including the Bisayan Islands, indicates that agriculture was widespread there early also.

We could use language as indirect evidence of Central Philippine agriculture, first by comparing a large set of words indicative of agriculture in several Central Philippine languages[2] and then examining these words in the light of an analysis of sound correspondences indicating relative times of separation from Central Philippine languages. If cognates for these "agricultural" terms were found to be widespread among Central Philippine languages, and if these cognates reflected the regular sound changes that had taken place after the splits of these languages from parent stock, we would have indirect evidence for Central Philippine agriculture before the split. We could run the same test on the descendant languages of Proto-Manobo. If Tasaday demonstrated the regular sound shifts common to other Manobo languages, then even though we could not find words strongly suggesting agriculture, we would have indirect evidence that the Tasaday are descendants of people who at one time had agriculture. Evidence of Proto-Manobo agriculture would be in conflict with the lack of evidence for Tasaday itself, since we have not found Tasaday words clearly indicating agriculture. The conservative nature of languages would indicate that agriculture had not been dropped recently by Tasaday, else we would find vestigial agricultural words. Preliminary steps toward this endeavor indicate that Central Philippine languages show long presence of agriculture. This still leaves open the possibility that some Proto-Manobo people may have been preagricultural. Though Yen and I both focused heavily on this domain in our questioning of the Tasaday, our observation of their work, and our listening to their conversations, the tiny vocabulary we were able to gather of terms related to the agricultural complex of other Philippine languages is hardly indicative of agriculture among the Tasaday.

Given Central Philippine language affiliation, one possibility remains that the Tasaday may be descendants of preagricultural peoples: it is possible that agriculturalists and preagriculturalists existed side by side in the Central Philippines, and that the Proto-Manobo people who migrated to Mindanao were preagriculturalists; this explanation is less plausible than the loss of agriculture explanation (see Table 2).

Yen searched for Tasaday words indicative of agriculture, but was able to find only *fəmula* (rather loosely translated as 'to plant') and *ləsung* ('mortar') and *sinong* ('pestle'), the latter two both associated with agriculture in other languages, but used by Tasaday exclusively for preparing betel chew. These three words hardly represent a lexical indication of agriculture in the present or recent past. Salazar (1971) suggested that 'grind' and 'grain' were implied as Tasaday words in Llamzon's report, but we searched in vain for such words among Tasaday speakers.

We first heard the term *fəmula* when, sitting with almost the entire group of Tasaday at the helipad (basking in sunshine but brooding over a recent Tasaday experience), I was suddenly distracted by a casual remark made by Bilangan. Doug Yen had been pointing out to me lowland weeds which had been introduced to the helipad by the wheels of the helicopter. In effect, we were continuing the ethnobotanical investigation there at the helipad while sitting with these people. We asked Bilangan what he knew about those plants. He responded that they were

TABLE 2

Tasaday Terms Related to 200 + Agricultural Terms in Other Philippine Languages[a]

filay	'to fell (tree)'	*dugi*	'thorn'
kali	'to dig (hole)'	*fanga'*	'branch'
kali biking, kalub	'digging stick'	*kayu*	'tree, wood'
kalu'	'disturbed soil around yam'	*kunul, lunit*	'bark, peeling'
tubu	'to grow'	*lubunan*	'woody stem'
fəmula	'to plant'	*lawa*	'tree trunk'
hinəmula	'to replant'	*da'un*	'leaf'
tana'	'earth, soil'	*kəli*	'exudate'
dəmuli'	'plant shoot'	*tugbun*	'leaf bud'
mələnək, nda' malaga	'immature'	*bulak*	'flower'
təgəlug	'immature yam'	*klu'on*	'plant (generic)'
bulbul	'hairy, of plants'	*dalem*	'seed'
bunga' dalem tana'	'edible root'	*dalid*	'root'

[a]Not included are 200 + Tasaday terms for plants, none of them domesticated.

new plants, confirming Yen's report. And then he pointed to another plant, a little tomato plant, saying that Fludi had planted it! (Fludi was one of Elizalde's aides.) I was astounded to hear the word *fəmula,* which means 'to plant' in surrounding languages. All of our concerted efforts (short of asking a leading question) had until this moment failed to elicit this word. Holding my breath and taking a quick glance at Yen, I quietly asked in Tasaday, "How did he plant it?" Bilangan replied that Fludi had been eating a tomato, and the seeds had dropped from his tomato. I then asked the big question: "What else can you *fəmula?*" He responded with information we had already heard (but with the word we had not yet heard up until the moment before), that after digging up a wild yam, they routinely toss the leaves back into the hole; this process is also called *fəmula.* They sometimes return after a few months to see if a new yam has grown, and frequently it has. After asking if there were other plants that could be "planted," and receiving a negative answer, I asked, "What are the ways in which one can plant?" Bilangan replied that there were only these two ways: tossing the yam leaves back into the hole, and (accidently) dropping the seeds on the ground. In neither case is the action deliberate, with the aim of getting a new plant.

As the language data continued to show separation from neighboring languages, my skepticism gradually diminished. That is not to say I no longer recognized that important questions remained unanswered. On the contrary, fundamental questions remained, such as why no agriculture? Why only 26 people? Why so little contact with neighbors so close by? Consistent with the language data were other experiences supporting the believability of the life-style of these people.

For example, my second visit to the Tasaday, in November 1972, was unannounced and came after the Tasaday had had some two months without any visits from outsiders. The helicopter breezed in over the forested mountains and dropped just four people at the hilltop landing: Dad Tuan, Fludi, Doug Yen, and me. We walked down to the stream and up the other side of the valley along the path through the trees to the tarpaulin overhang where the outsiders had been sleeping. Leaving our bags there, we went on to the caves. All of us were a little surprised that no Tasaday had come to greet us. At the caves the hearths were cold, but it was clear that people had been at the caves recently, for there were belongings and no accumulation of dust or debris that any breeze would have blown in. We called out, but heard no response. Back down at the stream, Yen and I decided to walk up it to look for people. Neither of us was so adept as the Tasaday at traveling along the stream. We had seen during the last visit that they moved swiftly and quietly, even while carrying little children and belongings, stepping and jumping from stone to stone, and only in the few places possible did they walk along the banks. We, in contrast, slipped on the stones now and then, splashing into the rocky but shallow stream.

After about a half hour (and perhaps an hour since arriving in the Tasaday's valley), we rounded a bend in the stream to encounter a group of seven Tasaday at a spot where many orchids grew. The Tasaday were hurriedly fashioning new orchid-leaf clothing and fitting them onto their bodies. As they greeted us, it was clear that we had interrupted them. But what was the clothing they were taking off? It too was of leaves. After completing their tasks, they greeted us again in their more usual effusive way (which we had grown accustomed to during our visits ending two months earlier). They told us that they had been near here when they heard the helicopter and, thinking Elizalde might be arriving, wanted to dress up for the occasion.

Conclusion

The hoax theory does not hinge on whether the Tasaday were completely isolated or not for the last several hundred years. In fact, John Nance, in his popular 1975 book *The Gentle Tasaday,* stated that they had baskets, cloth, knives, and other evidence of contact with neighbors. We know that the way dialects and languages emerge is by separation of speakers. That these people speak something real (not created) and believable as a Manobo language, indicates separation (not necessarily isolation).

Logically, it is very difficult to imagine that Elizalde or anyone else was clever enough to: (1) create a new language, with all the complexity of a real language, with expected divergence from neighboring languages; (2) recognize, then teach adults and children to avoid the myriad borrowings into other Philippine languages, many of which had been disguised over time; (3) coerce children to refrain from using their first language with their parents, and adults from lapsing into their usual language; (4) choreograph this language hoax with the complex of other cultural traits they displayed; *and* (5) coach these adults and children so thoroughly that they never slipped in their presentation to different investigators over a period of one-and-a-half years, even though they were usually interviewed when not all Tasaday were present, so they couldn't possibly keep track of each other's answers to questions.

My analysis has changed in these 18 years since I last saw the Tasaday, and since Oswald Iten's work (1986a, 1986b) was published four years ago announcing the hoax theory. First, I am more cautious about speaking of separation of the Tasaday speakers from other Manobos. I use the term "separation" rather than "isolation," especially within the last few generations. And second, I am struck as I was not then by the evidence of forest denudation in this century, and how it must have impacted on people accustomed to living entirely within its boundaries until recently.

Today the Tasaday find themselves subjected to a second wave of sensational reports about their culture. It is as if there were some need to view them only in black and white: either they are Stone Age primitives, as the journalists reported 18 years ago, or they are participants in some elaborate hoax, as we are being told today. This time, though, the tribe may actually have something to lose. The hunger for lumber in the Philippines is greater than ever. The majority of the country's timberland already has been denuded by U.S., Japanese, and Philippine logging companies. Compounding the problem is the intense population pressure being brought to bear on South Cotabato; the number of people in the province has increased from about 460,000 in 1970 to more than one million today. The forest of the Tasaday was declared a National Reserve for them by President Marcos in 1972. If the Tasaday are said *not* to be a distinct, anthropologically unique tribe, there will be no reason to treat them any differently from other natives. They, like others, may have to give up their land to loggers, miners, and developers.

Notes

1. I would modify the statement to read: "A small group of people calling themselves the Tasaday, and speaking a Manobo language similar to that of their nearest neighbors, lived in caves and the forest in the southern Philippines. They claimed that until the early 1960s they used only stone tools, they foraged for food in the stream and the forest, and they had no contact with agricultural peoples." The researchers had soundly dismissed in 1971 any claims that these people were Stone Age holdovers (from the earlier developmental age).
2. See Conklin 1957 for such a list, which includes many terms for garden and field preparation, plants, plant parts, harvesting, storing, and processing.

● *chapter eight*

The Tasaday: Some Observations

RICHARD E. ELKINS

In late 1971 Dr. Teodoro Llamzon, then President of the Linguistic Society of the Philippines, asked me to look at some data he had recorded from people of the recently discovered group called Tasaday. After spending a few minutes examining the material I said to him, "These people are Manobo; their language appears to be a dialect of what is called Cotabato Manobo."

At that time I had worked in the Philippines for 18 years, living among Manobo peoples and studying their languages. I had also spent considerable time with other Mindanao groups, notably the Tboli. My assessment of Llamzon's data was based on my own studies of the various languages which are members of the Manobo subgroup of Philippine languages. There are certain lexical features which are shared by all members of the Manobo subgroup of languages which are not found in the languages of other Philippine subgroups (Elkins 1971:32). These features were present in the Tasaday data. Also present were features that identified Tasaday as belonging to the particular Manobo subgroup called Southern Manobo of which Cotabato Manobo and Blit Manobo are also members (Elkins 1974:637).

A year later I was invited to join a research party on a visit to the Tasaday. A principal member of that party was Douglas Yen. I joined the group as a linguist to support him in his ethnobotanical studies as well as to pursue my own linguistic investigations. Because of a health problem I was able to stay only four days. During that time, however, I recorded a basic word list and was able to establish some rapport with certain of the Tasaday because of the fact that, being familiar with other Manobo languages, I soon began to participate in rudimentary conversations.

There are two points I would like to make here. The first is based on the linguistic data, which I feel suggest that the Tasaday, at the time of discovery, were a speech community which had developed, to some degree, separately from the other Manobo groups nearby. The second point is that certain aspects of Tasaday behavior were not typical of any other Mindanao tribal groups, including the Cotabato Manobo. This suggests that their cultural and social development was also separate from other nearby groups. If these two suggestions are indeed fact, it follows that the Tasaday were not picked at random from other groups and persuaded to perform for journalists and social scientists.

Observations Based on the Linguistic Data

A comparison of the Tasaday data (Elkins 1972; Molony with Tuan 1976) with
Cotabato Manobo dictionaries (Errington and Errington 1981; Johnston 1968)
suggests that the Tasaday represent a separate speech community, one which has
developed differently from the main body of Cotabato Manobo speakers. The difference is that Tasaday has been less conservative in its development with regard
to the retention of reflexes and meanings of reconstructed proto-forms. Also, there
are instances of semantic skewing between Cotabato Manobo and Tasaday cognate lexemes which seem to be consistent with, or reflect, the relative isolation
and simple life-style claimed for the Tasaday. Evidence for this is as follows.

Basic Vocabulary Differences

In both Molony's (Molony with Tuan 1976) and Elkins's (1972) word lists, comparisons between Tasaday and Cotabato Manobo indicate that a difference of
about 20% exists in basic vocabulary. For these two speech communities the 80%
shared vocabulary represents comparisons which, for all practical purposes, are
between identical items. The 20% represents comparisons of different, noncog-
nate items.

Retention of Older Forms

In a list of 21 comparisons of Tasaday and Cotabato Manobo words where only
one of the two words in any pair retained a reflex of a proto-form, Cotabato Manobo retained reflexes of 15 proto-forms (see Table 1) and Tasaday retained six
(see Table 2). The proto-forms cited are my own reconstructions, either Proto-
Manobo or forms reconstructed at a level which might be labeled Proto-East-Cen-

---

TABLE 1

Instances where Cotabato Manobo retained older forms

	Proto-form	Gloss	CTM	TAS
1.	*gaqena	'earlier today'	giqina	duginu
2.	*quled	'snake, worm'	quled	qefuy
3.	*pusung	'heart'	fusung	fusuq
4.	*duma	'accompany'	duma	sama
5.	*pigsa	'boil (sore)'	figsa	mebagaq
6.	*hiyup	'blow on'	hiyuf	yufyuf
7.	*mata	'eye'	mata	qighaqa
8.	*qaldaw	'sun, day'	qagdaw	fegloqon
9.	*bulan	'moon'	bulan	sebang
10.	*bituqen	'star'	bituqen	tubaliq
11.	*sekedu	'water pole'	sekedu	nefnef
12.	*gemen	'smile'	gemen	fetawa
13.	*genaw	'cold'	genaw	gemgem
14.	*langaw	'fly (insect)'	langaw	longed
15.	*himatay	'kill'	qimatay	hagtay

tral-Southern Manobo (Elkins 1973–74, 1974, 1984). I have regularized the spelling for the Tasaday data (mine and Carol Molony's) and also for the Cotabato Manobo forms. I have used *q* for glottal stop, *ng* for the velar nasal, *e* for the central mid vowel, and *é* for the front mid vowel.

The areal norms of Matteo Bartoli as cited by Bolinger (1968) may be relevant here. "It should be possible, he [Bartoli] thought, to correlate the past evolution of dialects with their positions relative to one another, and he expressed the correlations in a set of four areal norms." They are as follows:

1. Norm of the isolated area. An area that is cut off and shielded from communication tends to retain older forms.

2. Norm of the lateral area. Where a central area is wedged into the middle of a zone that presumably was once homogeneous, the edges tend to retain older forms.

3. Norm of the principal area. If the zone is split into two segments, the larger one tends to have the older forms. (This is in partial conflict with 1 and 2.)

4. Norm of the later area. An area that has been overrun, as by conquest, at a more recent date tends to have older forms. [Bartoli, as cited in Bolinger 1968:148]

Following the norm of the isolated area, our expectation would be that Tasaday, because of its presumed isolation, would tend to retain the older forms; but by stating that the norm of the principal area is in partial conflict with the norm of the isolated area, Bartoli seems to allow that the norm of the principal area may, in fact, be in effect in the case of Tasaday and Cotabato Manobo. The fact that the Tasaday were very much fewer in number may have ruled out the effect of the norm of the isolated area.

Retention of Older Meanings

Cotabato Manobo also appears to be more conservative than Tasaday in retaining older meanings intact (i.e., the meanings posited for proto-forms). A comparison of the Tasaday data with Johnston's and the Erringtons' Cotabato Manobo dictionaries, and with my reconstructions in Table 3, shows that in nine instances Cotabato Manobo retains older meanings (Table 4) while Tasaday retains them in only three instances (Table 5).

TABLE 2
Instances where Tasaday retained older forms

	Proto-form	Gloss	CTM	TAS
1.	*lambuq	'fat'	gebuq	lagbuq
2.	*(pa)laguy	'run'	letu	laguy
3.	*layag	'light'	legdaw	layag
4.	*qugat	'vein'	qégél	qugat
5.	*lipat	'forget'	lifeng	lifot
6.	*dangaw	'handspan'	selifo	dangaw

TABLE 3
The reconstructions with which the Tasaday and the Cotabato Manobo data are compared

1.	*beha(n)qan	'omen'
2.	*balaw	'fierce'
3.	*bugis	'Tinea corporis'
4.	*kakay	'older sibling'
5.	*baga	'ember'
6.	*ledak	'rotten'
7.	*layqang	'lie face up'
8.	*tapay	'beforehand'
9.	*taguq	'put away'
10.	*bekeleng	'throat'
11.	*tali	'string'
12.	*quman	'repeat'

TABLE 4
Instances in which Cotabato Manobo retains the older meaning

	CTM	Gloss	TAS	Gloss
1.	baqenan	'omen'	baqanan	'sneeze'
2.	balaw	'fierce'	balaw	'angry'
3.	bugis	'Tinea corporis'	bugis	'scabies'
4.	kakay	'older sibling'	kakay	'friend'
5.	baga	'ember'	baga	'to boil'
6.	ledak	'rotten'	ledak	'skin rash'
7.	liqiyang	'lie face up'	leqiyang	'upside-down'
8.	tafay	'beforehand'	tafay	'every'
9.	taguq	'put away'	taguq	'to hide'

TABLE 5
Instances in which Tasaday retains the older meaning and Cotabato Manobo does not

	TAS	Gloss	CTM	Gloss
1.	bekeleng	'throat'	bekeleng	'voice'
2.	tali	'string'	tali	'rope'
3.	quman	'repeat'	quman	'continue'

Semantic Skewing

In Table 6, the forms cited are identical in shape for both Tasaday and Cotabato Manobo. Only the meanings are different. As I stated earlier, certain meaning differences of cognate lexemes between Tasaday and Cotabato Manobo are not inconsistent with a theory of separate development of the two speech communities and perhaps a simpler Tasaday life-style. The difference between the Cotabato Manobo lexeme *kahung* ('swim') and its Tasaday cognate meaning 'float' is con-

TABLE 6

Instances in which words are identical in shape for Tasaday and Cotabato Manobo but meanings are different

	Form	CTM gloss	TAS gloss
1.	*bekut*	'to wrap something'	'sling for a baby'
2.	*belagkal*	'floor joist'	'cave or forest floor'
3.	*hagtay*	'cause to live'	'kill'
4.	*kahung*	'swim'	'float, of any object'
5.	*kadoqo*	'number'	'entirety'
6.	*legaq*	'trail food'	'cook'
7.	*mahoq*	'foul smell'	'swollen'
8.	*gemgem*	'shiver'	'cold'
9.	*sebat*	'shoulder strap'	'tie up something'
10.	*sebang*	'appear in the west, of a new moon'	'moon'

sistent with the fact that streams in the Tasaday area are too shallow for swimming but not for small objects to float. Also, the difference between the Cotabato Manobo lexeme *belagkal* ('floor joist') and its Tasaday cognate meaning 'floor of the forest or of a cave' fits the theory that the Tasaday were unfamiliar with houses.

Observations About Tasaday Behavior

During my stay with the Tasaday I noted several instances of behavior which suggested that they were free from, or ignorant of, certain inhibitions commonly found among other Mindanao groups such as the Tboli, the Blaan, and the various other Manobo groups. Two of those instances stand out in my memory.

Public Display of Affection

Among all the tribal groups in Mindanao with which I am familiar, affection between adults, especially between husband and wife, is never shown openly. Tasaday behavior in this regard was strikingly different. It was not uncommon to see married couples sitting arm in arm, something I have never observed in any other Manobo community in 36 years of living among them. The Tasaday teenage boy Lobo on several occasions sidled up to me or Douglas Yen with his hand on our shoulder or arm. On one occasion when Belayem and his wife Sindi came down from the caves, both of them, Belayem first and Sindi following, put their arms around me and gave me a sniffing Mindanao kiss on the cheek while saying my name. It appeared to be, for them, a casual act devoid of any sexual connotation. I was completely surprised because it was so out of character for other Mindanao peoples. Peter Wilson (1988:52) writes that one of the regular features of hunter-gatherer social life is the reliance on affection to sustain relationships. The Tasaday's apparent lack of inhibition in this regard seemed to bear this out.

Naive Response to a Potentially Dangerous Situation

During my visit the Blit Manobo trapper, Dafal, managed to acquire some liquor and became intoxicated. He began to shout and to gesture threateningly. In spite of the fact that he was armed with a shotgun and a bolo and was potentially dangerous, the Tasaday, including several children, clustered around him. They seemed surprised, curious, totally fascinated, and completely unconcerned about possible harm to themselves or their children. As I remember, none of them spoke to him. All of the surrounding groups in Mindanao are familiar with some form of alcohol and its effects. Tasaday behavior on that occasion seemed in sharp contrast with what might be expected of a similar Tboli or Cotabato Manobo group when confronted with an intoxication crisis. Women and children, at least, would have been kept away from him. Even if the Tasaday were "performers" they could easily have discretely kept at a distance without, as it were, "blowing their cover."

Summary

Comparisons of Tasaday and Cotabato Manobo lexical data with reconstructions of Manobo proto-forms indicate that Cotabato Manobo, presumably in accordance with Bartoli's "norm of the principal area," has a higher retention rate of older forms and meanings than does Tasaday. This fact, along with the 20% difference in basic vocabulary, suggests that these two speech communities, at least in their more recent history, have developed separately.

Certain striking differences in behavior between the Tasaday and other Mindanao groups, including the Tboli and the Cotabato Manobo, suggest that the Tasaday have also developed socially and culturally apart from those groups.

PART III

New Perspectives on Some Old Data

● *chapter nine*

A Nutritional Analysis of the Philippine Tasaday Diet

Barry Fankhauser

The cave-dwelling Tasaday of Mindanao, Philippines, used a large number of plant materials as sources of food (Yen and Gutierrez 1974). With the addition of hunting technology they supplemented their diet with meat from wild deer, pig, monkey, and birds. Yen recorded the amount of food brought back to their caves over a period of five days in August 1972. A nutritional analysis of this food along with a discussion of the problems associated with the collection of nutritional data has already been published (Robson and Yen 1976). It is my purpose here to present a reanalysis of the nutrition provided by the Tasaday diet as recorded by Yen. This analysis is based on recent nutritional research and recommendations. In addition, the absence of certain individuals from the Tasaday group is considered.

Food Collected and Its Nutritional Value

Table 1 gives the composition of the group of Tasaday for whom Yen (Robson and Yen 1976) recorded the amount of food brought back to the caves. The group

TABLE 1

Sex distribution, physiological status, and days absent for a group of Tasaday hunters and gatherers, August 1972.

Sex	Physiological status	Numbers	Adjustment for absence
Male	Elderly	2	-2
	Adult	5	$-(\frac{4}{5} + \frac{2}{5})$
	Adolescent	5	None
Female	Elderly	2	-2
	Adult	1	$-\frac{4}{5}$
	Pregnant and lactating	3	None
Male and Female	Breast-fed infants	2	None
	Toddlers under 5 years	3	$-\frac{4}{5}$
	5–12 years	2	$-\frac{4}{5}$

From Robson and Yen 1976 and Yen (personal communication).

125

numbered 26 but during the five-day period several individuals were absent for varying lengths of time (Table 1). For example, the elderly males and females were not present at all during the five days and the one adult female was absent for four out of the five days.

The proximate analysis of the foods is shown in Table 2. Identical foods vary in composition and the values given are, for the most part, based on the means of a large number of food samples. The meat and fish items represent the major source of protein, and the plant products are the source of carbohydrate.

The estimated quantities of food collected during five days and their energy and protein content using data from Table 2 are shown in Table 3. The total calculated energy agrees to within 1% with that of Robson and Yen (1976), but the total protein presented here is 22% greater, which is due mainly to the use of a different proximate analysis for deer. The deer meat supplies 80% of the total protein. The fruits *sufini* and *dalikan* furnish twice the protein and nearly twice the energy than that calculated previously because of the use of a different prox-

---

TABLE 2

Proximate composition of foods consumed by Tasaday hunters and gatherers (amounts/100g)

	Water	Protein	Fat	Carb	Fibre	Ash	Energy[a] kcal	Energy[a] kJ
natek (*Caryota* starch)[b]	14.5	0.6	<0.5	81.8	1.5	2.4	331	1385
biking (wild yam, *Dioscorea* sp.)[b]	62.7	2.0	<0.5	34.1	1.5	1.1	143	598
ubod basag (*Caryota* leaf bud) *ubod* (leaf buds of *Areca*, *Pinanga Heterospathe* palms[c]	86.4	3.3	0.3	9.0	—	1.0	43	143
dalikan (fruits of *Amomum* sp.) *sufini* (fruits of *Calamus* sp.)[d]	79.0	0.6	1.2	18.6	0.5	0.6	79	330
libuted (palm weevil grubs)[e]	—	16.3	6.7	0	—	—	130	544
fish[f]	73.7	20.0	1.3	0	0	5.0	97	406
tadpoles (frog)[f]	83.6	15.3	0.3	0	0	0.8	68	284
crab (refuse 62%)[f]	29.8	4.7	1.1	1.2	0	1.2	35	146
deer[g]	74.7	20.6	3.3	0	0	1.0	118	494

(—indicates no data available)

[a]The Atwater system of calculating energy values was used as shown in Merrill and Watt (1955).

[b]From Robson and Yen (1976). Energy values based on Atwater factors of protein = 2.78 kcal/g and carbohydrate = 4.03 kcal/g.

[c]No data for *Caryota* leaf bud, assumed to be the same as *Areca* buds, FAO/HEW (1972) item 411. Atwater factors: protein = 2.44, fat = 8.37 and carbohydrate = 3.57 kcal/g.

[d]No data for *Amomum* sp., assumed to be the same as *Calamus* sp., FAO/HEW (1972) item 994. Atwater factors: protein = 3.36, fat = 8.37 and carbohydrate = 3.60 kcal/g.

[e]From FAO (1954) item 219b cited in Robson and Yen (1976). Atwater factors for this and following items: protein = 4.27 and fat = 9.02 kcal/g.

[f]From FAO/HEW (1972) items 1282, 1082a, and 1244b, respectively. Atwater factor for crab carbohydrate = 4.11 kcal/g.

[g]From Scherz, Kloos, and Senser (1986:342).

TABLE 3

Estimated quantities of foods brought to Tasaday caves and their energy and protein content.

Food	Quantity kg	Protein g	Energy kcal	Energy MJ[a]
natek (*Caryota* starch)	12	74	39720	166.2
biking (wild yam *Dioscorea* sp.)	4	80	5720	23.9
ubod basag (*Caryota* leaf bud)	5	165	2135	8.9
Ubod (leaf buds of *Areca, Pinanga Heterospathe* palms)	7	231	2989	12.5
dalikan (fruits of *Amomum* sp.)	2	12	1580	6.6
sufini (fruits of *Calamus* sp.)	2	12	1580	6.6
libuted (palm weevil grubs)	1	163	1300	5.4
fish, tadpoles, crab[b]	2	267	1362	6.0
deer	20	4120	23600	98.7
Total	55	5124	79986	334.8

[a]MJ = megajoules.
[b]Equal quantities of these items assumed for the calculation of protein and energy.

imate analysis. However, these fruits contribute a negligible amount of protein and only 4% of the energy in the observed diet.

Protein and Energy Requirements

Table 4 lists the energy and protein requirements of the group considering the time that individuals were actually present during the five-day period. No values are given for breast-fed infants because their requirements are provided by human milk. However, additional energy and protein are required for lactation. Body weights and heights of individuals have not been used for protein and energy calculations because this information was not available. This may lead to some error in the estimation of requirements. The energy requirements for adults are based on 1.8 times the basal metabolic rates (BMR), which appear to be suitable according to the World Health Organization (WHO 1985:75–79).

Protein and Energy Intake

The total estimated energy intake from the food collected is 334.8 megajoules (MJ) (Table 3). The energy required, using information provided in WHO (1985), is 791 MJ (Table 4). Thus, only 42% of the energy required has been supplied by hunting and gathering activities. This value may actually be too low for several reasons: (1) Some food would be eaten in the forest (e.g., what happened to the remaining part of the deer?). (2) Group members were found later to be supplementing their diet with rice (Yen personal communication). (3) The actual energy requirements may be lower than those presented in WHO (1985). (This is discussed in Robson and Yen 1976.) If one uses the energy requirements proposed by Fox for Africa (Clark and Turner 1973) the available energy in the Tasaday diet comes to 57% of requirements. According to Clark and Turner the "FAO

TABLE 4

Energy and protein requirements for those present in a group of Tasaday hunters and gatherers.

Subjects	Person days	Energy required kcal/day	Energy required MJ/day	Energy required Total kcal	Protein required g/day	Protein required Total g
Male:						
Adult[a]	19	2600	10.9	49400	37.5	712
Adolescent[b]	25	2500	10.5	62500	47.5	1188
Female:						
Adult[c]	1	2100	8.8	2100	34	34
Pregnant and lactating[d]	15	2490	10.4	37350	46	690
Adolescent[e]	5	2100	8.8	10500	44	220
Male and Female:						
Toddlers under 5 years[f]	11	1450	6.1	15950	16.5	182
5–12 years[g]	6	1875	7.8	11250	24	144
Total				189050 (791 MJ)		3170

Note: All requirements are from WHO (1985)

[a]Requirements for 50 kg adult (1.8 BMR) from Table 42.

[b]Requirements based on average of 12–16-year-old boys from Table 48.

[c]Requirements for 45 kg adult (1.8 BMR) from Table 45.

[d]Additional energy and protein requirements (+ 390 kcal/day, + 12 g/day) based on average of pregnancy and lactation from Table 50.

[e]Requirements for 12–14-year-old girls from Table 48.

[f]Requirements based on average of 2–5 year olds from Table 49.

[g]Requirements based on average of boys and girls 5–10 years old from Table 49.

scale of calorie requirements for children is much too high. Fox's estimates in Africa are much lower. His scale is the more reliable" (1973:65). But there is still a large energy deficit even with Fox's requirements. No doubt a considerable amount of food was eaten in the forest during hunting and gathering activities, food which could not be calculated. This fact alone may have resulted in an adequate energy intake for the Tasaday.

The available protein is seemingly more than adequate. The protein required from Table 4 is 3,170 g while the protein available is 5,124 g (Table 3). These values are for protein with a digestibility and an amino acid score of 100%. Since most of the energy required by the Tasaday is for adults (and the amount of food eaten by each member is not known), no correction is needed for the amino acid score (cf. WHO 1985:120–127). However, digestibility of the protein must be considered and this was calculated to be 93% (based on WHO 1985:118–120). With a digestibility factor of 93% the actual available protein is 5,124 g × 93/ 100 = 4,765 g. The diet over the five-day period had 150% of protein requirements. However, if the energy needs are not met then protein is diverted to meeting the energy needs.

People who take adequate or more than adequate protein, but who are not able to utilize the protein for lack of adequate energy in the diet, obviously form a part of the protein deficient population. [Sukhatme 1975:64]

Only when the energy intake exceeds $1.5 \times$ BMR is protein fully utilized. Furthermore, protein needs are usually met when the food intake is sufficient.

Conclusions

The recorded quantities of food collected by the Tasaday over a five-day period would not have been adequate for energy needs. In addition, even though the available protein was 150% of that required, there would be a deficit because this protein would be diverted to meeting the energy needs of maintenance. If casual eating made up the energy needs, then the protein intake would be more than adequate.

● *chapter ten*

What Did the Tasaday Eat?

Thomas N. Headland

In 1971 the international news media broke the story of the discovery of a small group of 26 Stone Age, cave-dwelling people, referred to as the Tasaday, who up to then had been living, isolated and unknown to the outside world, in a rain forest in the southern Philippines. Fifteen years later, in 1986, there was a flurry of news reports that this story was a hoax.

For scientists, the general argument centers on whether the Tasaday people were living a pure foraging subsistence until the middle of this century, or not. I use "pure" here to refer to a people living a life-style close to what we would call paleolithic, that is, without iron tools (stone-using, but not necessarily Stone Age), but especially a group subsisting independently of cultivated foods. In the particular case of the Tasaday, the argument also centers on whether they had any contact with agricultural peoples. The main working hypothesis, then, is that there was a band of cave-dwelling people in the southern Philippines called Tasaday who followed a stone tool–using, foraging mode of subsistence, without iron, eating only wild foods, and having no contact with agricultural peoples until the 1960s.

The Wild Yam Question

At the Tasaday symposium in Zagreb, Yugoslavia, in 1988, I presented a statement which began with a query to the protagonists at that meeting. That statement was an empirical question, the answer to which should shed light on the puzzles surrounding the Tasaday controversy. The question is, if there was a population of hunter-gatherers living independently of produced foods in the South Cotabato rain forest in the recent past, *what did they eat?*

I have spent most of the last quarter-century living in a Philippine tropical rain forest with Agta hunter-gatherers. Perhaps the Agta are not too different from the Tasaday. At least John Nance reports that the Tasaday's "appearance and possessions were similar to other primitive Filipinos . . . [like] the Agta of Luzon" (1975:12).[1] During the decade of the 1980s, after years of studying the subsistence behavior of Agta bands, I developed a hypothesis which I refer to as "The Wild Yam Question" (Headland 1986:178–184; 1987; Headland and Reid 1989). The core of the argument is that tropical rain forest biomes in general lack sufficient wild starch foods to sustain human foragers on a long-term basis. Wild yams, especially, are so scarce and so hard to extract that pure hunter-gatherers could not live in such biomes without recourse to at least some cultivated foods.

To follow the argument, a proper definition of "tropical rain forest" is necessary here. Throughout the tropical world, there are two main types of tropical moist forest. One type is the seasonal forest (called monsoon forest in Southeast Asia), a deciduous forest with a marked dry season and a rainfall of less than 3,000 mm per year. The other type is true "rain forest," characterized as evergreen, nonseasonal, with an average annual rainfall of more than 3,000 mm, with no marked dry season, and with a biomass five times that of monsoon forest. In rain forests, very little sunlight penetrates to the forest floor, thus inhibiting (but not forbidding) the growth of wild plant foods accessible to human foragers. The Tasaday forest area is true rain forest (Philippine Atlas 1975:21, 25), with their cave situated at 6° 18' N. lat. and 124° 33' E. long., at an elevation of 1,200 meters, or 4,000 feet. There are of course at least 40 subtypes of tropical rain forest—five main subtypes in my research area in Luzon, plus several more microhabitats within those five (described in Headland 1988).

This carbohydrate-scarcity hypothesis is not restricted just to yams; it applies to all types of carbohydrates combined, as well as to lipids from animal fat. In my area of research (in Luzon) the rain forest has several types of edible wild carbohydrate foods, including fruits, wild bananas, caryota palm, honey, the hearts or buds of small palms such as rattan, and six types of wild yams. But all of these combined make up an extremely undependable resource because of their low caloric content, scarcity, and/or heavy labor involved in extraction or preparation. Honey is plentiful only when the dipterocarps blossom, which is only once every four to six years. I have discussed elsewhere the limitations of wild animal fat, and why it could not supply foragers in the Philippines with sufficient nutritional needs in the absence of starch foods (Headland 1987:483–485). Wild bananas (*Musa* sp.), it should be noted, are not like what we saw Tarzan pick and feed to Jane in the movies we viewed as children. The plant is common in Philippine lowland forests, but "the fruit is hardly edible" (Headland and Headland 1974:123); being small, full of large seeds, and with only a little, highly astringent flesh, it is unappetizing and very rarely eaten by Agta. The Tasaday are also reported to have considered the wild banana as "evidently not desirable" (Nance 1975:22; see also Fernandez and Lynch 1972:302), "more valuable as bait in monkeytraps [the Tasaday said] than for people to eat" (Nance 1975:277).

The hypothesis of course conflicts with the assumption, generally held until recently, that tropical rain forests are food-rich biomes for human foragers, that wild tubers were the staple of prehistoric hunter-gatherers in such environments, and that such peoples once lived completely independent of cultivated foods. Collins's (1990:92) *a priori* statement in his new book on rain forests, "Famine is unknown—the [rain] forest always provides" is, in my view, unwarranted.

Recent Studies that Test the
Carbohydrate-Scarcity Hypothesis

As I showed in my 1987 article, there is very little support in the literature for the null hypothesis to the yam question, that is, that tropical forests *do* provide sufficient wild starch foods for foragers. Significantly, there is another team of scientists who have recently raised this same question: Are wild starch foods the critical limiting factor in tropical forests? These researchers independently reached the same conclusion I did. (They knew nothing of my work, nor I of theirs, until our respective papers were in press.)

The first on this team to publish were Terese Hart and John Hart (1986), who argued that in the central African forests there is not enough wild food to provide the year-round carbohydrates needed by a hunting and gathering people (such as the Mbuti pygmies). Soon after, their colleague Robert Bailey published his study (Bailey and Peacock 1988; Bailey et al. 1989). Bailey's articles "test the hypothesis that humans do not exist and have never existed independently of agriculture in tropical rain forest" (1989:59). They found "no convincing ethnographic evidence and, with the possible exception of Malaysia, no archeological evidence for pure foragers [ever having lived] in undisturbed tropical rain forests" (1989:59).

One value of these four published studies (Harts', Bailey's two, and my 1987 paper) is that there is little overlap in the references cited in them. (Only 18 of the Harts' 74 references and only 29 of the 177 references in Bailey et al. 1989 are cited in my paper.) Their articles cite a high number of published items in their library searches that support the wild yam question that I did not find. Those wishing to do further research on the topic will find in the four bibliographies well over a hundred studies supporting the hypothesis directly or indirectly.

A number of scholars have recently addressed the wild yam question in response to Headland's and Bailey's papers. Colinvaux and Bush (1991) review paleoenvironmental evidence for an area in Panama which they argue refutes my and Bailey's hypothesis. Bailey's reply (Bailey, Jenike, and Rechtman 1991) points out the shortcomings in their argument. A recent volume edited by Harris and Hillman (1989) has three chapters which speak indirectly to the yam scarcity hypothesis: The first, by Dolores Piperno (1989) challenges the concept that hunters and gatherers were affluent in Central American tropical forests. Her conclusion is that such environments were "seriously deficient in available carbohydrates" (p. 543), and that the few wild resources available would have been "severely limited, unstable, and unpredictable" (p. 539). (Piperno cites Hart and Hart 1986; none of these three chapters cite Headland or Bailey.) In the second of these chapters, Chikwendu and Okezie (1989) state that "there is an abundance of wild yam species in the local forests" of southeastern Nigeria (p. 344), but that it was nearly impossible to dig them up even with iron tools, because of the "hostile thorns" and the maze of root tangles wedging in the tubers. While they consider that such roots could have been dug up with wooden implements sharpened to points (p. 356), they doubt that it would have been possisble to grub up yam tubers "with any stone tool that was known during the Sangoan [Stone Age] period" (p. 345). In the third chapter, Joyce White (1989) discusses her observations on wild and cultivated yams in a forest area in northeastern Thailand. The five species of wild yams in her area are readily available, even sold in the market in certain seasons. But her study area was a deciduous seasonal savanna-like forest (not a rain forest), and the tubers "become shrivelled and fibrous, and are not considered edible" during the rainy season (p. 156).

Darna Dufour (1989) has recently reported on the use of wild plant foods among Tukano horticulturalists in a rain forest in the northwest Amazon. She found, first of all, "a general absence of [wild] starch storage organs" (p. 8). The Tukano in her area did utilize "edible parts of some 31 different wild plants" (p. 4), but these were a very minor part of their diet, and most were available only seasonally. They consisted of fruits, nuts, seeds, and pulses, but no roots. Five of the seven seeds and nuts require detoxification before they can be eaten, and nonpoisonous nuts "tend to be protected by nut walls which are so hard that the seeds are virtually inaccessible" (p. 8). "Typically [the wild plant foods] are incorporated as flavorful additions" to their main foods, manioc and fish (p. 4). She estimated that wild plant foods contribute in most years about 2% of all food energy among the Tukano.

An indication of the growing interest in this carbohydrate-scarcity hypothesis was seen at the recent (November 1991) Annual Meeting of the American Anthropological Association, in Chicago, where four symposia focused several of their papers on the topic. These four sessions were entitled: "Forager Models: Genuine or Spurious?" organized by Alice Kehoe and Charles Bishop; "Hunting and Gathering in Lowland South America," organized by Anna Roosevelt and Stephen Beckerman; "Eating on the Wild Side . . . Implications of Using Noncultigens," organized by Nine Letkin; and "New Guinea Foragers?: Views from the Sepik Hinterlands," organized by Patricia Townsend and William Mitchell. Finally, the journal *Human Ecology* will publish a special issue on the topic in late 1992.

Finding Food without Iron Tools

Those of us who have watched the work involved when foragers have dug up wild roots using iron tools have to wonder how long it took to dig up tubers before such tools were available. Hurtado and Hill (1989) give us an idea. Their survey of studies of root-digging rates of *wild* roots leads them to suggest that women "would have to spend from 2.7 to the impossible number of 64 hours per day digging [wild] tubers with traditional tools" (p. 214) to feed a family of seven. They found that, among Machiguenga women, cultivated manioc can be harvested with wooden tools, although it takes two or three times longer than when using machetes. While this makes only a minor difference in the total time Machiguenga women spend in subsistence tasks, Hurtado and Hill's data indirectly support the assumption that it would take much longer to dig up roots with wooden tools than with iron tools. An earlier study by Colchester (1984) also suggests that iron tools greatly increase the efficiency of wild-plant food gathering.

We should note here, however, that stone tools *are* apparently adequate for cutting down and splitting sago palm *(Metroxylon* spp.; *Euggeissona utilis)* (Townsend 1969; Peter Brosius, personal communication). And it may turn out that exceptions to my starch scarcity hypothesis occur in the few tropical forest areas where sago palms are abundant, as in Borneo or the Sepik area of Papua New Guinea (Townsend 1990; but cf. Bailey 1990). This is an irrelevant issue, however, as concerns the Tasaday, because sago palms do not grow in their area and they claim that the inferior sago-like caryota palm *(Caryota cumingii)* in their area was not a part of their traditional diet before 1966.

Are the Tasaday an Exception to the Hypothesis?

Of course, the inquiry presently before us is not sago or Borneo, but whether the Tasaday might be an exception to the wild yam question. A careful reading of the reports on the Tasaday certainly supports the hypothesis, even though an early report based on a two-week visit among the Tasaday in May 1972 by Fernandez and Lynch stressed an abundance of food in the Tasaday subsistence system: "The kindness of their environment is such that the food supply is constant and ample for their present population; they need not seasonally trek after abundance north, south, east, or west; it surrounds them always (1972:287; see also p. 328, n. 9); "Food is abundant, constantly available, and found with little effort (p. 303); "Suffice it to say that the Tasaday live in plenty" (p. 309).

This judgment was made "on grounds of the short-term observations of Fernandez [Lynch was only there for one day, and Fernandez for ten days] . . . that the adult per-capita commitment to the food quest was about three hours a day" (p. 309). Similarly, a *National Geographic* reporter who was there at that time said he saw two men collect enough food in two hours to feed their family of seven "through at least a day" (MacLeish 1972:245). An even earlier Panamin report, based on just a few hours' contact—their *initial* contact—with the Tasaday at the edge of the forest on June 7, June 8, and June 16, 1971 (Elizalde with Fox 1971a:4), makes the following rather extravagant *a priori* claim:

> The Tasaday have absolutely no knowledge of rice, taro (gabi), the sweet potato, corn, cassava, or any cultivated plant. . . . They had never tasted salt or smoked tobacco!. . . . The Tasaday have no formal trade or recurring contacts with the outside world, living in almost total social and geographical isolation, an incredible fact. [pp. 1, 3]

What, then, did the Tasaday eat? Douglas Yen's impression, which was based on 38 days of observation in 1972 (Yen 1976b:x, 174), was that wild foods would have provided only marginal sustenance at best for a people living as the Tasaday were reportedly living before 1966. Yen refers to the Tasaday diet as "low-level" (p. 169), saying specifically that wild tubers were scattered, of low density, and that "if there is any great dependence on the tuber as a food, the foraging range has to be more than 25 sq. km" (p. 171). Yen states that yam harvest yields are low (p. 169, 171), that starch foods in general are in short supply (p. 174), and that in December Tasaday said they had to "travel long distances for food. . . . They had to walk 3 days to a far valley where there was plenty of [yams and caryota]'' (p. 171). He reckoned that yams would not be sufficient without caryota palm starch (p. 175), which the Tasaday began to eat only after they were so taught by the Manobo trader Dafal in 1966. As for *ubod* (the edible pith found in the terminal buds of wild palms and other plants), Fernandez and Lynch report that ''the collecting of this food item was also introduced by Dafal. . . . Dafal is emphatic in his claim that the Tasaday . . . when he met them [did not] collect *ubod*'' (1972:299; see also pp. 305 and 311).

Agta foragers in the rain forests in Luzon identify from six to twelve wild tubers, depending on the area, that are important dietary components to them. Most of these are *Dioscorea* spp. (Allen 1985:56, 58; Headland 1981:70–76). They eat these infrequently, however, for ''the labor they expend to obtain [them] is quite high for the small amount of starch they get, and the plants are not abundant in any of the five forest types of eastern Luzon'' (Headland 1987:466). The Tasaday, by contrast, reportedly ''knew of only one species [of yam in 1972], . . . referred to as *biking*'' (Fernandez and Lynch 1972:304).[2] If ''the Tasaday food quest centered on [just] one . . . species of wild yam *(biking)*'' in the pre-Dafal era (Fernandez and Lynch 1972:294; see also p. 304; Yen and Gutierrez 1974:105; Yen 1976b), it is not surprising that, as Dafal said when he first met them (around 1966), the Tasaday were ''thin creatures with . . . insufficient food'' (Nance 1975:5, see also p. 327). The logic breaks down here, because it would of course be impossible for a group of foragers, or any human population, to survive and reproduce themselves for centuries on insufficient food.

Unfortunately, Yen's field research was conducted under less than ideal circumstances (Nance 1975:308; Yen 1976b:163). There are three reasons why it was difficult for him, or anyone, to know what the Tasaday traditionally ate: (1) ''Yen's collecting of *biking* [wild yams] had involved an exchange for rice'' (Nance 1975:326). (2) The Panamin camp staff were—unbeknownst to Yen until late in his field study—secretly giving rice regularly to the Tasaday. Yen says, ''We did not discover the extent of these gifts until later'' (Yen 1976b:168, see also p. 163; ABC-TV 1986:6; Fankhauser 1989:1 and this volume; Nance 1975:257, 311, 442). It certainly must have been difficult for anyone to know what the Tasaday were eating because, as Yen (1976b:163) says, ''Meal-times were probably the only occasions during which our party was courteously unwelcome at the caves.'' Nance suspected that the reason the Tasaday did not want visitors present when they ate had ''to do with rice'' (1975:442). ''The Tasaday may have decided that rice was to be eaten in private,'' says Nance, ''because they knew that giving rice had become a sore point . . . when the anthropologists had disputed with Fludi over rice doles to the Tasaday'' (1975:442). Finally, (3) during Yen's second field trip (when Elizalde was not there), he did not know what they were eating because, as Yen is later said to have concluded, individual family units ''went out for several days without returning,'' and ''much . . . eating was done in the forest . . . not collectively at the caves'' (1975:398). In any case, as we shall see in a moment, the Tasaday were well into eating rice months before Yen arrived on the scene.

Yen is nobody's fool. He was aware of the carbohydrate-scarcity question before I was, for Nance (1975:270) quotes him as "expressing some doubts about the report that before meeting Dafal, the Tasaday's primary food was *biking* [wild yams]." Yen said this in 1972, shortly before he began his fieldwork with the Tasaday. At the same time,

> Yen said that in other forest areas in which he had conducted ethnobotanical studies, the wild yam *(biking)* was not plentiful enough to provide the everyday staple food. And even though the Tasaday were few in number and supposedly sedentary, it would be rather surprising if *biking* was sufficient for them to have relied upon it to the extent reported. "Perhaps *ubod* [palm leaf buds] or something else was used. Of course, I don't know. We'll have to wait and see." [1975:270–271]

Yen's skepticism did not change after he completed his fieldwork, for Nance reports that Yen was still "puzzled by the seemingly low caloric content of their diet. And, furthermore, if it was low now, what had it been before they had knives to get *natek* [caryota starch] and make animal traps?" (1975:398). A year later, Yen reportedly told Nance that, based on his analysis of his data, "It appeared that [their total wild food sources] . . . provided very few calories—conceivably no more than 1,000 to 1,500 calories per person a day" (1975:431). Elsewhere, Robson and Yen state:

> it would appear that the formal foraging of the group resulted in the production of food that would meet . . . only 27 percent of the energy requirements. . . . If there was no underreporting of the foods brought to the caves, then a three hour period of random snacking in the forest has to provide almost two thirds of the total daily intake of energy and protein. [1976:87, 88]

A later nutritional analysis of the same data collected by Yen came to essentially the same conclusion: "[Yen's] recorded quantities of foods collected by the Tasaday over a five-day period would not have been adequate for energy needs" (Fankhauser 1989:2). (Also see Fankhauser's chapter in this volume.)

Nance (1975:432) quotes Yen as saying, "The low estimates so far would lead you to think that they must be eating something else, something we haven't included." My own conclusion is, of course, that that "something else" was cultivated foods.

Fernandez and Lynch also hint that they may have had some second thoughts about food abundance when the Tasaday had only yams for their staple. They state:

> Biking [yams], the traditional staple, . . . is found in less abundance [than caryota palm starch and *ubod*], requires greater effort to gather, and yields much less in terms of food per unit of time and effort. Moreover, it makes a monotonous diet. [1972:311]

Yen and Gutierrez also reported that the yams in the Tasaday area are difficult to harvest,

> because of the depth to which the tuber grows into the soil substratum . . . [it] provides little bulk food for the amount of labor expended on its digging. . . .

> The largest specimen harvested during our field work . . . was only 1.5 kg, and
> its harvesting occupied a man and his waiting wife more than 50 minutes. . . .
> The largest harvest seen by us consisted [of] three roots whose total weight could
> not have exceeded 2 kg. [1974:105]

In fact, they wondered what the Tasaday ate in the pre-Dafal era, before Dafal
taught them in the 1960s how to secure mammalian food sources and caryota palm
starch. Their logical hypothesis that other wild food sources must have been in
use was not however supported by their field data. They state it this way:

> The possibility of feasible alternative bulk foods to wild roots like heavy-bear-
> ing-nuts of tree species that might have endowed the earlier Tasaday diet with a
> quantitative [food source] . . . was not realized in our study. [1974:125]

From this they conclude that wild roots "must have been the main staple plant
emphasis" (1974:126) before the arrival of Dafal in the mid-1960s. But since
such plants were "rather sparsely distributed in the vicinity of the cave dwell-
ings" at the time of their visit (1974:125–126), they reason that the Tasaday must
have had "a more extensive pattern of foraging in the time of pre-Dafal technology" (1974:126; Yen 1976b:176).

I agree. The Tasaday must have had a different pattern of subsistence than
the *a priori* one proposed by Elizalde after his initial few hours' visit to the Tasaday, and quoted above. The task before us is to attempt to reconstruct just what
that subsistence was.

I am not questioning at this time whether there was a group of people called
Tasaday living in a rain forest biome in southwestern South Cotabato. I *am* suggesting that wherever these people were living—and I think it probable that they
were living somewhere near this area—they could not have been subsisting completely on wild foods.

It should be noted that Yen is quoted in the May 6, 1989, issue of *Science
News* as stating that "Headland's 'wild yam hypothesis' is off the mark: the forest
provided [the Tasaday] with enough food of sufficient variety to subsist on" (Yen,
quoted in Bower 1989b:281). If Yen believes this, then I am disappointed that he
did not pursue his line of argument in his paper he presented at this Tasaday symposium later that year (Yen 1989). He pointed out his skepticism that the yam
hypothesis could apply to tropical forests in general, but the specific question I
am addressing here is, do the Tasaday support or contradict the hypothesis? Yen's
data, as analyzed by Fankhauser (1989, and this volume), show that the Tasaday
case supports it. As Fankhauser concludes, "[Yen's] recorded quantities of foods
collected by the Tasaday over a five day period would not have been adequate for
energy needs" (1989:2). We may assume that Yen had no disagreement with
Fankhauser's conclusion, since he not only made no negative comment about it
in his 1989 paper, but he included it as an appendix in his paper. When Harold
Olofson addressed his question to me recently in print (1989:15), "Why would
the people with whom Yen walked around the forest spend almost a whole month
'starving' themselves?" he was asking the wrong question. It should be clear from
Table 1 in this chapter that they weren't starving at all. They were, in fact, eating

rice. I have answered in detail elsewhere (Headland 1990a) the four questions Olofson raised in his paper.

As researchers seek answers to the Tasaday puzzle, then, they must look not only for ethnographic, archaeological, linguistic, archival, and genealogical evidence, but also for the botanical evidence. Specifically, how plentiful and how accessible are wild carbohydrate foods in the area around the Tasaday caves, and how accessible would such foods have been to a people without iron tools? Finally, we must ask, how likely is it that this population had subsisted alone as pure foragers for several hundred years in their present rain forest biome? My answer is, not very.

What the Tasaday Ate before June 1971

To go back, then, to the original question in the title of this chapter: until a thorough botanical study can be made of wild plant foods in the area to prove otherwise, I continue to argue that the Tasaday before June 7, 1971, were at least periodically dependent on cultivated foods. They either grew root crops in small gardens themselves, or acquired cultivars through trade, or both. Nance himself reports that "they evidently traded because they [already] had cloth and brass" (1975:14), metal-tipped arrows (p. 18), and bows, cooking tubes, and jew's harps made from *cultivated* bamboo (p. 23, emphasis added; see also Elizalde with Fox 1971a:8; Nance 1975:64; and Peralta 1987:66). They also had "bolos, baskets and clothes, . . . trade items obtained from a local hunter" (Terry 1989). Fernandez and Lynch (1972:300) also list these and other items, including glass beads and "several tins." Elizalde's 1971 report, written just one month after the initial June 7 contact, mentions several of these trade goods as well (Elizalde with Fox 1971a:vii, 8).

Whether or not all these goods came to the Tasaday solely through Dafal, as Nance (1975:23) and Elizalde claimed (Elizalde with Fox 1971a:vii), and as Yen obliquely questions (1976b:176), my point is that starch foods could easily have come by the same route. We need to remember that the Tasaday caves were not situated deep in a remote forest, certainly not a six-day hike as *National Geographic* reported (MacLeish 1972:222), but were only a three-hour walk from Blit, a "large agricultural settlement" of Manobo farmers (Yen 1976b:170). (The straight-line distance from Blit to the caves was 4 kilometers.) A matter we need to ponder is why Tasaday would choose to hike for three days to a valley where they could dig up a few wild yams, rather than take a three-hour walk to a village where they could secure rice, corn, sweet potatoes, and cassava, not to mention the trade articles they had when first seen by Panamin officials in June 1971.[3] It is clear, at least, that before 1971 nearby agriculturalists were eating meat from wild game that had been killed and smoke-dried by Tasaday (MacLeish 1972:237). Wild meat, of course, is a main trade item exchanged for cultivated foods by tropical forest hunter-gatherers all over the world. I see no reason to doubt that the Tasaday situation was any different.

Yen's Usual Question

On the BBC Horizon film on the Tasaday (Lerner 1989), Douglas Yen is filmed telling how, on a return helicopter flight from Blit to the caves in late August 1972, he took in with him a handful of freshly picked rice plants with mature heads of rice on them. He says,

> I was very skeptical about the isolation of the Tasaday, especially from their [Blit Manobo] neighbours, who are slash-and-burn agriculturalists. . . . I went to Blit [village] and got this (rice plants). But when I went back I was surrounded by 2 or 3 or 4 [Tasaday] kids and so I just pulled this [rice plant] out of the pack and I said, "What is this?," my usual question, "What is this?" Their expressions were of absolute surprise. They didn't know what it was, they didn't associate it with the polished rice they'd been given to eat . . . they didn't associate it with anything. Keep in mind they were children. This couldn't have been faked. [Lerner 1989:16]

It is interesting that the children did not recognize this rice in its natural unmilled form.[4] My question, however, is not whether the children were faking, but why Yen never bothered to show the plant to any Tasaday adults? It is clear from Molony's chapter in this volume that she and Yen were asking other questions to see if the Tasaday knew anything about cultivation. Why then didn't Yen ask at least one adult the same question he had asked the two children—the first question any ethnographer would ask when pursuing the hypothesis he and Molony were investigating—"What is this?" Would the adults have recognized the plant that Yen was carrying around in his pack? Yen was asking "What is this?" to Tasaday adults about all the other plants he was collecting that month. He collected some 200 plant species and, by asking his usual question, elicited 210 Tasaday names for those plants (Yen and Gutierrez 1974:124). It is amazing to me that he failed to ask his usual question to any adult about the rice plant he had picked that same month from a Blit Manobo field just four kilometers away. Eliciting local plant terms from native informants is a complicated business with pitfalls, as I have discussed elsewhere (Headland 1985). Multiple informants should be interviewed in separate sessions, and children should be used only secondarily; children are not normally reliable informants, not only because they are shy before strangers, but because they do not know the plant world near as well as their elders do.

What the Tasaday Ate after June 1971

As to what the Tasaday ate after June 7, 1971, and especially from March 23, 1972, when the Panamin teams began living adjacent to them at the caves (this latter period includes the 38 days when Douglas Yen was there), the answer seems quite clear from Nance's (1975) book: from the beginning one of their important foods was rice. We know that by March 28, 1972, the Tasaday were cooking rice in bamboo tubes in their caves (p. 159); bamboo "cultivated in the lowlands" (p. 23, 64; Elizalde with Fox 1971a:8; Peralta 1987:66).[5] This was only six days after the Panamin team of 41 people had first moved into their camp by the cave site to begin their field investigation. By April 18, the Tasaday were well into eating rice

(Nance 1975:202, 204–205, 311). This was three months before Yen began his fieldwork among them on July 29. "Large amounts of rice were regularly being given to the Tasaday" throughout the time Panamin had their camp at the cave site (p. 311), sometimes "at least twice and possibly three times every day" (p. 257).[6] Table 1 below provides several quotations from Nance, Yen, and Elizalde documenting the use of rice in the Tasaday diet during the period they were being studied by scientists in the early 1970s.

Panamin anthropologist David Baradas also reported that cooked rice was being sneaked into the caves without his knowledge during his period of Tasaday fieldwork in May 1972 (ABC-TV 1986:6). He stated on public television in 1986, "Our repeated request not to dole out food in order for us to get a more real view of their daily activity fell on deaf ears" (ABC-TV 1986). Of course, they had been given large amounts of rice by the Panamin exploration team almost a year earlier than this, one sack of rice on June 7 and 8, and two sacks on June 16, 1971 (Elizalde with Fox 1971a:vii, viii).[7]

Conclusion

No scientist, nor anyone on the Panamin team, ever saw the Tasaday living on wild foods. While it was appropriate for the early investigators to propose the hypothesis that these people were subsisting totally upon wild foods, today, 20 years later, the accumulation of evidence as set forth here leads us now to soundly reject that hypothesis.

TABLE 1

Direct quotes that talk about rice being given to or eaten by Tasaday while scientists were studying their wild food foraging and eating habits.

References from Nance 1975:

Inside were a full bag of rice. . . . [p. 87]. . . . Elizalde gave the Tasaday a piece of white cloth, salt, rice, and a whistle. [p. 101]. . . . He gave them rice to make up for their inability to gather food, as had been done on earlier occasions, and the Tasaday cheered up. [p. 231]. . . . The Tasaday were jovial the next morning, pleased with the rice. [p. 232]. . . . Fernandez and Baradas reported that, without their knowledge, rice had been given regularly and to such an extent from the beginning of their visit that it had distorted their research on Tasaday gathering habits and economy. Baradas estimated that the Tboli had given rice at least twice and possibly three times every day until the anthropologists discovered it. [p. 257]. . . . Fludi had suggested that giving rice was the only way to keep the Tasaday at the caves, otherwise most of them would have gone away. [p. 257]. . . . The anthropologists said it had been expressly understood that there would be no such disruptions, and that this one, like the giving of rice, had thrown the Tasaday far off their normal behavior. [p. 257]. . . . The Tasaday had learned to like rice, Mai said, though it was given to them seldom. [p. 271]. . . . What he had done was make a strong pronouncement to Mai and Fludi against gift giving after Carlos Fernandez and David Baradas discovered that large amounts of rice were regularly being given to the Tasaday. [p. 311]. . . . One evening, Yen had discovered the Tasaday were still getting rice from the tribesmen at the camp: when Dad delivered the rice to them for *biking* [yams] received that day, he found that they had already got rice in the morning. It turned out that Dafal and some of the Tboli camp staff helping Yen and NBC had been giving them rice regularly. Yen and Manda [Elizalde] asked them again not to do this, but they now realized that it was extremely difficult for the tribesmen to see anything wrong with giving the Tasaday rice— there was plenty, the Tasaday liked it; what harm could it do? I [Nance] had been surprised that rice doles continued despite the strictures against it, but soon found out for myself that it was not easy to stick to that rule. [p. 311]. . . . Another message arrived from Elizalde in Tboli, reminding me that there should be no gift giving; rice was permissible, depending on the circumstances. [p. 322]. . . . Fludi looked at me and said, "Should we give them rice?" [p. 323]. . . . If we give rice Etut probably will stay . . . if he would like to have some rice. . . . "I'm not asking for rice, but if you want to give it I'm happy to receive it" [said one Tasaday]. [p. 324]. . . . We had been amply reimbursed for the rice we had given them that same morning. . . . Yen's collecting of *biking* [wild yams] had involved an exchange for rice. [p. 326]. . . . We asked Bilangan if he would like to take her some rice in the meantime. [p. 343]. . . . Bilangan was given enough rice for everyone. . . . He took the rice himself. [p. 344]. . . . As the newborn baby lay in her lap, covered by a rice bag, . . . [p. 345]. . . . The Tasaday told Yen that when they passed by the empty camp it made them feel lonely. Yen suggested to us, however, that it might not be loneliness so much as a longing for rice. [p. 397]. . . . Now the low estimates [of available wild foods] so far would lead you to think that they must be eating something else, something we haven't included [in our list of their foods]. [p. 432]. . . . because of a bag of rice brought to them by Fludi's team. [p. 438]. . . . They did not want us present when they ate. Why? We had seen them eat before. I wondered if it had to do with rice; Fludi had given them rice before the rest of our party arrived and the Tasaday might assume that we did not know about it. Giving rice had become a sore point during an earlier visit, when the anthropologists had disputed with Fludi over rice doles to the Tasaday. This led to a cut in the amount given and also caused antagonism among the visitors. To avoid a recurrence, the Tasaday may have decided that rice was to be eaten in private. . . . Later, he reported that after we left the cave the Tasaday did eat rice. [p. 442]. . . . Even in the short period of contact [in 1971], the Tasaday had learned new words. Rice, for instance, they called *bigas,* a Tagalog word, not *begas,* as in many closer dialects. [p. 21] [Editor's note: If the Tasaday used the word *bigas* for 'rice' in 1971, why did they call it *natek* (literally, 'palm starch') in 1972, as shown in the quotes below?—TNH

[The following quotations (also from Nance 1975) come from English translations of a recording of Tasaday conversations in 1972. The conversations were said to have been recorded on a hidden tape recorder in the cave when no outsiders were present. The first of these statements was recorded on March 28, 1972, only six days after the Panamin team began their field investigation at the cave site. Notice that in 1972 the Tasaday were reported here (below) to be using the word *natek* for 'rice', whereas in 1971 they were reportedly using the term *bigas* for 'rice' (as shown in the sentence directly above in this table).]

Find bamboo to cook the *natek* [literally 'palm starch,' but here 'rice'] of MDDT [i.e., Elizalde]. [p. 159]. . . . The *natek* [starch, i.e., 'rice'] of MDDT [i.e., Elizalde] is starting to taste very good. [p. 202]. . . . All of us have tasted the *natek* of MDDT [i.e., Elizalde]. [p. 204]. . . . I ate plenty of MDDT's [i.e., Elizalde's] *natek.* [p. 204]. . . . I like the taste of this *natek* of MDDT [i.e., Elizalde]. [p. 204]. . . . This *natek* of MDDT [i.e., Elizalde] is white. . . . We will now again eat the *natek* of MDDT. . . . It's good that we have the *natek* of MDDT. . . . Even if we do not go out, we have MDDT's *natek.* . . . He knows that we cannot go out to make our own *natek* so he gives us his. . . . He gives us his own *natek.* . . . Now we are eating his *natek.* [p. 205]

References from Yen 1976b:
One tangible factor . . . is the occasional giving of rice . . . to the Tasaday by Tboli and Blit assistants. [p. 163]. . . . We did not discover the extent of these gifts [of rice] until later. [p. 168]

References from Elizalde with Fox 1971a:
Material Culture Received by the Tasaday. . . . First Visit of PANAMIN (June 7–8, 1971)
1 sack of rice and sample of sweet potatoes. [p. vii]. . . . Second Trip of PANAMIN (June 16, 1971). . . . 2 sacks of rice. [p. viii]

Notes

1. At least the Agta are similar to, and better at, making fire by friction than the Tasaday. *National Geographic,* in its glowing depiction of the primitiveness of the Tasaday, said they can create the "miracle of fire . . . after ten laborious minutes" (MacLeish 1972:228). If *National Geographic's* statement on the same page is correct that "Other Philippine tribes have all but forgotten this ancient technique for making fire," the Agta have not. With dry sticks, Agta men take an average of only 114 seconds to make a fire by friction once they begin rubbing the sticks across each other, followed by an average of 88 seconds of gentle blowing before the smoldering tinder bursts into flame. When I submerged the sticks of their fire-making kit in the river for several seconds and then asked them to do it, their average time for the same two steps extended to 5.5 minutes (Headland 1976 personal field notes), still only half the time it reportedly took the Tasaday.

2. Yen and Gutierrez (1974:104, 105) later found two more species of wild *Dioscorea* recognized by the Tasaday (named by the Tasaday as *mabanal* and *banag limukan*). They report that these two yam types had "lesser importance" in the Tasaday diet, and were "rarely sought."

3. The Tasaday were wearing cloth, not leaves, when first contacted by Elizalde in June 1971 (Elizalde with Fox 1971a; Nance 1975:12, 14, 18, 50, 55, 110; Terry 1989). They switched to leaves at the specific request of Elizalde (Nance 1975:50, 55, 112, 469; Terry 1989). It was the *National Geographic* team which erred, not Panamin, when they stated in their now-famous magazine article that the Tasaday had "no woven cloth; leaves serve as clothing" (MacLeish 1972:242). The Panamin reports clearly stated otherwise (Elizalde with Fox 1971a; Fernandez and Lynch 1972:300; Nance 1975). Unfortunately, Nance's (1981) "photo novel" on the Tasaday enforces the public's view of these people as leaf-wearers. All but four of his 325 photographs of Tasaday show them as wearing only leaves. The exceptions are the four photographs (pp. 211, 212, and 216) taken of the Tasaday woman Etut covering herself with a Panamin rice sack at the time of her child's birth in August 1972.

4. There are some discrepancies between Yen's and Nance's (1975:319) report of this incident. Nance says the plant was millet, not rice. Yen said in his chapter for this volume (which he later withdrew) that he questioned two children who were Lobo and Udo (or Odoq), but Nance says they were Adug and Lolo, two of the other Tasaday children.

5. If the Tasaday knew nothing of cultivation and were not trading with outsiders, where were they getting cultivated bamboo? Not from the forest, for as Peralta states (this volume), "The species of bamboo required did not grow there." Yen and Gutierrez identified this bamboo as *Dinochloa* spp. (1974:117; see also pp. 104 and 126 of the 1976 edition of their paper). Fox said the bamboo was "probably *Bambusa vulgaris*

Schrad., which is planted by man and *not* found in the forest environment of the Tasaday'' (Elizalde with Fox 1971a:8, emphasis in the original).

6. The camp of the 41 people on the Panamin staff, and where the researchers lived, was situated out of sight of the Tasaday caves at an elevation 60 meters lower than that of the caves (Fernandez and Lynch 1972:290).

7. This was milled rice. The national standard sack of rice in the Philippines measures by volume 75 liters and by weight when milled 58 kg (Philippine Yearbook 1977:ix).

● *chapter eleven*

The Tasaday Language: Is it Cotabato Manobo?

E. CLAY JOHNSTON

At the 1989 symposium entitled "The Tasaday Controversy: An Assessment of the Evidence," Thomas Headland presented a working hypothesis which read, in part: "A small band of people known as Tasaday lived . . . in the southern Philippines . . . having no contact with agricultural peoples until the 1960s" (Headland 1989d, and Chapter 1 of this volume).

One test of this hypothesis would be to measure the degree of similarity between the language spoken by the Tasaday and that spoken by the Manobo agricultural peoples living nearby. This chapter describes my method of taking that measurement, and what I subsequently concluded about the Tasaday speech.

Specifically, I attempted to discover some indication of the degree of similarity between Tasaday speech and the language known as Cotabato Manobo by evaluating reactions of speakers of Cotabato Manobo to the following: first, an audio tape recording of Tasaday speakers made in 1972 by Carol Molony and, second, to selected words from a Tasaday word list taken in 1972 by Richard Elkins (1972). I conducted my evaluation during a field trip to the Cotabato Manobo language area January 2–9, 1989.

Background

The language known as Cotabato Manobo is an Austronesian language spoken by an estimated 12,000 people who live scattered in the mountains of the province of Sultan Kudarat, which is one of four provinces comprising what was formerly the province of Cotabato. Cotabato Manobo is one of more than 20 languages making up the Manobo subgroup of the Southern Philippine language family (Elkins 1974, 1977, 1983; Harmon 1979; McFarland 1980:62). Every subsequent mention of "Manobo" in this chapter, unless otherwise noted, refers to the Cotabato Manobo language and the particular ethnic group that speaks it, not to the other Manobo languages and groups.

Since 1957 the Cotabato Manobo language has been studied almost continuously by field linguists of the Summer Institute of Linguistics (SIL) in the Philippines. Various features of the language have been described by them (Barnard, Lindquist, and Forsberg 1955; Errington 1979a, 1979b, 1984, 1988; Errington and Errington 1981; Johnston 1975, 1979; Kerr 1965, 1988a, 1988b; and Lyman

144

1971). It has been compared with other Philippine languages by Reid (1971, this volume) and Walton (1979). Elkins (1971, 1972, 1973–74, 1974, 1977, 1983, and this volume) and Walton (1979) compared it specifically with Tasaday.

From September 1963 to May 1968, and again from September 1973 to May 1978, my wife and I lived about 40% of our time with the Manobo in the municipality of Kalamansig, where we were engaged continually in linguistic research and literacy efforts among them under the auspices of SIL. During this ten-year period I became fluent in Manobo, though I have not actively studied or used the language since 1978 except for two brief visits to the Manobo area in 1988 and 1989.

Method

In January 1989, I played Molony's 1972 tape recording of Tasaday speakers for small groups of Manobo speakers in the villages of Elem, Belanga, and Kelusoy (see Figure 1). The Manobo listeners were not given any information about the source of the recording. They were first asked if they could identify the speakers. Then they were asked whether or not they considered the speakers to be speaking "their" language. Finally, they were asked to make a guess about where these people—the speakers on the tape—might live.

In Elem and Belanga, Manobo informants reviewed with me each of the selected words taken from Elkins's Tasaday list. In Kelusoy, only words from that list that had completely different phonetic forms from known Manobo words were reviewed.

Also, in Belanga, Dasul Masot, who has frequently worked as my informant in the past, helped me transcribe a section of Molony's tape that describes the making of edible starch from the wild caryota palm *(Caryota cuminggi)*. That transcription appears at the end of this chapter (see Appendix).

Manobo Responses to the Tape Recording

Of the Manobo people who listened to the recording, no one ventured a guess as to the names of the speakers. When asked if the people were speaking their language (i.e., Cotabato Manobo), the response in each community was the same: "Yes, but. . . . " The people in Elem said that the *godoy*, "tune," was different and the speech was *melayat*, "having gaps" or "spread out with gaps between," as a person's teeth might be. They also commented on the fact that Manobo people in different communities speak differently. They made no comments that indicated that what they were hearing was outside of acceptable limits for people whom they considered to be fellow Manobo.

In Belanga, the people described the speech on the tape as *megligboyot*, "clumsy, awkward." They, like the people in Elem, suggested that the speakers might be from Beluwan, a Manobo community to the east and closer to the Tboli language area. (I do not know the specific location of this community.)

In Kelusoy, which is in the interior and nearer to the Tboli area (about 25 km [16 mi] from the Tasaday caves), as the people listened to the tape they identified

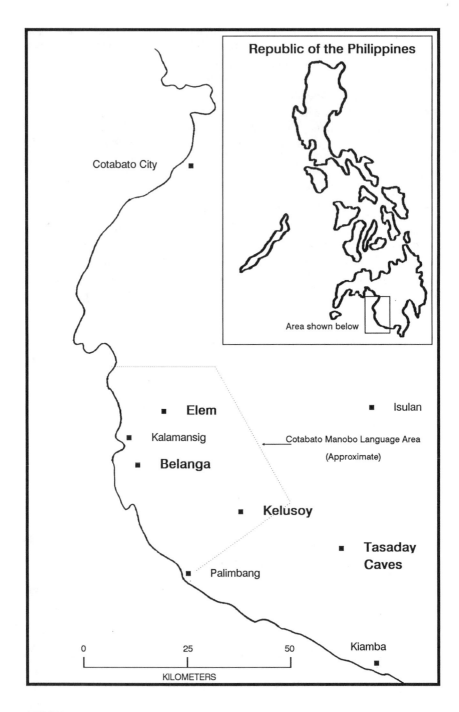

FIGURE 1
Southwestern Mindanao

the word *supéng* 'clamp' (sentences 23 and 24 in Appendix) as Tboli. They suggested that the speakers were probably from a Manobo community where Manobo and Tboli people intermarry. Vivian Forsberg of SIL has confirmed that this is a Tboli word meaning 'fork of a tree or branch' (personal communication).

None of the Manobo people for whom I played the tape indicated any difficulty in following the speaker's narration even though there were words they did not recognize as Manobo.

Manobo Responses to Selected Words in the Tasaday Word List

Elkins's (1972) Tasaday word list has 263 entries that he recorded. I immediately recognized 217 of them (83%) as being identical with the Manobo lexicon known to me. I then compiled a list of the 46 words I did not recognize (17%) in order to review them with Manobo people. (This list, along with my notes, is displayed in Table 1.)

Of these 46 words, 9 turned out to be Manobo words that were correctly entered in the list but were unknown to me. Of the remaining 37 unrecognized words, 22 were Manobo words that have different meanings in Manobo from those assigned in Elkins's Tasaday list. It is my opinion that 12 of these are elicitation mistakes since the Tasaday word in Elkins's list matches a Manobo word that is related semantically in some obvious way to the English meaning of the word being elicited; for example, specific for generic, effect for cause, or appearance for quality. (These 12 words are listed preceding Table 1.)

Of the remaining 25 words, 15 did not match any known word form in Manobo. The other 10, while similar in form to known Manobo words, seemed completely different in meaning.

The Tasaday language, then, according to my best judgment, is approximately 90% (238/263) the same as Cotabato Manobo. It is noteworthy that this matches my intuitive guess based on my first hearing of Molony's Tasaday tape. I communicated this estimate to her by letter on November 28, 1988, before any of the preceding evaluation was made.

In further support of this conclusion (that the vocabulary of the two speech communities is 90% identical), the transcribed text in the Appendix contains 99 different word forms, only 12 of which (including the particles) differ from Manobo. That is, 88% of the words in the text are identical.

Some Notable Word Form Differences

A few novel idiosyncracies occur in the data (not included in the preceding counts or in Table 1). One is a reversal of the word forms for 'alive' and 'dead'. The Manobo word for 'dead', *nematay,* is entered in Elkins's list for 'alive.' The word *nehagtay,* which means 'alive' in Manobo, is entered for 'dead'. Also, the words for 'sun', 'moon', and 'stars' are very different from their Manobo counterparts and from the forms found in other Philippine languages. (For comparisons, see Reid 1971:67, 105, 139.)

TABLE 1

Tasaday words not immediately recognized and Manobo informants responses to them

In January 1989, I reviewed Richard Elkins's (1972) Tasaday list. Table 1 is a list of the Tasaday words I did not immediately recognize as part of the Cotabato Manobo lexicon. The notes in righthand column of the table are based on discussions of each word with several different speakers of Cotabato Manobo in the villages of Elem and Belanga in January 1989. I have used the following notations:

UNKNOWN means that the Manobo speakers did not recognize the form as part of their lexicon.

SAME means that this word was recognized by the Manobo speakers as part of their lexicon with a similar meaning to that recorded by Elkins. Sometimes there were vowel variations between the form in Elkins's list and what the Manobo speakers considered to be correct. These variations are enclosed in slashes, e.g., /lunut/, along with other notes.

Words *not* labeled UNKNOWN or SAME were known words in Manobo but having a different meaning from the one given in Elkins's list. If I knew the Manobo word that corresponded to the gloss in the list, I include it in the notes in column 3. Single quotes mark my glosses for word forms in Cotabato Manobo based on my discussions with Manobo speakers in January 1989. The Manobo orthography (as described in the Appendix) was used for all the Tasaday and Manobo word forms in the list and in the notes.

Words from Table 1 that I suspect to be elicitation mistakes:

4. anger	29. boil (skin)	62. count	71. deep
115. floor	170. liver	172. lonely	224. rain
239. roof	271. smell	274. snake	311. thirst

Meaning Gloss	Tasaday Word	Notes based on Manobo
4. anger	*eqpebalaw*	'to cause to be bold/fierce'
5. ankle	*peningtingan*	SAME /peningtingen/
14. bark	*lunet*	SAME /lunét/ alternate form /lunut/
17. betel pepper leaf	*lawingan*	SAME
29. boil (skin)	*mebagà*	'swollen'
38. buttocks	*pundang*	UNKNOWN
47. chicken	*melok*	SAME 'wild chicken'
52. cloud	*paway*	UNKNOWN
62. count	*eg-isa*	SAME? /eg-esà/, in counting, /isa/ is the Manobo word for 'one'
64. crow	*meites*	UNKNOWN
67. day	*pegleun*	UNKNOWN—in Manobo /agdaw/ is 'sun' or 'day'
71. deep	*keladayan*	'smooth water' as in a river where there are no rocks/ turbulence; /medalem/ is word for 'deep'

(Continued next page)

(Table 1 continued)

Meaning Gloss	Tasaday Word	Notes based on Manobo
83. dull (knife)	*bulinak*	UNKNOWN
115. floor	*belagkal*	'floor support' or 'joist' in house construction
118. to fly	*lipad*	UNKNOWN—/*eglayang*/ is 'to fly/glide'
120. forget	*kelipot*	'to pretend not to hear', i.e., 'to feign sleep'
125. full, satisfied	*egtegitegi*	UNKNOWN—/*nebesug*/ is word for 'full' in Manobo
142. house	*ilib*	'rock face', i.e., a cliff /*dalesan*/ is 'house'
154. knee	*igbukug*	'hunchback' or 'stooped' /*lulud*/ is 'knee'
166. lightning	*bukyaw*	UNKNOWN—/*silà*/ in Manobo is 'lightning'
170. liver	*bagà*	'lungs' in Manobo
171. loincloth	*bangi*	UNKNOWN—/*baeg*/ in Manobo
172. lonely	*egkebenges*	'to become sad'
181. moon	*sebang*	/*egsebang*/ 'to rise in the west at sunset'—used only with 'moon' as the implied subject—western horizon is called /*sebangan*/
184. mosquito	*tagenek*	SAME /*tegenek*/
199. noon	*nekepakang*	SAME—alternate form is /*nekebugsang*/
205. old person	*lukesan*	SAME? /*lukes*/ means 'old person'—/*eglukes*/ means 'to oversee responsibly' /*lukesan*/ normally means children who are 'overseen' by elders
216. wild pig	*usa*	SAME 'wild pig or deer'; not generic for other animals
221. pull	*gawes*	/*eggawes*/ means 'to forbid'
224. rain	*dames*	'rainstorm with wind'
225. rainbow	*taladtad*	same form is used for small plant leaf used as ingredient in betel nut chew
227. rat	*tekubung*	SAME—specific for large variety of rat—/*ungeh*/ is more common

(Continued next page)

(Table 1 continued)

Meaning Gloss	Tasaday Word	Notes based on Manobo
232. rib	*kumabus*	SAME
239. roof	*bunbun*	'cover for protection from sun or rain'—/atep/ is common word for 'roof'
248. scar	*lakesan*	UNKNOWN /eglakes/ means 'to splint,' e.g., bind a new post to an old weak one
271. smell	*habhab*	'to sniff,' e.g., a dog
274. snake	*epuy*	a specific variety of poisonous snake—/uled/ is generic for harmful snakes
275. sole of foot	*paked*	SAME? /taked/
277. sour	*mesupelet*	'causing choking'—an adjective used for food which catches in throat
279. 8″ span	*dangawan*	'good person' or 'good-thinking person'
280. spider	*keluwating*	UNKNOWN
285. star	*tubali*	name of specific star, /bituen/ is generic
287. to stick to	*igkelet*	UNKNOWN—/egdeket/ means 'to stick to'
311. thirst	*egbuelen*	'to drink to wash down food'
342. water container	*nepnep*	SAME /napnap/ a small variety of bamboo sometimes used as a temporary water container
344. waterfall	*etas*	UNKNOWN

I first suspected, on the basis of proximity and the reaction of Manobo speakers, that the unknown word forms would turn out to be borrowed from the Tboli or Blaan languages. A cursory comparison with the word lists compiled by Reid (1971) did not support this assumption. In fact, only one of the unknown words, *dangawan*, 'hand span', appeared similar to Tboli and Blaan. Another word, *lakesan*, 'scar', may possibly be associated with *laas*, 'scar' in Blaan.

Some Notable Phonological Differences

One feature I missed in listening to the Tasaday tape was some phonological differences between the verb- and noun-marking particles of Tasaday and the verb- and noun-marking particles of Manobo. These were called to my attention by my informant, Dasul Masot. I have marked them with double asterisks (**) in the interlinear transcription in the Appendix.

In the case of verb-marking particles, in Manobo languages these particles are usually single-syllable words that modify the meaning of the verb as to completion, intention, or assertion. Two of the forms in the Tasaday text, *dò* and *duu,* occur in Manobo but are used differently. The way they were used in the Tasaday text was considered strange by Masot. Two other forms, *do* and *de,* are not found in Manobo and seemed to be used where we would have expected the form *dé,* which can be translated 'already', meaning the action is completed. Note, however, that the Manobo form *dé* does occur in several places in the Tasaday text in a manner consistent with its use in Manobo.

In the case of noun-marking particles, these particles sometimes identify the noun as the grammatical topic of the sentence. Sometimes they seem to be a matter of the speaker's style. Two such particles in the Tasaday text are not found in Manobo: *sadu* and *sado.* They occur where Manobo would expect *sa* or *sak.* I cannot distinguish any meaning difference in these Manobo forms. Note, however, that Manobo *sa* and *sak* both occur in the Tasaday text.

In the Appendix is a limited description of the Manobo orthography used in transcribing the Tasaday text and word list. Reid (1971) gives a complete listing of the phones of the Manobo phonemic alphabet.

Defining the Terms "Language" and "Dialect"

Before I try to answer the main question posed in the title of this chapter, I must define some terms. What do we mean when we say "same language," or "dialects of the same language"?

McFarland (1980:1–10) discusses criteria for describing the relationship between the speech of two different communities. In his view, the test is mutual intelligibility; that is, if people from the two groups can communicate, even with some difficulty, they may be considered to be speaking the same language. Also, McFarland (p. 10) feels that a shared vocabulary of 75% or more is an indication of probable intelligibility between the speech of any two groups. If the people can communicate but notice differences between their speech and that of the other group, they may be considered to be speaking dialects of the same language.

Conclusion

Based on the McFarland definition, the data presented in this article, and everything I learned in evaluating the data with Manobo speakers, it is my assertion that Tasaday is clearly the same language as Cotabato Manobo.

The shared vocabulary between the Tasaday group and the Manobo speakers I interviewed is very high—about 90%. I found nothing in the reaction of the Manobo listeners or in my understanding of what we heard on the tape to call into question the mutual intelligibility of these speech communities. Both are close dialects of the same language, or, if we assume the language spoken by the larger group to be primary, Tasaday is a dialect of Cotabato Manobo.

This conclusion does not ignore the differences between the speech of these two communities. The two dialects are not identical, as evidenced by Manobo reaction to what they heard on the Tasaday tape recording. Vocabulary differ-ences between the two dialects are significant and unusual in that several of them represent very common objects. Furthermore, the Tasaday words for these objects are not similar to those in other Philippine languages.

Appendix: A Tasaday Text

With the help of a Manobo informant, Dasul Masot, I transcribed the following Tasaday text in January 1989. The audiotape from which it comes was recorded by Carol Molony in 1972 at the Tasaday caves. This section of the recording is a monologue about the procedure for extracting edible starch from the caryota palm.

Words in the text that were not recognized as Manobo are marked in three different ways: (1) Words whose meaning could be deciphered from the context are glossed in all caps (e.g., CLAMP). (2) Words whose meaning could not be deciphered are glossed "Unknown." (3) Noun-marking and verb-marking words whose function is clear but whose forms are different from those found in Manobo are glossed with a double asterisk (**).

The alphabet used for transcribing the text is Manobo. In Manobo most of the consonants match their phonetic values. Those that differ are /p/ and glottal stop. For these, /p/ is used for the bilabial fricative which sounds like /f/; glottal stop in word-final position is written as a grave accent on the last vowel (e.g., /kedagì/); in word-initial position, it is not written (e.g., /uton/); inside of words it is written as a hyphen when it occurs syllable-initial following a consonant (e.g., /meilag-ilag/), and it is not written when it is syllable-initial following a vowel (e.g., /humaa/ which has an unwritten glottal stop before the final /a/).

Vowel sounds correspond to the initial vowel sounds in the following Stan-dard American English words:

/a/	as in *bottle*
/u/	as in *boot*
/i/	as in *beet*
/e/	as in *but*
/é/	as in *bet*
/o/	as in *both*

Sentence 1
eglagbet   ké   basag.
search-for   we   caryota-palm
We look for the palm.

Sentence 2
hinaa   ké   dé   basag,   duen   palas   di
saw-it   we   already   palm   there-is   appearance   its

duen   keli   di.
there-is   STARCH its
When we saw the palm, it had the appearance of having a good amount of starch.

Sentence 3
na, kuwaen da   sa pais   basag, pinilay da.
next get-it they   CHOPPING-INSTRUMENT palm   fell-it   they
Next, when they get the instrument for cutting the palm, they chop it down.

Sentence 4
hinaa   da diyà   bukag   di   (diyé?).
saw-it   they at   core   its   (that's-true?)
They looked at its core. (Aside to others present "Isn't that so?")

Sentence 5
tigesa   ma diyà bukag   di   amuk duen   keli   di.
different also at   core   its   if   there-is STARCH its
Its core will be different in appearance if it has starch.

Sentence 6
amuk   melenek,   endà.
if   soft   no
If it (the core) is soft, it does not have starch.

Sentence 7
amuk   metegas, duen.
if   hard   there-is
If it is hard, it does have starch.

Sentence 8
duen   kagi   wayeg di, duen   eluk   wagey di.
there-is word/speech water its there-is sloshing-sound water its
It has the voice of water, it has the sloshing sound of water.

Sentence 9
peedung   dalem supà   di diyà pesu   di (ohò),   iya sa dinegen.
cause-to-begin inside UNKNOWN its at   base its (yes)   that thing-heard
Beginning with UNKNOWN at its base (that's right), that what is heard.

Sentence 10
amuk mepion sa kedagì   wayeg di,   duen   keli   di.
if   good   to-be-sounding water its there-is STARCH its
If there is a good sounding of its water, it has starch.

Sentence 11
amuk mepion dagì   wayeg di,   lumagbas pumilay.
if   good   sound   water its   will-pass-he will-fell-he
If its sound of water is good, he will go ahead and chop it down.

Sentence 12
hê,   ataw nga   mepilay   da   dò dahiya,
next/then or   UNKNOWN to-fell-involuntarily they ** there
egtebuk da   dé   diyà teliwadà   lawa di.
to-split they already at   middle   body its
**Then look, or if they happen to fell it there, they will split its body open in
the middle.**
Sentence 13
tinagped da   dò diyà taman   keli   di.
cut-off   they ** at   until   STARCH its
They will cut it off at the place which is the extent of its starch.

Sentence 14
nadò   taman   keli   di, iya taman di kenà   ta egtagped
UNKNOWN until   STARCH its that   until   its place we cut-off
sadu basag.
**   palm
Up to the extent of its starch, that is the place we will cut off the palm.

Sentence 15
ubus   sa ketagped ta, uwiten   ta dalem   wayeg.
finish   cutting-off our will-take-it we into   water/river
When we are finished cutting it off, we will take it into the river.

Sentence 16
uwiten   ta   dalem wayeg,   itenà   ta de dahiya.
to-take-it we   into   water/river to put-it we ** there
When we have taken it into the river, we will put it down there.

Sentence 17
langun sado   kedoo   di eg-ugpà   diyà palas
all   **   having-become-many its to-stay/stay-put at   UNKNOWN
kenà   ta egsakul,   sạdu medapag diyà wayeg, diyà ilis
place we to-scoop   **   near   at   water   at   edge
gunaan   di.
strainer/press its
**All of its pieces will be resting near our place for scooping up water, at the
edge of the strainer.**

Sentence 18
ubus   da   do iya, baelan   da de   gunaan.
finished they ** that will-make they ** strainer
**When they have finished that (taking it all to the river), they will make a
strainer.**

Sentence 19
kuwaen ta de lunét kayu.
will-get we ** bark tree
We will get the bark of a tree.

Sentence 20
ubus dé sak lunét kayu, baelan dé sa gunaan dahiya.
finished already bark tree will-make already strainer there
When we have finished getting the tree bark, the strainer will be made.

Sentence 21
ubus duu gunaan, itaen ta de sado lunét kayu.
finished ** strainer to-put-under we(inc) ** ** bark tree
When the strainer has been made, we put the tree bark under it (to catch the starch that falls through the strainer with the water).

Sentence 22
tueg sadu lunét kayu.
to-roast ** bark tree
The bark of the tree will be roasted in the fire (i.e., to seal the ends together to make a trough for the water and starch).

Sentence 23
ubus dé iya, baelan supéng di sadu lunét kayu
finished already that will-make-it CLAMP its ** bark tree
When the roasting of the bark is finished, its clamp will be made from tree bark.

[break in discourse]

Sentence 24
amuk duen sadu belagen, polot ta duu sadu supéng di.
if there-is ** rattan-vine will-bind/tie-it we ** ** CLAMP its
If there is some rattan available, we will bind the clamp with it.

Sentence 25
amuk duen ma polot dahini, duen ma sadu ugpu di.
if there-is also binding here there-is also ** end its
If there is binding here (i.e., at one end), there will also be binding at the other end of it.

Sentence 26
sadu polot ma diyà uman ta igpolot, daedò dema
** binding also at every-time we have-bound-it there again
sadu ugpu di.
** end its
Whenever we bind it also with that binding, there we are again at its end (meaning not clear).

Sentence 27
pelesen daedò elê daedò, endà uman di, endà egtebow sadu
to-tighten-it there UNKNOWN there not again it not to-arrive **
wayeg di.
water its
It will be tightened in that place—it will not happen again—its water (i.e., the water and starch squeezed out of the palm) will not run out.

Sentence 28
ubus   dé   iya, sumakul   ki de.
finished already that will-scoop/scrape we **
When that is finished, we will scoop out the core of the palm.

Sentence 29
ubus   ké sumakul,   duen   sadu lubulubu.
finished we will-scoop/scrape there-is **   scrapings
When we have finished scooping out the palm, there is a pile of scrapings.

Sentence 30
na,   kuwa ta de sadu lubu,   ugpà
now/next to-get we ** **   scrapings to-stay/stay-put
ta   de diatas   sadu gunaan.
we ** above/on-top of **   strainer
**Then, when we have gathered the scrapings, we put them on top of the
   strainer/press.**

Sentence 31
gumunà   ki de.
to-strain-with-pressing we **
We press and strain it (the palm shavings).

● *chapter twelve*

The Role of the National Museum of the Philippines in the Tasaday Issue

In 1971 the National Museum of the Philippines was working on the Early Man Project in the Cagayan Valley of Northern Luzon. The project was a Pleistocene archaeological research effort headed by Robert B. Fox, then Chief of the Anthropology Division of the National Museum, with the author, then a graduate student at the University of the Philippines, as one of the staff members.

Prior to July of that year, Fox, then in the Cagayan Valley with the author, received a telegram from Panamin (Presidential Assistant on National Minorities, headed by Manuel Elizalde, Jr.), informing him of the discovery of a group of people in South Cotabato and requesting that he come to Cotabato to verify the discovery. (Fox was then a consultant of Panamin.)

He received the wire with skepticism, as he did subsequent telegrams. He discussed with his staff the issues that could be raised regarding the initial items of information, e.g., the stone tools, the question of isolation, the use of sago, the presence of baskets, etc. He then went to Cotabato in response to the request and to see the reported group.

When Fox returned to Manila from Cotabato, he held a follow-up discussion with us, presenting the information that he had obtained. He then asked me to go with him to Cotabato to see the group. We made the trip in July 1971.

For reasons that only Fox knew, when I arrived in Cotabato I was introduced to Elizalde as a "scientific illustrator," though my official position in the National Museum at that time was museum researcher. I, however, acted the role since I assumed that Fox might have wanted an observer who was unknown to Panamin at that time. In this guise, I collected data in piecemeal fashion, obtaining the services of the available interpreters intermittently.

At the same time that I was at the edge of the forest with the Tasaday, formal interviews were being conducted by the Panamin staff, by various correspondents, and by people from the Institute of Philippine Culture of the Ateneo de Manila University. Since I was not a part of the formal interview process, I moved about the clearing to observe other Tasaday in a nearby hut. I there saw one male individual sharpening the end of a stick with a piece of stone that looked like a thumb-nail scraper. I asked to see the piece of stone. It was an opaline quartz high-angle scraper with stepped working edge. I then gave the tool back to the man and returned to the main group where the interviews were in progress.

I listened to the interviews quietly until Elizalde showed the two hafted stone tools to the group, saying that these were the only tools that they had found in use among the Tasaday. It was then that I interrupted, saying that I had just seen another stone tool in use in the other hut. Elizalde insisted that they had already gathered all the stone tools that they had found. I insisted that I had seen an opaline quartz high-angle scraper in use. Fox then asked me what it was and I explained that it was something similar to the paleolithic-type tools we had been encountering in our archaeological work in the Cagayan Valley. At that point, Elizalde asked one of his men to get the tool for Fox to examine. After examining the tool, Fox agreed with my finding.

I wish to point out here that nobody in the whole group, not even Fox, was aware of the existence of the high-angle scraper until I brought it up. Nobody else in the group except Fox and I could recognize this type of tool, because of the quantities of similar materials we had excavated in the Cagayan Valley.

After this, I was asked to sketch illustrations of the tools. Reproductions of the drawings I made in my field notebook are appended below. To my knowledge, these three are the only tools found among the Tasaday that were examined by National Museum personnel. (I was told later that these tools were sent to then First Lady Imelda R. Marcos in Malacañang Palace in Manila.) These tools were never seen again.

Other Tasaday stone tools were subsequently displayed in the Panamin Museum in the Nayong Filipino Complex and photographs were published of them. But these were items specially made by the Tasaday to demonstrate to newspaper correspondents how they made hafted stone tools.

Later I was able to talk with Balayam, one of the more vocal of the Tasaday group members, and I asked him (through Igna who interpreted for me) to let me tape-record his playing of the bamboo Jew's harp. Before recording the music, I asked him what he calls his group. He stated, "Manobo Tasaday."

More and more questions were coming to mind. So when meetings were held in the Panamin camp in Kemato, I asked what they thought might be the origin of the Tasaday's basketry and the Jew's harp. (The Jew's harp could not have been made without the use of metal tools.) I also raised the issue concerning the improbability of their being able to extract palm cabbages or to maintain a sago-making technology with the tools they had. All the replies to these questions were reduced to the same answer: the items had been introduced by the Manobo hunter Dafal.

The next day I was no longer included in the group that went back to see the Tasaday at the forest edge. Being ignored, I felt that I was unwanted because of the sensitive issues I had raised. I returned to Manila to report back to work at the National Museum.

The Three Stone Tools

The Scraper

The scraper was made of opaline quartz, approximately 2.1 cm by 1.4 cm by 0.8 cm in size (see Figure 1). The striking platform, bulb of percussion, and point of percussion were evident. The edge of the ventral side opposite to the bulb of percussion exhibited invasive and stepped flaking on the edge opposite that of the striking platform. The use-wear was evident on this edge.

The typology of the tool conformed with the unifacial flaked stone tool technology found in the premetal archaeological sites in the Philippines and the rest of island Southeast Asia. The patination and use-wear indicated long-term use.

The Hafted Edge-ground Tool

The hafted edge-ground tool appeared to be made of sandstone. It was approximately 9 cm by 6.5 cm by 1.8 cm in size (Figure 2). The total length of the tool including the handle was 20.5 cm. The body of the stone was lashed to a rattan (*Calamus* sp.) handle. A segment of the stone approximately 5 by 2 cm was exposed from the hafting. This exposed segment had a working edge of approximately 3.5 cm. The grinding of this edge was bifacial. The edge showed bruise marks.

The form of the tool was rather unusual; such a shape had not been encountered in any other group nor in any archaeological site in the country. Usually edge-ground tools in the Philippines are tabular in form with the ground edge oriented to one end. The working edge of this tool was not found in either of the terminal ends of the longitudinal axis, but was instead perpendicular to this. The lashing of the hafting, however, has ethnographic analogies even in the ethno-

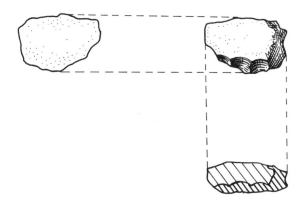

FIGURE 1

The Tasaday stone scraper of opaline quartz; size approximately 2.1 cm by 1.4 cm by 0.8 cm (shown here actual size) (sketch by Jesus Peralta 1971)

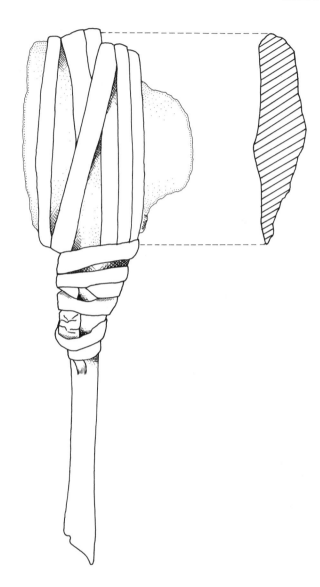

FIGURE 2
The hafted edge-ground tool; size approximately 9 cm by 6.5 cm by 1.8 cm; length including handle 20.5 cm; stone was lashed to a rattan handle, as shown here (sketch by Jesus Peralta 1971)

graphic collections of the National Museum. The patination and use-wear on the stone and the hafting indicated long-term use.

The Hafted Stone Hammer

The hafted stone hammer was of an undetermined kind of stone (possibly andesitic) measuring approximately 11 by 6 cm (Figure 3). The thickness was not mea-

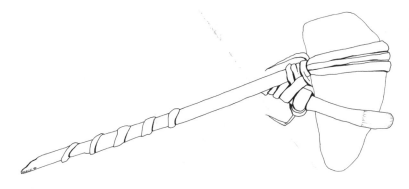

FIGURE 3
The hafted stone hammer; size approximately 11 cm by 6 cm; length with handle was 28.5 cm (sketch by Jesus Peralta 1971)

sured. The total length of the tool including the handle was 28.5 cm. Bruise marks were evident on the working end of the tool.

Stone hammers of this type have been found in ethnographic and archaeological contexts in the Philippines, although without the hafting. The patination and use-wear on the stone and the hafting suggested long-term use.

In sum, it is my judgment that these three tools were actual tools that had been used for an undetermined length of time and that they had been made using mental templates canalized through distinct cultural imperatives. This is especially true of the flake tool.

The 1986 Controversy

When the controversy surrounding the Tasaday became public in 1986, Carlos Fernandez asked me to accompany him and others to visit the Tasaday. We stayed from April 17 to April 24, 1986. Fernandez, of course, was one of the original ethnographers of the Tasaday in 1972. My report describing that visit was read in the Indo-Pacific Prehistoric Association meetings held in Osaka and Tokyo, Japan, in 1987 (Peralta 1987).

At that time (mid-1986), the National Museum's position on the controversy, as stated by then Assistant Director and Officer in Charge, Alfredo Evangelista, was that the weight of the available ethnographic literature supported the authenticity of the Tasaday. While the existing ethnographic data were insufficient due to the short time spent studying the group, the basic data indicated the existence of a subgroup of the South Cotabato Manobo in the area of the Tasaday mountain. Continued study of the group was recommended. An investigation of the case by the Committee on National Cultural Communities, the Philippine House of Representatives, and the Congress of the Philippines supported the findings of the ethnographers. In November 1988, Philippine President Corazon Aquino, in a public address to the International Festival and Conference on Indigenous and

Traditional Cultures, stated the Philippine government's position recognizing the Tasaday as an authentic ethnolinguistic group.

The 1986 Visit

As I stated in my 1987 report, a large group of Tasaday were congregated at the mouth of the cave when we arrived in April 1986. A quick inspection of the cave complex showed that "Cave III" (Fernandez and Lynch 1972) and the immediate areas were completely clean-swept, except for tiny pieces of paper, foil, and other debris apparently from previous visits of people with market commodities.

Tasaday Dress in April 1986

The adults were dressed in loin coverings and skirts of leaves of the same plant they used in the 1970s *(Curculigo capitulata)*. But beneath these could be seen well-worn clothing, almost completely covered by the leaves. When we asked why they wore the leaves over their cloth loin covering, they replied vaguely that the leaves were stronger and afforded better protection. They also stated that the cloth and leaves were equally good and they had no preferences. They evaded the issue of the use of leaves over the cloth.

The implication, at least to this author, was that the Tasaday were putting on the leaves for the benefit of outsiders who had come to see and photograph them, having been conditioned to this in the past. The less reticent among them even knew what was wanted of them in terms of action and poses. It appeared that they were conscious of the image that was wanted of them and, in fact, they were putting on a visual and even an auditive performance. There was no indication from any of the dialogue that they had been asked to attempt this seeming deception. It appeared rather to be a spontaneous attempt to maintain an appearance because of the economic benefits that it brought.

When they were made to realize that Elizalde might no longer return to see them, and that they should learn to live their own lives without depending on the return of Elizalde, they declared a *magto kagi* (literally, 'new word') emphasizing their liberation from the past. At this point the idea that they should wear whatever they wished was injected. We also suggested that they could dress the way they normally did when other people were not around. Igna, our interpreter, also suggested to them during their private conversations one evening that they should not put up an appearance but just wear what they ordinarily wear.

The next morning came as a revelation.

He woke up that morning in Cave III with visitors in the persons of Gintuy, Labo, and Bilangan. They were wearing cloth loin coverings, tattered pairs of red trunks, *Curculigo* leaves, soiled T-shirts, and other motley clothing. The women in Cave I were in different kinds of cotton skirts and blouses. The leaf skirt was totally absent. The adolescent males and young boys wore only *Curculigo* leaves as loin coverings.

The Population in April 1986

From 1972 to 1986 there was quite an increase in the population due to subsequent intermarriages between Tasaday and Blit Manobo. There were now 17 Manobo women and two men who had married into the Tasaday group. Including the newly born children of the Manobo-Tasaday unions, there were 41 Tasaday and 20 Manobo, bringing the entire forest population to 61. (During the previous 15 years there had been seven deaths and one case of abduction of a Tasaday woman.) It is highly probable that there were other individuals in the group who were not included in our count, since the brevity of our visit did not allow for verification of the census information. We calculated there were 16 nuclear units in all. (These are listed by name in Peralta 1987:64.)

The Subsistence and Technology in April 1986

During our visit, the food we observed, apart from that brought in by our party, included caryota palm hearts, rattan fruit, caryota (sago) starch, tadpoles, crabs, and wild yams. The palm starch was said to have deer fat in it. Their quantity of food did not appear to be sufficient to sustain the group under ordinary circumstances. The large amount of caryota hearts gathered suggested this to be emergency rations—to supply the food needed to enable them to stay in the caves while the visitors were around.

The bow and arrow seemed now to be an important piece of equipment. Deer, monkey, and pig were said to be the animals hunted. All married adult men had a bow and arrows, except four of the younger males. We counted a total of 12 sets, including two belonging to the two Manobo men. All of the bows and arrows were made by the Manobo and given to the Tasaday. These could not be made in the Tasaday area because the species of bamboo required did not grow there.

As to subsistence mode, the Tasaday as we observed them had remained food procurers. No cultivation of any kind was noted, though informants said that some Tasaday had helped various Manobo cultivate swiddens in the recent past.

There were indications as well that the in-married Manobo women and men occasionally brought in food from the Manobo village of Blit in exchange for forest products and other economic benefits not defined to us. Thus there was in April 1986 considerable alteration from the earlier reported diet of the Tasaday.

Conclusion: Tasaday Culture Change

The most dramatic catalyst for culture change among the Tasaday since the 1972 inroads was the establishment of intermarriage with the Blit Manobo. The in-marriages of 19 Manobo have doubtless precipitated major upheaval. Not only was the Tasaday's problem of spouse unavailability solved by this, but opportunities have been opened up for them to have a more direct and reliable supply of outside goods. The Tasaday are now desirous of and dependent upon products such as rice, tobacco, salt, cloth, etc. Further, the presence within the population today of individuals who have come from a horticultural society posits the potential for further change to food production.

It seems highly likely that the interaction between the Manobo and the Tasaday will intensify in the near future, and will probably develop into a convergence of culture and language. There are only 12 adult individuals still steeped in the values, beliefs, and other cultural traits of the Tasaday, so the more abstract aspects of the culture will likely disappear within the next generation, and the Tasaday will remain only as so much ethnographic data.

PART IV

Comments from Outside Scientists

● *chapter thirteen*

Making Sense of the Tasaday: Three Discourses

RICHARD B. LEE

In making sense of the Tasaday, evaluating the ethnographic evidence is only part of the story. We have the obligation to frame the problem within at least three discourses: the Tasaday themselves, the Tasaday in the Philippine context, and the Tasaday case and its role in Western consciousness. The most remarkable feature of the Tasaday affair is that issues which seem cut-and-dried in one discourse dissolve and recombine to assume quite different meanings in other discourses.

The complexities are compounded when we pose the nonquestion: Are the Tasaday "real"? Of course they are real. But the nature of their "reality" depends on which discourse we are engaging. They may well constitute an ethnic group that has lived by foraging. But that is only a starting point. What they are not is a Stone Age relict population locked in a time warp out of contact with the rest of the world for hundreds of years.

Discourse One: The Tasaday Themselves

The first discourse attempts to locate the Tasaday historically and socially within their immediate context. The task here is to evaluate the claims to antiquity and isolation originally put forward by their "discoverers." Six lines of evidence lead to the conclusion that the original claims cannot be sustained, and the Tasaday to this extent are a hoax.[1]

1. *The Middens:* No one has found a trace of archaeological deposits in or in front of the famous Tasaday caves. I find William Longacre's argument (this volume) convincing: if there are middens, it would not take long for a trained archaeologist to find them, and conversely, their absence would be a powerful support for the hoax view. This would be the simplest and most elegant way of resolving the issue of time-depth authenticity.

2. *The Diet:* How foragers live in the rain forest without access to cereal crops or root crops of neighboring cultivators has become an area of increasing focus in hunter-gatherer studies (Bailey et al. 1989; Headland 1987, 1989a). It seems unlikely that the Tasaday would walk for three days into the forest to dig tubers and ignore much closer resources available at neighboring agricultural villages. Thomas Headland's arguments on this point are compelling.

3. *The Proximity of Villages:* Even if the dietary sources in the forest were adequate, it seems highly unlikely that people like the Tasaday would ignore their neighbors living three hours' walk away. Although the frontier of settlement has moved closer in this century, it would be interesting to trace the proximity of agricultural settlement in relation to the Tasaday caves 50 or 100 years ago, to see how many villages would have been found within the radius of a one-, two-, or three-day walk.

4. *The Tools:* The "heirloom" stone axes produced by the Tasaday in 1972–73 could not have sustained any meaningful use in production. The status of these tools remains unclear. In the meantime what did their nonmetal tool assemblage consist of and would it have been sufficient to have sustained life? Robert Carneiro's observations (this volume) on this point are hard to dispute.

5. *The Other Groups:* Two purported "other" groups similar to the Tasaday—the Sanduka and the Tasafang—were claimed to have been the source of the wives of the Tasaday men. Neither of these groups has ever been found. Even had they existed there is no evidence that they were as isolated as the Tasaday were claimed to be. Thus, if the Tasaday women married into groups that were part of the wider world, then in what sense were the Tasaday "isolated"? If on the other hand the three groups constituted a closed breeding deme of under 100 people, it would have been below the minimum size threshold of breeding deme viability (as reviewed in Headland 1990a:26–27), making long term survival unlikely.

6. *The Immunology Question:* If the Tasaday were out of contact with the wider world for several hundred years, then the initial "contracts" in the late 1960s should have produced evidence for infections, epidemics, and higher mortality for the Tasaday. That this did not occur strongly indicates that the Tasaday *were not* isolated from the wider world.

Taken singly or in pairs each of the six preceding arguments might not constitute an overpowering case for the hoax theory. Together they make some form of hoax extremely difficult to discount. But at this point we need to be clear: If the Tasaday story is a "Rain Forest Watergate" (Berreman, this volume), we must acknowledge that it is Elizalde's Watergate and not the Tasaday's.

The most likely scenario—discounting the argument that they were local peasants hired as actors for the job—is that the Tasaday are a Manobo-speaking people, possibly a distinct ethnic group, possibly foragers or part-time foragers who have maintained regular contact with other peoples. They are not isolated and certainly not "Stone Age," whatever that may mean in this context. From internal evidence they appeared to be practicing sharing and egalitarian principles characteristic of the foraging or communal mode of production (Lee 1981, 1988). The point is that this description would apply equally well to some 20 or 30 South Asian or Southeast Asian foraging peoples who hunt, gather, share food, trade with their neighbors, cook in iron pots, wear Levis, and listen to transistor radios. I wonder whether the National Geographic Society, which made the story so famous with their television film and their magazine cover story in 1972 (MacLeish 1972; National Geographic Society 1972), would have given a second glance to the Batek, Hill Pandaram, Agta, Naiken, or other forager or semiforager group, yet every one of these cases has yielded more useful information on foragers in context than we have on the Tasaday (see, for example, Bird-David 1983; Brosius 1990; Eder 1987; Endicott 1979; Griffin and Estioko-Griffin 1985; Headland 1986; and Morris 1982).

Discourse Two: The Tasaday and Philippine Reality

Whether or not the Tasaday are ''real'' foragers (whatever *that* means) is only one and perhaps not even the most interesting of the discourses spawned by *l'affaire Tasaday*. While the Tasaday exist as a small and embattled ethnic group in a corner of the Philippines, they also exist as regional and national celebrities (and pawns) in a wider world. What role have the Tasaday assumed in Philippine national consciousness in the Marcos and post-Marcos era? Here the David and Goliath imagery of gentle Tasaday and rapacious outsiders becomes refracted through a series of mirrors. The view of the Tasaday as relics of the Stone Age is backed by some of the most powerful elements of the Philippine ruling oligarchy. And those who oppose this view of them are in many ways courageous dissidents who have spoken out often at great personal risk. At least one of these dissidents has died under mysterious circumstances and many have been threatened and intimidated.[2] The Tasaday's recent lawsuit against some of these critics was filed from the offices of the Philippines' most prestigious law firm.[3]

When we try to make sense of the Tasaday in a regional context, sharply contradictory images undermine any sense of coherence. What the world regards as a remote paradise and stronghold of Stone Age culture is seen by the South Cotabato Provincial Chamber of Commerce as a booming area ripe for development (Duhaylungsod and Hyndman, this volume). Not far from Tasadayland 10,000 miners are honeycombing the Tboli hills searching for alluvial gold. Multinational corporations (including U.S. Weyerhauser) are competing for logging concessions, and a major influx of Filipino immigrants from the Visayas are in the process of colonizing this fertile corner of Mindanao. Add to this the antigovernment activities of the Moro National Liberation Front (MNLF) and the New Peoples Army (NPA) and we begin to get some idea of the complex terrain on which the Tasaday drama is being played out. One of the most disturbing elements of the Tasaday story is the dramatic militarization of South Cotabato since the Aquino regime came to power.

Duhaylungsod and Hyndman correctly draw attention to the realities of life in Cotabato today and the role of Panamin, the agency charged with the protection of tribal Filipinos. During the Marcos era Panamin had an ambiguous character to say the least (Rocamora 1979). Some benefits did accrue to indigenous peoples, the 48,000 hectare Tasaday Reserve being one example. But even when the agency was not a vehicle for personal gain, it always functioned as means for establishing the state's presence and hegemony in the most remote areas of the country. Today Panamin's successor agencies provide a bulwark for the Philippine state and state elite against the increasingly restive indigenous peoples and emerging national minority elites of the country.

At the same time these ''Panamin'' spheres of influence, such as the Tasaday Reserve, may paradoxically provide protection for indigenous peoples against the expansionist designs of local elites. At the Washington meeting it was pointed out that the 50 Tasaday now share ''their'' reserve with several thousand Blit Manobo and Tboli cultivators, whose future and livelihood are closely bound up with the fate of the Tasaday on the world stage.

In some scenarios the ''exposure'' of the Tasaday as a hoax will lead inevitably to the abolition of the reserve and the opening up of its virgin acres to development. This possibility has galvanized a substantial body of opinion committed to preserving their ''authenticity'' at all costs. This may explain, in part, why the Tasaday myth has proven so tenacious in the face of contradictory evidence raised in Discourse One. And why thoughtful people continue to defend the legitimacy of the Tasaday's original story.

Discourse Three: Tasaday and the West

The third discourse in which knowledge of the Tasaday is embedded is their reception in the Western media and popular imagination. Unlike most scholars who have tended to treat the original Tasaday story with skepticism and to hold the Tasaday at arm's length, the public in North America and Europe accepted the story with unreserved interest, fascination, and enthusiasm. While this was due in no small part to the packaging and mass dissemination of the story by the *National Geographic* and other media, it was clear that there was an enormous emotional response to the Tasaday story, especially among children. I still remember the sense of awe and wonder in my own children's response to the original story, the TV specials, and to John Nance's gracefully written books.

The strongest indication of the public's need for the kind of primitivist fantasy conjured up by the Tasaday is the worldwide success of the recent popular films *The Gods Must Be Crazy* and *The Gods Must be Crazy, Part 2*. Here we have the same kind of misrepresentation of the foragers with a timeless and beautiful vision of simplicity and natural harmony crowding out the far less pleasant realities of life among former foragers in the 1980s.

Why the publics in the Western mass societies need the Tasaday and ''the gods'' is an important question of alienated cultural consciousness in Late Capitalism. It has been insightfully addressed by Jean-Paul Dumont (1988) and Leslie Sponsel (this volume).

However, I want to address here a different issue: the public perception of anthropology and the impact of the ''unmasking'' of the Tasaday. All anthropologists should be deeply concerned with the savagery with which the media jumped on the Tasaday case. Effortlessly passing from one discourse to another, they reported the story in a number of ways: from weird goings-on in strange locales (''Anthropologist Weds Headhunter Chief,'' ''South-Sea Natives Claim Lyndon Johnson as Cargo Cult Messiah'') to the debunking of anthropological paradigms for the purpose of exposing the fallibility of science and scientists. (The Margaret-Mead-in-Samoa story is an example that comes to mind.) The latter discourse resonates in curious ways with critical currents *within* anthropology generally lumped under the rubric "Postmodernism."

Titles like the following in the popular and semipopular press convey a sense of the debunking discourse by juxtaposing images of ancient and pristine purity with streetwise sophistication and disillusion: "The Tasaday—A Stone Age Swindle"; "A World that Never Existed: Reassessing Hunter-Gatherers"; "The Tribe That Never Was"; ". . . Rain-Forest Phonies." *U.S. News and World Report* summed up the journalistic kernel of this approach in the lead-in to their coverage of the Tasaday story (Brownlee 1990): "If Only Life Were So Simple," read the headline, followed by, "Anthropology: Why are we so fascinated with the notion of noble primitives? They never hold up under scientific scrutiny."

The third discourse, therefore, is one in which Western opinion makers take the raw materials of the primitive "Other" and seek to construct hegemonic ideologies that mirror the temper of the times and reinforce prevailing values. And in the era of Reagan, Bush, Gorbachev, and Yeltsin, ideologies centering on the loss of innocence and shattered illusions seems particularly apposite. It is appropriate and necessary that we go through the process of self-criticism, open debate, and house cleaning represented by the chapters in this volume. We must review the evidence, draw conclusions, and put our house in order. What we must resist is the temptation to jump on the debunking bandwagon and wallow in the cynicism and world-weariness that is so characteristic a feature of contemporary consciousness. The Tasaday and their neighbors of South Cotabato are fortunate to have powerful advocates for their interests in provincial capitals, in Manila, and even in Washington. But who speaks for the dozens of other band and tribal peoples throughout South and Southeast Asia and elsewhere? Often anthropologists have played crucial roles as lobbyists and activists defending the rights of tribal peoples against expropriation and disenfranchisement. (Similar points have been made by John Bodley and Gerald Berreman in this volume.)

We must not allow the Tasaday case to be used as a vehicle either for delegitimating anthropological studies of hunters and gatherers, or as a vehicle for delegitimating the foragers themselves, by calling into question their cultural autonomy or claims to authenticity—and by implication their rights to survival as cultural entities.

Notes

1. Note that to document the hoax, it is not necessary to invoke the two lines of evidence that generated the most discussion both at the Zagreb and the Washington meetings: the linguistic data and the genealogical data.
2. [Editor's note: The author is here referring to the reported violent death of Filipino Elizer Boone in 1987. For other references to Boone in the present volume, see the index—TNH.]
3. The two defendants against whom the lawsuit was specifically filed (in October 1988) are Jerome Bailen and Zeus Salazar, both professors of anthropology at the University of the Philippines (Mydans 1988). Both scholars have tried repeatedly over many years, against political suppression, to voice their views questioning the authenticity of the Tasaday story. (For details, see University of the Philippines 1987.)

● *chapter fourteen*

The Tasaday "Stone Axes"— What Do They Tell Us?

Robert L. Carneiro

A t the outset, I would like to make it clear that I have never done fieldwork in the Philippines. Nor have I made a close study of Philippine ethnology. Thus, as a commentator on the Tasaday, I lack the credentials of other scholars represented in this volume. But I do have a special interest in stone axes, having studied their manufacture and use in Amazonia (my own area of specialization) and elsewhere. And I have published on the subject, both alone (Carneiro 1974, 1979a, 1979b) and in collaboration with others (Kozák 1972; Kozák et al. 1979).

It was because of this special interest of mine that, in 1988, I was asked by Judith Moses to look closely at the photographs of Tasaday stone tools in John Nance's *Discovery of the Tasaday* (1981), and to express an opinion about their authenticity. Moses had produced an ABC television documentary on the Tasaday in 1986 for the program *20/20*, much of it filmed on location (ABC-TV 1986). Her request to me was prompted by the fact that she was working on a book dealing with the entire issue of whether or not the Tasaday were a hoax. The letter I wrote to Moses containing my views on Tasaday stone tools was later, unbeknownst to her, published in the *Manila Times,* and attracted a certain amount of attention. Thus, willy-nilly, I found myself in the midst of the Tasaday controversy. I welcome this opportunity to express myself more fully on these implements and what they suggest about the Tasaday.

The Nature of the Evidence

The evidence available on which one can now base an opinion about the Tasaday's stone tools is relatively limited. It seems desirable, therefore, to summarize it briefly before proceeding to discuss its implications.

The first encounter with the Tasaday occurred in June 1971 at the edge of their forest habitat in South Cotabato Province, Mindanao. Among the persons who met the Tasaday on that occasion was Robert Fox (now deceased), an archaeologist at the National Museum of the Philippines. The Tasaday had not brought along any stone tools, but during the five days Fox was with them they described and imitated the making and using of their stone implements (Fox 1976:3). Ac-

172

cording to Fox, no tribe in the Philippines had used stone tools during the last 300 years; so as he watched the Tasaday, he became, John Nance later wrote, "increasingly excited by what he was learning." Indeed, according to Nance, this demonstration "convinced him [Fox] that their practical knowledge of these ancient implements was genuine" (Nance 1975:23).

It was not until March 1972 that a party of outsiders was flown by helicopter into the middle of the Tasaday's forest and actually visited the group at the cave where they were said to live. This party included anthropologists Carlos Fernandez and Frank Lynch, as well as John Nance, who was then an Associated Press correspondent in the Philippines. The Tasaday showed these men three stone tools, already made and hafted, which they kept in their cave. These are the artifacts that have been referred to as the Tasaday's "heirloom" tools.

Intrigued by these implements, the observers asked the Tasaday to show them how they made and used them. The Tasaday obliged, and as they worked, Fernandez, Lynch, and Nance wrote down and photographed what they saw. Thus, altogether, we have three firsthand descriptions and discussions of Tasaday stone tool–making and use: Fox (1976), Fernandez and Lynch (1972), and Nance (1975, 1981). Since stone tools were never again seen being made or used by the Tasaday,[1] these four publications constitute virtually the sole body of evidence we have, or are ever likely to have, on which to assess those tools.[2]

The remarks that follow are based on a reading of these sources and on an examination of the photographs and drawings contained in them. My underlying aim is to shed light on the ultimate question: Regarding whether or not the Tasaday are a hoax, which way does the evidence of the stone tools point?

Differences in Tool Types

During their visits to the Tasaday in 1971 and 1972, observers reported seeing several types of stone tools, including scrapers. However, I will restrict my analysis to their so-called stone axes, that is, those implements which, whatever their actual use, were hafted like axes. Whether they were in fact axes has been debated. Fernandez and Lynch (1972:296) did not hesitate to call them such, but Fox objected strongly to their being characterized in that way. I will deal with this question later.

A distinction was made by the observers of the Tasaday between the "stone axes" they actually saw being made, and the so-called heirloom axes, which the Tasaday had in their cave and which they said had been made by their ancestors. (Illustrations of the three "heirloom" axes are found in Fernandez and Lynch 1972:Plate 2 and Nance 1981:70–71.) These heirloom axes were not taken to Manila, as were those that were made to order for the observers, but remained behind in the cave. They have not been seen since.

Fox (1976:8) wrote that the stone tools the Tasaday produced at the request of their visitors were "roughly made when compared with the 'heirloom' tools." But the praise this implies for the "heirloom" tools is certainly unwarranted. Indeed, in photographs of them, the "heirloom" tools also appear extremely crude and simple. Nance (1975:14) says of them that "the stones were harder, smoother, better shaped, and more sharply honed than the ones made to order." One cannot judge hardness from a photograph, but their greater smoothness and "better shape" says more about the natural condition of the stones from which they were made than about the work lavished on them. If anything, they seem to be even less worked than the tools hastily made by the Tasaday for their visitors. In fact, one can hardly detect any work on these "heirloom" tools at all. And as far as their being more sharply honed, this certainly is not what the photographs show. For purposes of analysis, then, there is no need to distinguish between the two sets of tools. One can safely consider both as having been made by the same hands.

The status of these "heirloom" tools is not without importance. Were we to judge the authenticity of the Tasaday solely on the basis of the few "demonstration models" made especially for Fernandez, Lynch, and Nance, it could be argued that such a judgment was unfair. The extreme crudity and amateurishness of the latter tools might be said to reflect the fact that, by 1972, the Tasaday had pretty well forgotten the art of stone axe making, as they themselves conceded. However, the Tasaday's also having had in their possession these "heirloom" tools which they claimed had been made by their ancestors who still ostensibly retained the art of stone axe making, gives us more solid grounds on which to judge whether the Tasaday really are a "Stone Age" people.

Without further ado, then, let me turn to an assessment of the Tasaday lithic implements. Since at times, at least, they have been called "stone axes," I first want to evaluate them as such, before considering what other functions they served and how well they served them.

Shape of the Axe Heads

The Tasaday stone axe heads shown in various published photographs are unlike stone axe heads found elsewhere in the world. Not only do they lack a definite and consistent shape, they appear to be almost unworked, not only in terms of their edge, but also as to their general form. Referring to this amorphousness, Fernandez and Lynch (1972:294) remark that "form . . . was not important" to the Tasaday. This, I would say, is a distinct understatement. Moreover, the alleged lack of interest in the form of their stone axes certainly sets the Tasaday apart from other stone axe makers.

Several Tasaday axes shown in the photos not only have unworked sides, but can hardly be said to have a cutting edge. An axe head Fernandez and Lynch saw being "sharpened," was merely rubbed back and forth on a piece of stone for ten minutes. Then, after hafting, it was rubbed "a few more strokes against the flat rock [to] give the edge a final honing" (1972:Plate 3). A close-up photo of this axe, however, shows that those few minutes of grinding failed to produce anything like an effective cutting edge.

Referring to this specimen and to the other two made at the same time, Nance (1975:140–141) wrote that "The honed edges of all three tools were sharp enough to saw through a vine." That may well be, but sawing depends on the ability to abrade by repeated reciprocal motions, which in turn depends on the roughness of the edge, whereas *cutting,* the true function of an axe, depends on the sharpness of the edge.

There is one artifact (see photo in Nance 1981:74) that, unlike the others, appears to have the general shape of a stone axe head. And it does seem to narrow at the bit to something like an edge. At first I thought this might have been an actual specimen of a stone axe that had been found in a streambed by the Tasaday. (Its dark cortex suggested the absence of recent use.) But a closer look at the photograph convinces me that its similarity to a genuine stone axe is purely adventitious, and whatever edge it may appear to have comes solely from the natural shape of the rock. The photo referred to shows a slightly lighter area around the bit, which may have been caused by a desultory attempt to sharpen it. However, the result, as far as I can tell from the photo, was far from an effective cutting edge.

Making the Axes

When, at the request of their visitors, the Tasaday made a few stone axes, it took them between 12 and 15 minutes per axe (Fernandez and Lynch 1972:297; Nance 1975:140). This included not only grinding the bit but hafting the axe head as well. Even for a people who claimed to have partially lost the art of stone working, the results of these few minutes of labor were anything but credible specimens. As Nance himself wrote, "The speed with which these implements were constructed suggested that they were used and tossed aside" (Nance 1975:141). That is not the way stone axe makers elsewhere in the world treat their axes.[3]

In making their stone axes the Tasaday were not only fast but brusque. Thus, Fernandez and Lynch (1972:297) report: "Sometimes the process [of axe making] may begin with the fracturing of a large slab by dropping or hurling it against a boulder. If the outcome is right (by chance) there may be no need for further dressing of the stone, for the fracture may be such as to yield a fragment suitable for immediate hafting and use." But this hit-or-miss process of axe making runs the risk of inducing small cracks in the stone to be used, which may later lead to the fracturing of the implement made from it.

Type of Stone Used

As they appear in the close-up photographs, the stones used by the Tasaday for their axe heads have a very rough texture. Some of them contain large crystals, readily visible to the naked eye. Stones of this type are generally unsuitable for axe heads. They contain too many weak spots at which an axe could readily fracture if used for heavy chopping. Stone axes are thus almost always made from cryptocrystalline rocks which are dense and homogeneous and in which the crystals cannot usually be seen with the naked eye. Thus, even if the Tasaday had ground their stone axes to a sharp edge, the stones chosen by them for the purpose were such that they would not have made a reliable cutting tool for very long.

Hafting

The hafting on Tasaday stone axes does not appear well suited to holding an axe head firmly in place. The handles attached to the axes made especially for their visitors are particularly flimsy, almost ludicrously so.[4]

Nance (1975:141) wrote of this hafting that while it might be firm enough to serve for a tool used as a hammer or pounder, it "would not do for heavy work." Moreover, a few days after the hafting had been done, he observed that "the vine lacing stretched as it dried, so that the stones loosened, making the tool unusable."

The hafting of the "heirloom" specimens was more carefully done. Indeed, it impressed Nance (1975:141, 306) sufficiently for him to speak of the "uniform excellence of the rattan lacing," and again, to say that the lacings "were so neat and uniform." But what this "excellence" and "uniformity" amounts to is only a regular wrapping of the split rattan around the handle, just below the axe head. The part of the hafting that grips the axe head, though, does not look very substantial and could hardly have kept the head in place for long during heavy cutting. If these axes were put to serious use in chopping, either the lashings would break, or, more likely, the axe head would come out of its haft.

Yet another question can be raised about the hafting. The materials used for lashing the axe head to the handle were lengths of vine or of split rattan. Sometimes the handle itself was "made of . . . a piece of rattan bent double over the stone" (Fernandez and Lynch 1972:297). "However," Fernandez and Lynch continue, "cutting this plant is a relatively difficult task for the stone axe." Zeus Salazar (1989) goes further, maintaining that Tasaday stone axes were incapable of cutting rattan. How, then, he wonders, were the Tasaday able to put handles on their axes before they acquired the steel bolo?

In summary, then, as axes, the stone tools the Tasaday had in their possession in 1972 simply fail to measure up to acceptable standards.

Other Uses of the Stone Tools

However, as mentioned earlier, Robert Fox objected to calling these tools axes at all. Consequently, he thought they should not be compared to the Neolithic axes found archaeologically in other parts of the Philippines, whose primary use was to fell trees. "Despite their being hafted," Fox wrote, "there is no evidence that the edge-ground tools of the Tasaday were used as an axe. . . . the only use which the writer saw for an edge-ground tool among the Tasaday was as a scraper" (1976:8). However, it must be noted that Fernandez and Lynch, who had occasion to observe the Tasaday for a longer period than Fox, wrote:

> a principal practical function of the stone tool was to sharpen . . . [the digging stick used for digging up wild yams]. Stone tools were also used to hack at wild-banana stems and trunks; to crack and crush the shell of the ripe wild-ginger fruit; to mash betel nut; to pound the bark of trees; to split or chop firewood that could not be snapped in two or broken over the knee or head; to sharpen bamboo tools and wooden fire drills. . . ; and to scrape tinder from the bark of the wild palm. [1972:294]

We thus are faced with a quandary. For certain uses to which the Tasaday put their stone tools, such as hacking at banana stems or chopping firewood—uses that were certainly axe-like—a strong haft would have been highly desirable, if not downright necessary. Why, then, were Tasaday hafts so insubstantial? On the other hand, for several other uses observed by Fernandez and Lynch, for which a handle was not really appropriate, why were these stone tools hafted at all?

To crack nuts with a stone, for example, it seems more convenient to simply hold the stone, unhafted, in the palm of the hand and pound with it. This is the way primitive peoples generally use nut stones. Moreover, for cracking nuts it is more efficient to use a round stone that fits nicely in the hand than a flatish, angular one as the Tasaday employed. One has to wonder, then, why the Tasaday would bother to haft stones they used for pounding, cracking, and scraping.

Linguistic Evidence

Certain linguistic evidence strikes me—as it has others (e.g., Salazar 1989)—as relevant to the authenticity of Tasaday stone tools. Fernandez and Lynch (1972:294) say that the name the Tasaday gave to the bolo knife, which was said to have been introduced to them by a Manobo Blit hunter named Dafal, was *fais*, meaning 'striker'. Their stone axe, on the other hand, they called *fais batu* 'striker of stone'. This seems anomalous to me. One would expect the Tasaday, if they were indeed a Stone Age people, to have called their native stone axe *fais*, and the introduced bolo, '*fais*-made-of-metal', or '*fais*-of-a-new material', or something of the sort. The way the Tasaday actually designated these tools is thus much more consistent with the stone axe being the novel tool and the bolo the familiar one.

Comparisons

Speaking of Tasaday stone tools in general, Fernandez and Lynch raise the following question: "What known type of series of Philippine stone implements do they approximate? A simple answer would be none" (1972:294). Two pages later they again say, "The Tasaday axes are certainly completely unrelated, both in form and technique of manufacture, to the painstakingly made ground-stone tools, mostly adzes, found elsewhere in the Philippines" (1972:296). What does this uniqueness in the character of Tasaday stone implements imply?

It is possible, of course, that the Tasaday's skill in making stone tools might once have been the equal of other Philippine tribes. And perhaps their axes were once similar to others in form as well, so that their present uniqueness reflects only degeneration through time. But the degeneration theory poses certain problems. Since the Tasaday are supposed to have lived in isolation for centuries, with no metal tools at all, and thus been forced to rely entirely on their stone artifacts for cutting, chopping, pounding, cracking, and crushing, one would expect that such a heavy reliance on a lithic technology would have been reason enough for them to keep it functional, rather than allowing it to decay.

The typological uniqueness of Tasaday stone tools, then, added to their crudeness, makes them even more aberrant. And these two facts together argue against their being part of a genuine, effective, and functional lithic tool kit.

Fernandez and Lynch themselves seem to suggest this when they say of the Tasaday, "They do use stone tools, but the role of these implements in their technology is so restricted, and their appreciation of them within that small sphere so utterly pragmatic, that we did not even include the descriptive tag stone-tool-using in the title of this paper" (1972:294). In other words, Tasaday stone tools appeared to Fernandez and Lynch more like an anomaly than a credible central element of their culture.

Conclusion

Why, then, did the Tasaday possess these implausible implements? Might they have fashioned them in a crude attempt to recreate an artifact of which they had been told but about which they knew little, in an effort to convince outsiders that they really were the Stone Age people they were supposed to be? Fernandez and Lynch's assertion that "It is almost certain that the only axes they have made and hafted are those they produced at the request of outsiders like ourselves" (1972:294) serves to strengthen this belief.

In view of all the foregoing evidence, it seems to me that, in so far as the Tasaday's stone tools bear on the issue of the group's authenticity, they point toward the Tasaday being an artificially constituted group, hastily brought together and haphazardly equipped, rather than an authentic, pristine representative of a Stone Age people.

Notes

1. After Oswald Iten reported in 1986 that the Tasaday were a hoax, an expedition including Carlos Fernandez and Jesus Peralta of the National Museum of the Philippines was organized and flown to South Cotabato Province, where, from April 17 to 24, 1986, they visited the Tasaday in their caves. While the report of this "revisitation team" (Peralta 1987) mentioned the changes that had taken place in Tasaday subsistence, not a word was said about their stone tools—either that they were still in use, or that they were at least to be seen, or that they were no longer in evidence. I find this failure to say anything at all about these famous implements rather surprising, especially since Nance informed me that the Tasaday "have told me within the last year that despite having metal knives they continue to occasionally make stone implements when a situation demands it" (personal communication 1988).
2. [Editor's note: A fifth publication with some further information on Tasaday stone tools is provided by Jesus Peralta in this volume. Peralta's paper was not available to Carneiro at the time he wrote this chapter—TNH.]
3. Anyone wishing to learn how much work is actually involved in making a stone axe—the hours of laborious pecking, grinding, and polishing, and the careful fitting of a haft—can do so by reading Vladimír Kozák's detailed account of this process as seen

by him among the Héta Indians of southern Brazil (Kozák 1972; Kozák et al. 1979:399–403).

4. Contrast this with the wooden pounders used by the Tasaday to loosen *natek*, the sago-like flour obtained from the split stem of a caryota palm *(Caryota cumingii)*. These pounders appear, from photographs (Nance 1981:102–103), to be well made, with the two parts of the implement firmly attached together.

● *chapter fifteen*

The Tasaday Language: A Key to Tasaday Prehistory

LAWRENCE A. REID

In this chapter I examine two bodies of linguistic evidence in order to determine whether there was a systematic attempt to deceive investigators as to the true identity of the Tasaday.[1] First, I will look at the linguistic material gathered from the Tasaday during the 1971–72 contacts by outsiders; second, at the linguistic evidence that has become available since then. I will test the claims of the 'hoax' proponents regarding the identity of the Tasaday against the form of the Tasaday language.

New linguistic evidence now available in papers by Johnston (1989 and in a slightly revised form elsewhere in this volume), Elkins (1989, this volume), and Molony (1989a, this volume; Molony with Tuan 1976) makes it possible to draw conclusions regarding a possible hoax.[2] I will address the following issues: the nature of language versus dialect; the position of the Tasaday speech variety vis-à-vis other Manobo speech varieties; implications for whether the Tasaday are a hoax; and the extent to which the Tasaday may have been isolated from other Manobo communities.

Critical Evaluation of the Data

The most prominent claim hoax proponents make regarding the true identity of the Tasaday is that they are Tboli people who are bilingual in Manobo. This position is taken by Duhaylungsod and Hyndman (1989),[3] as well as by Salazar, who presented genealogical evidence for such a scenario.[4] The only non-Tboli is said to have been Balayam (alias Tinda), a speaker of Blit Manobo. I proceed on the assumption that if the Tasaday were really Tboli, they would most likely speak Blit Manobo, characterized by one or more of the following features: (1) the sporadic appearance of uniquely Tboli terms, (2) Tboli cognates of Manobo terms, and (3) Manobo terms spoken with a Tboli accent pattern. I further assume that if the hoax proponents are correct, the first two of these features would probably result in some variation between the two sets of terms (Tboli and Blit Manobo) as they were recorded by different investigators.

A number of problems arise when we try to interpret the linguistic data that have become available. First, there is a fair amount of variability for some terms among the lists; that is, different investigators have recorded different Tasaday terms with the same meaning. Second, the researchers' phonetic transcriptions for even the same lexical item frequently do not match. While it is true that even within a small linguistic community there is often variation in the pronunciation of certain lexical items, it is also true that with any linguistic fieldwork, unless one is a skilled phonetician, there are invariably errors of recognition and transcription during the first stages of elicitation. Thus the researcher may introduce variation where none actually exists.[5]

Still another problem in interpreting the data is the lack of substantial information from certain speech varieties spoken in the immediate geographical vicinity of the Tasaday. There are four fairly substantial unpublished dictionaries of Southern Manobo languages, each prepared by a member of the Summer Institute of Linguistics after many years of residence in the area. Two of these dictionaries (Johnston 1968 and Errington and Errington 1981) are for the Manobo spoken in Kalamansig, Cotabato (referred to hereafter as MbKC), some 25 km west of the Tasaday caves. Another dictionary (DuBois 1988) is for the Tagabawa Manobo spoken on the southern and southeastern slopes of Mt. Apo in Davao del Sur. The fourth (DuBois n.d.) is for the Sarangani Manobo spoken on the east coast of the Sarangani Peninsula and on the San Agustin Peninsula of southern Mindanao. But all that is known of the Blit Manobo speech variety is the brief list in the comparative lists of Fox (Elizalde with Fox 1971a), Llamzon (1971b), Yen (1976a), and Molony (Molony with Tuan 1976).[6] Nor is there anything available from any of the other supposedly Manobo-speaking communities close to the caves, such as Barrio Ned.

Also lacking is a substantial body of lexical material from those languages generally referred to now as the Southern Mindanao languages. There is a vocabulary of approximately 1,500 words of the Tboli (Tbl) used in Sinolon, Alah Valley (Forsberg and Lindquist 1955). There is also a 6,000 word lexicon of Tiruray spoken in Cotabato Province, north of Kalamansig (Schlegel 1971). But for the other Southern Mindanao languages, Koronadal Blaan and Sarangani Blaan, there are only the word lists in the studies of Reid (1971) and, for Ubo, of Yap (1977).

Fox's Word List

A list of approximately 110 words was collected by anthropologist Robert Fox on June 16 and 17, 1971, about two weeks after the first reported Tasaday contact (Elizalde with Fox 1971a:Appendix I). That Elizalde included Fox in the first group of scientists to visit the area suggests that Elizalde did not attempt to exclude anyone who might be able to detect a Tasaday fraud. Fox, a highly respected anthropologist and former director of the Philippine National Museum, had considerable ability and experience not only in archaeology and ethnographic description but also in recording the languages of tribal peoples in the Philippines.

In this instance, according to Nance (1975:21), elicitation was conducted through a multiple translation process, from English to Tboli to Blit Manobo to Tasaday. The equivalent forms in the intermediate languages were also in many cases recorded by Fox. Presumably these are the terms which the translators Mai Tuan and Dad Tuan (for Kemato Tboli) and Igna (for Blit Manobo) used. It was Fox who first recognized the apparent similarities between the speech of the Tasaday and that of what he was told was Blit Manobo.

As we carefully examine each of the terms collected by Fox in the light of what later researchers recorded and compare them with lexical material from surrounding languages, we soon distinguish two sets of data that differ from what we would expect. The first set are what might be called probable elicitation errors, that is, misidentifications of what are probably the actual meanings of terms. They include:[7]

1. *èbang* 'moon' (recorded by Peralta and Elkins as *sèbang;* cf. MbKC *sèbang* 'to rise, of the moon')
2. *bukuwan* 'arm' (lit., 'place of the joint')
3. *dáoy* 'leaf' (possibly a typographical error, recorded as *daun* by later researchers)
4. *kamèl* 'hand' (but note Tagalog and Kapampangan *kamal* 'a large handful', MbKC *kemel* 'finger, toe', Western Bukidnon Manobo *kamel* 'the binder ring on the handle of a bolo', also *kemer* 'finger, toe').
5. *lablab* 'wild pig' (Western Bukidnon Manobo 'male pig, either wild or domestic', Tbl *leblab* 'wild male pig')
6. *loós* 'teeth' (MbKC 'gums')
7. *nafnaf* 'small bamboo mortar for betel' (Sarangani Manobo and MbKC 'a kind of thin-walled bamboo', Tbl *naf* 'type of bamboo from which baskets are made')
8. *sèladang* 'deer' (MbKC 'buck, male deer', Tbl *sledeng* 'male deer')

There are also a number of unique items in this list, forms that appear to have no cognates in related languages. Some were recorded only by Fox, others by other researchers as well. They include the following:

1. *kálel* 'smoke'
2. *kamfí* 'T-string'
3. *laás* 'monitor lizard' (but note MbKC *pelaes* and Western Bukidnon Manobo *pelaas* 'monitor lizard')
4. *lágas* 'vulva'
5. *lingaw* 'tusk of wild pig'
6. *nasagbung* 'local group'
7. *salumfíng* 'beard'
8. *sètaláwmin* 'family'
9. *túmas* 'dog'
10. *bukíyaw* 'lightning' (also recorded by Elkins)
11. *búgèd* 'bamboo container for Jew's harp' (also recorded by Molony)
12. *ingkúlan* 'river' (also recorded by Llamzon)

How is one to account for these unusual forms? Fox was a competent and careful scholar; he recorded what the translators told him and what he presumably thought he heard uttered by the Tasaday person who was being queried. There is a remote possibility that one or more of the translators attempted to make the language sound more exotic than they knew it really was, but for such a scheme to succeed, the Tasaday themselves must have been in on it. But I think either (or both) of two other explanations is far more likely.

The first alternative explanation is that the translation process was so new to the Tasaday that they missed the point of many of the questions and gave terms semantically unrelated to what was being asked. How did the translators ask for terms for 'local group' and 'family', for example? It also seems unlikely that a term for 'vulva' could have been successfully elicited so soon.

Unfamiliarity with the translation process would also account for at least some of the 'elicitation errors' mentioned above. The use of terms such as *dinagán* 'ear' (lit., 'hearing place') instead of *telinga*, *bulawan* 'arm' (lit., 'place of the joint') instead of *bèlad*, and *'igha'a* 'eye' (lit., 'the thing that sees', recorded by Elkins) instead of *matá*, suggests that in these early elicitation sessions, the Tasaday had not yet grasped what it was that was being asked of them. It seems that they were interested in describing the functions of the body parts being pointed at, rather than the name they had for the part.

The second alternative explanation is that the terms given may in fact have been genuine terms in the Tasaday language for the meanings that were supplied.[8] This raises the interesting possibility that the different forms that were recorded later for the same meanings were the result of language adaptation by the Tasaday to the Blit Manobo with whom they were by then frequently interacting. (The Blit Manobo language presumably would have had a higher status than the earlier form of their own language.)[9]

One unique term in the Fox list suggests that this latter explanation may have some validity—*weél* 'water'. This term is apparently a reflex of Proto-Philippine **waiR*. The presence of a final *l* in the Tasaday word marks it etymologically as a Southern Mindanao term (possibly a very early borrowing into Tasaday). All Manobo languages, on the other hand, reflect **R* as g. But in none of the available word lists of the southern Mindanao languages does the word appear in this full form *weél*. Either the initial consonant has been lost (as in Koronadal Blaan *'e'el*), or the first syllable has been lost (as in Tbl *'el*). It is highly unlikely that any of the Tboli people or other outsiders present during that first language elicitation session would have been aware of the etymologically correct initial consonant in the form. The term recorded by later researchers is invariably *wayeg*, showing the appropriate Manobo reflexes of **waiR*.

There is only one term in Fox's list that seems to be shared only with Blit Manobo and was not subsequently recorded by other researchers. It is *balangús* 'nose' (cf. Blit Manobo *blèngús* 'nose'). This is hardly what one would expect if the Tasaday were either Tboli poseurs who were all bilingual in Blit Manobo, or were themselves native speakers of Blit Manobo.

Peralta's Word List

A list of approximately 100 Tasaday terms was collected by Jesus Peralta (1971a), presently Chief Researcher at the Philippine National Museum, during short visits on July 20 and 21, 1971 (Nance 1975:47).[10] Peralta is an archaeologist, not a linguist. The list available to me is an unpublished photocopy of Peralta's original fieldnotes, a series of words and phrases that appear to have been jotted down often without semantic connection during the course of his anthropological investigations. They do not appear to be the result of systematic language elicitation, but simply a casual listing of overheard items. The terms collected are generally the same as those gathered by other researchers, but where the lists differ, it appears to be because of Peralta's method of data collection, and because of the fact that he was not a skilled phonetician. This resulted in a number of incorrectly transcribed words as in these forms in which Peralta used *u* to transcribe schwa: *humiguf* 'sip' (cf. *humigèf* 'sip' recorded by Molony); *maidúb* 'sharp' (probably a misidentification of *maidèb* 'pointed' as recorded by Molony, or *maedáb* 'sharp' as recorded by Llamzon; cf. MbKC *meideb*). There were also a number of forms whose meanings seem to have been misidentified. They include:

1. *bukal* 'leaf' (recorded by Yen 1976a:140 as a kind of plant)
2. *hinaa* 'catch a person' (recorded by later researchers as a form of the verb *haa,* 'to see')
3. *laha* 'penis' (MbKC 'scrotum', recorded as such by Molony)
4. *nèkabugsang* 'sun' (recorded by Llamzon as *nakabugsáng* 'noon' and by Molony as *nakèbugsang* 'perpendicular'; cf. MbKC *bugsang* 'to pass over the center of some expanse', used with nonvolitive *naka-* to indicate the noon position in the sky)
5. *sulo-lisan* 'rooster', possibly a reference to a cock's spur (recorded by Molony as *sulu lisèn* 'toenail'; cf. MbKC *sulu* 'nail', *lisèn* 'leg, including the foot')
6. *tudu* 'finger' (cf. MbKC *todo'* 'directed toward', *tinudu'* 'point with the finger, aim a weapon'. Tbl *tdok* 'finger')

The following appear to be unique terms occurring in Peralta's list, not found in other languages. These may be true Tasaday forms, especially in those instances where other researchers also recorded the same forms, but they may also have been misheard or misidentified forms.

1. *igsakag* 'full' (also recorded by Llamzon)
2. *lètu* 'ant'
3. *makètú* 'satisfied' (recorded by Llamzon as *makáttu* 'satisfied')
4. *nukitan* 'trail' (recorded by Llamzon as *nukitán* 'road')[11]
5. *lugilak* 'tongue' (cf. Tbl *dilak* 'tongue')

Forms which Peralta collected that have cognates in geographically distant Philippine languages are as follows:

1. *dad-duma* 'other(s)'. Although the term *duma* 'other, companion, spouse' is found in other Manobo languages, the plural form recorded by Peralta is not. It is unusual both in the vowel of the prefix and in the geminate medial consonant. To my knowledge, it is only in Ilokano that the word occurs in exactly this shape.

2. *dafúg* 'lime' (also recorded by Llamzon as such). Later researchers recorded the expected Manobo term *'afug*. The term *dafúg* appears to be a reflex of Proto-Philippine **dapuR* 'ash', which is not reflected in any other Manobo language or in any of the Southern Mindanao group of languages, but is found in various Bisayan languages such as Cebuano. It is possible that Tasaday is the only Manobo language to retain a reflex of the protoform.

3. *dangot* 'root' (also recorded by Llamzon as *dángut*). To my knowledge this term is found elsewhere only in Blit Manobo and in Ubo (which is not a Manobo language). Either language could have been the source of the term. It could have been introduced into Tasaday by Igna, or by one of the other speakers of Blit Manobo during the language elicitation sessions. Later researchers recorded the expected Manobo term *dalid* 'root'.

4. *èfak* 'frog'. Recorded by all other researchers as *bakbak*, the term appears to be a borrowing of the word for 'frog' found in the Southern Mindanao languages. (Tiruray has *efak;* Tbl, Blaan, and Ubo have *fak*.) It was also recorded by Molony for Blit Manobo. It could have been introduced by Igna.

5. *sakat* 'foot'. This term has no equivalents in any Manobo or Southern Mindanao language. It is possibly another Maranao borrowing (Maranao *sakat* 'to step up') with a misidentification of the meaning.

6. *tuod* 'knee'. A cognate of this form appears only in Agusan Manobo *tuhod*. MbKC *tuèd*, and its cognates Dibabawon Manobo *tuod*, and Tbl *tuhod* mean 'stump'; *tuod* 'knee' occurs elsewhere in Mindanao only in Mansaka.

Llamzon's Word List

Teodoro Llamzon compiled a Tasaday word list of about 200 items, some 65 of which are acknowledged as being recorded by Fox and used with his permission (Llamzon 1971a, 1971b). Collected at about the same time as Peralta's list (see note 10), a number of the items which were either misidentified by Peralta or otherwise appear to be unique in his list, also appear in Llamzon's list. These include the forms for 'full', 'lime', 'root', 'satisfied', and 'trail'.

In his discussion of the data that he collected Llamzon (1971b:1) indicates that he used the translation procedure previously also used by Fox (i.e., from English or Tagalog, to Tboli, to Blit Manobo and then to Tasaday, and back again). (Although he did not explicitly say so, this must also have been the route via which Peralta got his data.) The same translators were probably used by both Llamzon and Peralta, and it is possible that at least some of the problematic forms that are shared by the two lists were introduced by the translation process.

Llamzon's list has its share of problems too. Possibly misidentified forms include:

1. *taling* 'go' (recorded by Molony as 'wander, roam around')
2. *tuduk* 'mountain' (MbKC 'mountain range')

Unique forms include:

1. *fenágen* 'drive away'
2. *loongèn* 'fly'
3. *segelé* 'stick (v.)'
4. *tifang* 'roof'

Again, I find nothing in this list that would suggest that the Tasaday were actually Blit Manobo, or that they were Tboli who were bilingual in Blit Manobo. The irregular forms are all the result either of insufficient time to adjust to the phonological structure or to the semantics of the language, and are precisely what one would expect given the nature of these early contacts and the elicitation techniques used.

Elkins's Word List

Richard Elkins, a linguist and Bible translator who had by 1972 lived with various Manobo groups for many years, spoke Western Bukidnon Manobo, and was a specialist in the historical development of the Manobo languages, spent four days at the Tasaday caves in August 1972. During this period he elicited some 263 Tasaday words (see Elkins 1972), choosing the items from the 372 words in my word list (Reid 1971).

Elkins's list has a number of forms that are probably incorrectly identified, some of which follow. [12]

1. *bagá* 'liver' (recorded by Molony as *baga'* with the expected meaning 'lungs')
2. *bunbun* 'roof' (recorded by Molony as meaning 'ceiling, e.g., of a cave')
3. *dames* 'rain' (MbKC 'typhoon, rain and wind of long duration')
4. *igtigbas* 'right (hand)' (lit., 'the one used for cutting')
5. *igha?a* 'eye' (lit., 'the thing used for seeing')
6. *nekepákang* 'sun,' perhaps used metaphorically to refer to the heat of the sun (cf. MbKC *pakang* 'to pound, to split by pounding')
7. *pedú* 'heart' (recorded by Molony as *fèdu* 'mind, feeling', cf. MbKC *pedu* 'gall bladder, the seat of the emotions, mind, thought')

There are a few unexplainable forms in the Elkins list (as in the lists of earlier researchers). These include:

1. *lipad* 'to fly'. There are phonetically similar forms in several other Philippine languages (e.g., *lupad* in Kalagan and Tausug, and *lèpad* in Botolan Sambal and Mamanwa), but nothing similar is recorded for Manobo or Southern Mindanao languages.
2. *paway* 'cloud'

Elkins records one form which, because of its final vowel, is probably Tboli in origin, *kelipot* 'forget'. (Tbl has *klifot* 'forget', Western Bukidnon Manobo, Maranao, Ilokano, and others have *lipat*.) Molony records the expected Manobo form *kèlifong* 'forget', which Tasaday shares with Cotabato Manobo.

Linguistic Affiliation of the Tasaday

Language versus Dialect

In discussing the linguistic affiliation of the Tasaday, we must understand how the terms *language* and *dialect* are being used. Considerable confusion has surrounded this matter, primarily because some of those who have written on the Tasaday lack linguistic sophistication. From a linguist's point of view, the term *dialect* refers to a speech variety that is distinguished from other mutually intelligible dialects by restricted lexical, phonological, or syntactic features (whether restricted geographically or socially). So everyone (the Tasaday included) speaks a language and, depending on the features that are commonly used, a specific dialect of that language.

A variety of techniques have been used by linguists to measure degree of mutual intelligibility in order to draw language boundaries between more distantly related dialects and, conversely, to unite as one language those that are more closely related. Presumably then, when the question arises as to whether the Tasaday have an "independent language," the issue is whether or not the Tasaday speech variety is mutually intelligible with some other speech variety. The answer to this will depend upon the measure that the linguist uses to determine mutual intelligibility. There is no unequivocably correct answer to such a question.

Questions of whether Tasaday speak an "older" language than some other group are meaningless, since all languages change from one generation to the next and are therefore only as old as the generation that speaks them. Neither is it appropriate to speak of Tasaday as being an "offshoot" of some other presently spoken language, since such terminology implies that Tasaday is somehow younger than the dialect to which it is related. Such ways of thinking and talking about language (and culture) reflect the erroneous view that traditional peoples, particularly more isolated peoples, are purer or more pristine or less changed from some earlier state than "modern" groups, or looking at it from the opposite side, that the dialect of an outmigrating group is a corrupted version of the group from which they split. This is not to say that peripheral or isolated areas do not tend to be more lexically conservative than central areas; they do, but they cannot be considered to be "older" than nonrelic areas.

The Position of the Tasaday Speech Variety vis-à-vis Other Manobo Speech Varieties

Johnston's review of Elkins's word list and of the tape sent to him by Molony provides clear evidence that the Tasaday dialect is probably more closely related to the Manobo speech spoken in Kalamansig (MbKC) than to other Manobo dialects.[13] There is no question that they are mutually intelligible by anyone's measure and therefore constitute close regional dialects of a language that has been called Cotabato Manobo. The number of linguistic features that Tasaday appears to uniquely share with the Kalamansig dialect of Manobo (MbKC) establishes the relationship between them.[14]

Still problematic is the relationship between this language and that spoken in
Blit, from whence, according to some, the Tasaday "poseurs" were recruited.
From present evidence, which as I mentioned above is minimal because of the
paucity of Blit Manobo language data, it would seem that Blit is either a separate
language (judging from the comments of Blit Manobo people who claimed to be
unable to communicate with the Tasaday),[15] or it is a more distantly related dialect
of Cotabato Manobo (i.e., of MbKC).

As has been pointed out by others, the Tasaday language is more closely related to geographically remote regional dialects than to the dialects that are geographically closer. The actual degree of relationship between Tasaday and Kalamansig Cotabato Manobo (MbKC) is partially contingent on whether the terms in
the Elkins list that Johnston claims were elicitation errors were in fact errors or
whether they have undergone semantic change as is claimed by Elkins. That some
of Elkins's data is in error is certainly possible. However, several of the forms
were also recorded by Molony with the same meanings as those provided by Elkins, and these are almost certainly the result of semantic change. These (given
with Molony's fuller meanings) include: *keladayan* 'deep, e.g., of a river or valley'; *bèlagkál*, 'floor, e.g., of a cave or forest'; *ègkèbèngès* 'lonely'; *bunbun* 'ceiling (e.g., of a cave)' (Elkins had 'roof'); *habhab* 'to smell'; *ègbuèlèn* 'to have
thirst'. Similarly, Elkins's *mebága?* 'boil (infection)' appears in Mansaka as
baga? with the same narrowed meaning. Ultimately whether Johnston or Elkins
is correct makes little difference: Tasaday and MbKC would still be very closely
related to each other, and more closely related to each other than either is to Blit
Manobo.

Implications for Whether the Tasaday Are a Hoax

I believe that any linguist reviewing the available Tasaday data could only conclude that the Tasaday language has undergone a differentiation from any other
Manobo speech variety. This is not to say that the Tasaday speak a different language from their neighbors, but there certainly appears to be at least a dialectal
difference.[16] There are considerable differences, for example, between the ethnobotanical terms collected by Yen and their Blit equivalents. Whether the differences are as great with equivalent terms used in other Cotabato Manobo dialects has, to my knowledge, never been examined. There are also a number of
unique lexical items from the basic vocabulary that are not shared by Manobo or
by Southern Mindanao languages. Some of these terms have cognates in other
Philippine subgroups and could have been introduced by translators bilingual in
one of these languages, but at least one term (*weél* 'water') cannot be so explained. There is no evidence that the speakers of the language were bilingual in
Tboli or in any other language.

Johnston (personal communication) also claims that the lexical accent in the
Tasaday tapes to which he has listened indicates that the speakers were probably
not Tboli speakers who were speaking a Manobo dialect as a second language.
The accent patterns of Tboli are clearly distinct from Manobo accent patterns, and

the Tboli accent patterns would probably have been carried over into the pronunciation of Manobo words had these people been Tboli.

Extent to Which the Tasaday May Have Been Isolated from Other Manobo Communities

All languages change, but the changes tend to affect different language subsystems at relatively different speeds. Following geographical separation and subsequent reduced intercommunication, two kinds of change soon become apparent. One is lexical. Some words, although unchanged in pronunciation, come to be used in slightly different ways than in the home community. Such semantic shifts are often motivated by the different environment in which the breakaway community is living. (The changed environment also stimulates the development of unique lexical items, words which would not exist in the original home community.) The second kind of change that is quickly apparent is a shift in intonation.

Other types of change take place over much longer periods. For example, systematic shifts in the pronunciation of the segmental phonemes take longer. So do changes in the functional morphology, affecting pronouns, demonstratives, verbal morphology, and so on. Discernible changes in the syntax typically take longer still.

The types of differences that Johnston notes between MbKC and Tasaday suggest a relatively short period of separation and subsequent differentiation. For all intents and purposes the two dialects are still mutually intelligible. There appear to be no systematic sound changes that distinguish Tasaday from MbKC. Phonologically (apart from intonation) they appear to be identical. There are a few morphological differences between Tasaday and MbKC (outlined by Johnston), but whether these morphological features are shared by Blit Manobo is unknown. Neither, as far as I can tell, has there been any syntactic change.

Early studies such as Llamzon's placed too much value on glottochronology to measure the period of time that the Tasaday may have been separated from their neighbors. This method assumes that core vocabulary is replaced at a constant rate in all languages; therefore, the period of differentiation is measurable. It does not measure isolation. But because everybody believed the Tasaday's claims that they had not had contact with outsiders (apart from Dafal), it was assumed that Llamzon's calculation of 571 to 755 years of separation reflected the length of their isolation in the rain forest.

It should be remembered moreover that glottochronology has long since been discredited as a tool for dating periods of linguistic differentiation,[17] although lexicostatistics continues to be used by some as a rough measure of the degree of relationship shared by genetically related languages. In fact, the basic assumptions upon which the method relied has been shown to be untenable.[18]

Can we say anything at all then about the possible period of time since the Tasaday group moved away from their closest linguistic neighbors? Certainly it was not of the order of several hundreds of years. There is insufficient linguistic differentiation to allow for such a period of time. I think it more likely that differentiation has been taking place for no more than five or six generations at the

most, perhaps for 100–150 years.[19] Is such a short period of time sufficient to lose
a knowledge of agriculture?[20] Given the high elevation, the mountainous terrain
hostile to agriculture, and an absence of metal tools to clear the terrain and prepare
the soil,[21] the loss of agriculture could have taken place in a very short period of
time, even within a single generation. In this case, terminology associated with it
would quickly have been lost also. A single generation would have been sufficient.[22]

Salazar (1988) has discussed several Tasaday terms in an attempt to show
that the Tasaday were not unfamiliar with houses. However, his explanation of
the Tasaday word *lawi* 'lean-to, shed, shelter in forest' (Molony) as a metathes-
ized form of Maranao and Magindanao *walay* 'house', is simply not right. The
form (with a final glottal stop) is found in MbKC *lawi'* 'lean-to, any temporary
shelter without floor', and is probably a reflex of proto-Philippine (PPh) **lawiR*
'hut', with irregular development of the final consonant. (Compare Maranao *laoig*
'hovel, hut' [McKaughan and Macaraya 1967:203], apparently borrowed into
Tboli as Tbl *lowig* 'field shelter'.) Similarly, his account of the development of
Tasaday *tifang* 'roof' (Llamzon) as being related to Bikol *atop*, Tagalog *atip*, Iva-
tan *atep* (PPh **qatep* 'roof') by metathesis, runs into problems since there is no
Manobo language with an *i* reflex of PPh **e*, and no source for the final velar
nasal.

But even if Salazar's etymologies were correct, these do not tell anything
about whether or not the Tasaday were cave dwellers, or how long they might
have spent isolated from other communities.

Conclusion

In conclusion, then, I argue that there is nothing in the linguistic data to suggest
that the early researchers on the Tasaday were participants in, or victims of, a
conspiracy to deceive the general public as to the true identity of the subjects of
their research. To the contrary, the evidence clearly indicates that Tasaday respondents were linguistically unsophisticated and unfamiliar with the translation
process. The data collected represent a dialect of Manobo that is not spoken elsewhere, but is closely related to that known as Cotabato Manobo. Furthermore,
from the linguistic evidence presently available, I conclude that the Tasaday may
well have been living in near isolation from other groups, as they have consis-
tently asserted, but that the isolation may have lasted for only a few generations,
possibly no more than 150 years. Otherwise, greater differences would be apparent between the Tasaday speech variety and that of its closest relatives.

Postscript

After this chapter had been submitted for publication, I had the opportunity to do
fieldwork with the Tasaday for a period of eight days (March 7–14, 1990) in Surallah, Allah Valley, Cotabato. A group of Tasaday, including Dul and her husband Udelen and four of their children, Maman, Okon, Klohonon, and Fakel;
Lobo and his second wife, Funding; Natek and Dego (sons of Bilangan and Etut);

and Adug, had temporarily left the Tasaday Reserve and were staying at the house of Mayor Mai Tuan in Surallah. Also present at various times during my visit were several speakers of Blit Manobo, including Datu Mafalo Dudim and his sister Bol; Igna Kilam, a speaker of Sdaf Manobo; Juanito Balimbang, a speaker of Cotabato Manobo; and a considerable number of speakers of Tboli. Lexical and syntactic data were gathered for each of the Manobo dialects for which speakers were available, and I have begun comparative studies on the material. The main Tasaday assistants were Dul and Lobo.

Preliminary analysis confirms that the language spoken by the Tasaday is in no way similar to Tboli and is not mutually intelligible with it. It is clearly a Manobo language and is perhaps less similar to Cotabato Manobo than has been described by Johnston (1989 and this volume). Some of the lexical distinctiveness described by Hidalgo and Hidalgo (1989) has been confirmed, but their characterization of the language as a pidgin form of Manobo is not confirmed. The language has undergone certain syntactic changes which distinguish it from Cotabato Manobo and from Blit Manobo. Evidence for these statements will be presented in a forthcoming paper.

Notes

1. I make no apology for using the term *Tasaday* as an ethnonym for the group under discussion, even though Iten claimed that "it would be quite an exception, if in the Philippines an ethnic group would name itself after a mountain. Tribal names generally mean *'people, human being'* in their language" (1989:19). This is quite without foundation. The use of prominent landmarks is a much more common ethnonymic practice in the Philippines than the use of the local word for 'person.' Examples are the various communities that surround Lake Lanao in Mindanao, including the Maranao, Magindanao, and the Iranon and, similarly, the Bukidnon and Igorot 'mountain people,' the Itneg, who live along the Tineg River in Abra, Northern Luzon, the Matigsalug Manobo who live along the Salug River, and so on. To my knowledge the only groups in the Philippines who use their word for 'person' as an ethnonym are the Negritos of Northern Luzon, and in these cases the term refers only to 'Negrito person,' not 'person' in general.

2. I wish to express my thanks to Richard Elkins and Clay Johnston for reviewing my comments on Manobo lexical items and to Vivian Forsberg for providing me with Tboli cognates for some of the Tasaday terms discussed.

3. Duhaylungsod and Hyndman (1989:13) state that apart from the man Balayam ('the only Manobo made into a Tasaday'), all other Tasaday are Tboli who regularly speak Manobo.

4. This evidence has been convincingly refuted by Amelia Rogel-Rara and Emmanuel Nabayra (1989).

5. These errors are not necessarily eliminated if one already speaks a Philippine language. A native speaker of Tagalog, for example, will have difficulty distinguishing sounds such as schwa or geminate consonants, neither of which occurs in Tagalog. Knowledge of a closely related language obviously reduces the margin of error, but may not eliminate it entirely if the phonology is at all different from that to which one is accustomed.

6. There has also been recent linguistic research by Cesar Hidalgo and Araceli Hidalgo among the Tasaday and surrounding Manobo groups, but their data were not available to me during the preparation of this chapter.

7. All forms are cited precisely as they occur in the source documents, except that *è* represents schwa [ə] and *ng* replaces [ŋ]. In the cited Tboli forms, *e* represents schwa and *o* represents [ɔ].

8. Such an explanation is available for terms such as *finíngting* 'grandmother' (cf. *fè-nengtingan* 'ankle' [Molony]), and *lúlud* 'grandfather' (cf. 'knee' [Molony]). The apparent inconsistency in the meanings of these terms as recorded by Fox and Molony disappears when one knows that body parts such as 'knee' and 'ankle' are used in many Philippine languages, including Manobo languages, to refer to different generational levels.

9. This is apparently the position Hidalgo and Hidalgo have taken to explain the relatively large percentage of unique forms occuring in the Tasaday data that they recently elicited.

10. The chronology here is questionable. Nance (1975:70) implies that Llamzon and Lynch's visit postdated the visit by the group that included Peralta; yet an unpublished typed copy of Llamzon's word list states that it was compiled on July 16–17, 1971, which would have been several days prior to the date when Peralta visited the Tasaday.

11. Johnston (personal communication) notes, "The [MbKC] verb root *-ukit* means 'to pass through/over/by'. I suspect the form [*nukitan*] should be *inukitan,* where *in- -an* combine to mean 'past- -site,' i.e., 'site or way over which we passed'. The form *ukitan* is common for 'road' or 'trail'."

12. Elkins used an orthography which approximates that used by Johnston. *p* is used to represent the bilabial fricative since there is no contrasting bilabial stop. Other researchers represented the sound as *f.* In addition, Elkins used *e* to represent the central vowel [ə]. Molony was consistent in using ə for this sound (transcribed here by me as *è*), but other researchers, including Peralta and Llamzon represented it inconsistently, sometimes with ə, and sometimes with *a.* (It should be noted that there may have been other incorrectly identified terms in Elkins's list. Johnston 1989 cites some that he feels are incorrect; also see Johnston in this volume.)

13. The linguistic nature of the so-called Sanduka and the "Tao Mloy" (Duhaylungsod and Hyndman 1989:12) is not relevant to determining the linguistic affiliation of the Tasaday. The former groups may well be Tboli. We know already that this is a Tboli area, but until the Hidalgos make their linguistic data available one should reserve judgment on even this fact. And to claim that the area was the Tboli "homeland" is to lay claim to a knowledge of prehistory that is simply not available either to the Tboli or to anyone else.

14. Salazar suggests that Malay may be "closer" to Tasaday than even Blit Manobo is, because his count of cognates between the languages showed Tasaday sharing 40% of its cognates with Malay, but only 28% with Blit Manobo. This is not good linguistics. Subgrouping cannot be based on the number of shared cognates, but rather on the distribution of shared innovations in phonology, morphology, and syntax, as well as lexicon. Most of the items listed by Salazar have good Austronesian etymologies and are shared retentions in the two languages. This tells us only that both languages are Austronesian, nothing more. Neither has Salazar made any attempt to distinguish true cognates from similar forms that are the results of borrowing.

15. According to Nance, "Dudim told Mai he couldn't talk to these people, he didn't know their language and could do no good here. . . . Igna had difficulty understanding even half of the words he uttered" (1975:12).

16. This despite Iten's statement about scientists "who, even now, claim that the Tasaday speak a separate language, a thesis supported by questionable scientific standards" (from Iten's chapter in this volume). Only Olofson, an anthropologist, is making such claims today (Olofson 1989:6).

17. Despite Olofson's (1989:6) claim that "[glottochronology] is the most modern we have for reconstructing the evolution of languages," no reputable linguist ever used glottochronology to replace the comparative method that has been used for over a hundred years to establish genetic relationships between languages. Even Dyen, who is one of the few remaining proponents of lexicostatistics as a linguistic tool for subgrouping, looks to traditional use of exclusively shared innovations for qualitative evidence to confirm or disprove subgrouping hypotheses first established using quantitative evidence (Dyen 1970). Olofson's attempts to respond to some of the uninformed linguistic comments that have appeared in the literature is laudable, but in so doing he has misspoken himself in several places, including his reference to Proto-Manobo as an 'extinct' language. Extinct languages leave no daughter languages. Protolanguages are no more extinct than the languages of our grandparents. They are alive and well in the languages of succeeding generations.

18. See Blust (1983) for a review of literature and a convincing study that shows considerable variation in retention rate, at least among the Austronesian languages, of which Tasaday is a member.

19. In this I agree with Salazar: "If separation or isolation there was, it took place quite recently—not more than six or seven generations ago. And it did not involve a great number" (1971:36).

20. According to Llamzon (1971b:8), Frank Lynch proposed that the Tasaday probably never had agriculture, since "571–755 years . . . would hardly have been time enough for the Tasaday to lose this knowledge."

21. They probably had metal tools when they first moved away from their earlier homes, but given the environment they were in, such tools could not have lasted more than a generation or two, at the most. Without access to a new supply, the development of a stone-tool technology would have been the most reasonable adaptive strategy. That this technology was relatively primitive is further evidence that it was a relatively young technology.

22. It has been only around 20 years since New Zealand switched to decimal currency from its earlier pounds, shillings, and pence. Nevertheless, there are probably very few young New Zealanders today who could, without referring to a dictionary, say what /heypni/ (halfpenny), /kwɪd/ (quid, one pound), or other such formerly common terms used to mean.

● *chapter sixteen*

Cave Archaeology: A Possible Solution to the Tasaday Problem

WILLIAM A. LONGACRE

hose of you who have read these chapters are well aware of the emotions surrounding the topic of whether the Tasaday are a hoax or for real. I compliment the authors of the chapters and, especially, the editor of the volume, Thomas Headland. I know he spent many hours of his time organizing the original symposium and editing this book.

I realize I am a discussant and not a jury. My role is not to vote for hoax or for real Tasaday. I will, however, offer a solution to the problem.

Clearly this is an emotional issue. I am struck with the nonscientific arguments brought forth in some of the presentations. I guess it affirms the fact that anthropologists are real people with human responses after all. But it gets us no closer to an answer!

Professor Berreman (1989 and this volume) casts the "Tasaday for real" group as displaying the behaviors of the "True Believers" in a well-written and well-argued essay. But one could turn this around and make the identical case for the "Tasaday as hoax" group as well. He also made a point of examining the motives of the "for real" group. But he ignored an appraisal of motives in the opposition camp. There's a lot of money to be made by journalists who can sell sensational accounts to the tabloid market about the "Great Tasaday Hoax!" Clearly there's no parallel market for a story about the Tasaday for real!

Let us also note that in the early 1970s, when the Tasaday were first "discovered," then-President Marcos was having a lot of trouble with the University of the Philippines (UP). Student demonstrations had made him angry. With typical spiteful arrogance, he would not allow any UP anthropologists direct access to the Tasaday. Instead, he permitted only the anthropologists at the National Museum of the Philippines and at Ateneo de Manila University to visit the Tasaday area. Can we be surprised that the UP group claims hoax?

Are the Tasaday a hoax or for real? Can we arrive at a decision? I would say, yes and no. Without question, there was a hoax. The public at large was sold on the notion that the Tasaday were a "Stone Age tribe." I know of no anthropologist who believes that. The implication is that, somehow, this small group of people survived over countless millennia from the Ice Age in the forests of Mindanao.

194

My comment on that is the Tagalog slang word *bola*! ('deception'). It sold lots of magazines and TV specials, but it was a shameless hoax on the public at large.

On the other hand, were the Tasaday temporary actors, recruited and trained to play a foraging band for the benefit of the gullible press and anthropologists? I'm not sure we have enough evidence to come to an absolute answer. I am impressed by the linguistic evidence that supports the "for real" argument (see chapters in this volume by Elkins, Johnston, Molony, and Reid). And I am persuaded by the new data provided by Rogel-Rara (1989 and this volume) on kinship, genealogy, and social organization. Here we have a fine ethnographer undertaking extensive fieldwork of the sort called for by several of the authors of other chapters in this volume. Her data firmly support the "for real" conclusion.

Something else needs to be said here as well. Several fine, experienced anthropologists who were among the original team of investigators are no longer with us to discuss their Tasaday research. In particular, I am thinking of Frank Lynch and Robert Fox. Both were solidly trained social anthropologists with extensive field experience in the Philippines. In addition to extensive ethnographic experience, Fox also directed numerous archaeological excavations in the Philippines. Perhaps his best known work was at Tabon Cave, a deeply stratified rockshelter site on Palawan (Fox 1970).

But though further discussion with them is not possible, I cannot believe that such anthropologists could be hoodwinked by a group of people posing as tropical forest foragers who had been somewhat isolated over many generations. Even if the fieldwork were carried out only for a few weeks at a time, scholars of this stature could not be fooled by such a group of amateur players. I also share that belief about those authors who conducted fieldwork among the Tasaday and have presented their conclusions in this volume.

I am impressed with Fox's comments on the stone tools and their use based upon his field observations. In particular, his discussion of the use of flake tools (1976) by the Tasaday in his earliest observations are of interest.

The much-discussed stone axes that are in museum collections are not real tools. I understand that they represent a collection of hafting styles done by the Tasaday for the anthropologists, using convenient stones from the riverbed. They are not stone axes per se.

But, predictably, given the "True Believer" syndrome already discussed, neither the "hoax" group or the "for real" group will back away from their claims. So what can we do? Little will be accomplished by people arguing with one another or accusing each other of applying bribes to obtain the data to support their pet position.

I would like to offer here some hope for an objective appraisal of untapped evidence that should provide a powerful argument in support of one or the other camp. I speak as an archaeologist. That perhaps explains why I am a discussant of the Tasaday question in the first place, since some may protest, "He's an ethnoarchaeologist working in Luzon and Cebu—not only has he never seen a Tasaday, he has never even been to Mindanao!"

That is true; and there might even be some advantage to my lack of vested interest here. Nevertheless, as an archaeologist I am convinced that the solution to the problem might lie in the rock-shelter site itself. Think about it. If a group of two or three dozen people live in a suite of rock shelters over a period of several generations an archaeological record reflecting that fact will accumulate. I don't care how carefully the inhabitants swept out the debris from the cave floor, there will be a clear and informative record to the trained observer. I submit that it would take a competent archaeologist only a short time—a matter of hours—to determine if such a record exists. It would be fairly easy to determine whether people had inhabited the rock shelter for generations or for days only as a sham.

In 1987, I suggested to Jerome Bailen at the University of the Philippines that a "blue-ribbon" team of well-known and respected archaeologists be invited to visit the Tasaday rock-shelter site and conduct just such an appraisal. I had in mind people with considerable experience in the archaeology of cave and rock-shelter sites or in tropical archaeology, such as C. Melvin Aikens at the University of Oregon, David Hurst Thomas at the American Museum of National History, William Ayres of the University of Oregon, and Thomas Lynch at Cornell, to name only a few American examples. I argued that the individuals should *not* be involved in Philippines prehistory nor have any plans of ever getting involved.

I am convinced that it would be impossible to fool such a team—there is no way one could fake such evidence to trick a team of skilled, experienced archaeologists. If one could assemble such a team, get them in to the site for a couple of days and safely out again, then I think the Tasaday question might be solved. Well, *maybe* it would be; there is still the "True Believer" syndrome to confront.

At the least, it would bring a new dimension of evidence to bear upon the problem. Perhaps, added to the extant linguistic and sociological data, it would result in an appraisal. Clearly, not everyone would believe in such an appraisal, but we might well be closer to the truth than today.

Lastly, I would ask, is this whole controversy a healthy one for our profession? I would answer, yes. It is embarrassing—airing our dirty linen, so to speak, in the great debates at Zagreb and at the University of the Philippines conferences in 1986 and 1988, and at Annual Meeting of the American Anthropological Association in 1989. And this volume provides its share of discomfiture as well. But I think it all underscores the commitment to reveal the truth, to get to the bottom of this controversial episode in the history of anthropology.

Developing objective means of appraisal and judgment would greatly assist in reinforcing anthropology's credibility in the world today. If we approach the problem as scientists and try to discard as much of our emotional baggage as possible, then we have a chance at credibility.

Again, I salute the authors in this volume for taking a major step in that direction. Their well reasoned, careful presentations provide an important contribution toward a solution. I am optimistic that such a solution can be developed that will be accepted by the great majority of scholars in our field. We are not quite there yet, but we are well on the way.

● *chapter seventeen*

The Tasaday Debate and Indigenous Peoples

JOHN H. BODLEY

will limit my remarks to the implications of three key terms which have frequently been used in the Tasaday debate: contact, isolation, and Stone Age. I do not wish to imply that anyone has misused these terms and I am not passing judgment on their direct applicability to the Tasaday. My concern is that their use in the Tasaday debate may influence how these terms are used by those concerned with the larger question of the future of indigenous people in the world. The Tasaday case forces us to reconsider how we frame our discussion about the human rights of indigenous peoples and the debate about appropriate policies toward them. It bears on what are the most important issues for indigenous peoples.

The interrelated concepts of "contact" and "isolation" are key issues in the discussion of the Tasaday case and also in the debate over appropriate policy for many highly self-sufficient indigenous groups, such as the Yanomamo, especially in Amazonia. There is a problem with these concepts, however. They muddle the human rights issue of the territorial and cultural autonomy of indigenous peoples, because it is widely assumed that autonomy requires isolation, if not "pristine" status. Depending on how one interprets the Tasaday case, it can be taken as proof that there are no isolated peoples, or that "isolation," while it may have existed for the Tasaday, cannot possibly be maintained by any indigenous groups today. Either view places too much importance on the slippery concept of "isolation." Either view could also seriously reduce the political options for many threatened groups by lending support to the inevitability argument—the assumption that tribal groups cannot maintain their independence in the modern world. I would argue that, in relation to indigenous people, "isolation" is a false issue, as is the question of whether or not a given people are survivors of the "Stone Age."

Overemphasizing "contact" gives it an almost magical quality that masks the political nature of the interaction between peoples. It attributes an undue fragility to indigenous culture. Indigenous cultures do not mysteriously melt away upon exposure to alien cultures, although they can, of course, be damaged when their political autonomy and natural resources are reduced by invasion and conquest. So although metal tools can bring dramatic changes, in themselves they need not "destroy" an indigenous culture. It is quite possible for people to acquire metal tools (guns, for example) without undergoing much disruption, and then use them to defend themselves against unwanted intrusion. To stress "contact" is to imply a certain ignorance on the part of "isolated" peoples, suggesting that they lack technologies such as metal and farming because they simply don't know about them yet. Actually, in order to maintain their independence and physical security, many groups may *choose* to reduce their interaction with threatening outsiders.

Isolation must be recognized as a relative concept and a matter of degrees. It need not be present or absent in any absolute sense. It reveals more about a group's political and economic autonomy at a given moment than about its prehistory. Indigenous groups have maintained contacts of various sorts with outsiders at different points in the past. Peoples can move in and out of contact in different generations.

In the current debate, when the term *contact* is used, only contact with Europeans or citizens of the national society is in view. But, by definition, *contact* refers as well to interaction with related indigenous groups. Such contacts are often ignored. For indigenous peoples themselves, the important concern is not whether isolation is real or not, but who decides both the degree and the quality of contact that takes place between groups. In important respects, isolation is a matter of the degree to which a group controls its territory. The most ideal national policy toward indigenous groups would be for the group itself to have the freedom to decide the terms of interaction with outsiders. This is certainly what indigenous political organizations such as the World Council of Indigenous Peoples seek, and it is endorsed by the United Nations's Universal Declaration of Indigenous Rights.

Historically, there have been many "first" face to face "contacts" between Europeans and "isolated" indigenous groups. However, referring to such events as "discoveries" and emphasizing the "first" aspect reinforces the image of indigenous people as ignorant, if not "lost." This sort of terminology masks the fact that they know perfectly well where they are and they probably have a good idea of what lies beyond them. It masks the possibility that they may be deliberately choosing to avoid contact with threatening outsiders.

In 1975 I referred to the Tasaday as an example of peoples who were actively avoiding disruptive contacts with outsiders by deliberately maintaining their own isolation (Bodley 1975). I should perhaps emphasize that "active avoidance of contact" is a very real phenomenon in which indigenous peoples take action in their own defense. In my unpublished report to the Tasaday Commission (Bodley 1986) I suggested that the possibility of such "active avoidance" made the original descriptions of the Tasaday more believable. Whether the Tasaday in 1971 were in fact avoiding contact is not my concern here, but in the original reports they did appear to be a "refugee" group.

The issue of the status of the Tasaday as a Stone Age people raises two further difficulties. If the Tasaday *are* Stone Age, then they reinforce the widespread, but misplaced objections to so-called human zoo cultural preservation schemes. (The media parade to the Tasaday cave in the early 1970s certainly fostered the "zoo" image.) But if the Tasaday are *not* Stone Age, then many people who were led by the popular media to believe that they were, but are now told that they are not, may conclude that these "indigenous peoples" are simply rural peasants with no legitimate claim to cultural uniqueness or special human rights as groups.

Anthropologists are certainly aware of the technical implications of labeling any contemporary people as Stone Age in an archaeological sense. We may be quite sensitive to the nuances of meaning when we talk about the comparative method and use ethnoarchaeology to reconstruct the past. But in the popular media the term "Stone Age" carries its own connotations. Focusing attention on whether or not an indigenous group such as the Tasaday can legitimately be considered Stone Age is unfortunate for several reasons. In the first place, being Stone Age would suggest to many policy makers that a culture is delicate, an anachronism, doomed to disappear unless preserved in a human zoo. The image of a mere two dozen Tasaday certainly reinforced the concept of such vulnerability. The apparent fact that their small "reserve" has not proven inviolable might also seem to support the inevitability argument that "integration" is the only feasible policy.

Deciding whether or not a given group is Stone Age in any technical sense, is a question of technology. (The possibility of direct, unbroken continuity between people like the Tasaday and their ancestors who may have lived in the archaeological Stone Age is not the focus.) But emphasizing the absence of metal and farming may encourage in policy makers a certain technological and evolutionary arrogance. They might conclude that exposure to "modern technology" will, like contact itself, magically destroy "underdeveloped" cultures. They might even conclude that if indigenous cultures are that delicate, then there is no point in trying to "save" them, no point in granting them special political consideration.

In fact, only a few places would fit the definition of Stone Age in its strictly technical sense of autonomous, nonstate cultures operating within a world of similar cultures: Australia before 1789 and interior New Guinea and Amazonia before 1930. The Stone Age in that sense ends when independent tribal groups are conquered by states, but it is certainly possible for indigenous cultures to coexist with national societies and still retain their unique distinguishing features.

Whether any indigenous group practices "pure" gathering, hunting, herding, or farming, or mixes these activities with cash-cropping and wage labor, is irrelevant to their claim to special human rights as indigenous people. The characteristics of indigenous groups that are most significant in the contemporary political context are that they are culturally distinct, territorially based, small-scale communal societies that are self-governing and primarily dependent on local resources. They need be neither "Stone Age" or "isolated" to self-identify as indigenous peoples and to claim their internationally recognized rights. The real issue is political control over territory and resources.

● *chapter eighteen*

Our Fascination with the Tasaday: Anthropological Images and Images of Anthropology

Leslie E. Sponsel

> In this anthropological "experiment" which we initiate, it is not they who are
> the ultimate objects but ourselves. . . . we reflect on ourselves studying others,
> because we must, because man in civilization is the problem. [Diamond
> 1974:100]

> In order for an anthropologist to function as what I would call an authentic an-
> thropologist, he or she must study the cultural tradition in which the anthropo-
> logical inventions are used. Anthropologists must study the needs and concerns
> of their society to interpret why their inventions make sense to their audience,
> how and why their inventions fit in their society. Above all, anthropology must
> address the following question: what is the meaning of discourse on the human
> other in the Western tradition? [Pandian 1985:112]

Our Fascination

In 1971, the Tasaday were a group of only 24 people living in a remote forested
mountain area, yet they attracted the attention of the media, the public, and anthropology in the Philippines, the United States, and the world. At least 16 scientists from several countries have observed the Tasaday, although most for only
a few days (John Nance, personal communication). Moreover, in excess of four
dozen other persons have visited the Tasaday, mainly journalists, photographers,
and filmmakers. Even celebrities have viewed the Tasaday, such as aviator
Charles Lindbergh, actress Gina Lollobrigida, and the granddaughter of the Spanish dictator Francisco Franco.

Among other publications, these visits have yielded three books by journalist
John Nance (1975, 1981, 1982), who spent more time with the Tasaday than anyone else, about 125 days (John Nance, personal communication). One of the
books is specifically for children (Nance 1982). Nance is also currently working
on a new book about the Tasaday.

In addition, the Tasaday presented a superb photo opportunity. They were
filmed by Central TV, BBC, ABC, NBC, and the National Geographic Society,
among others, and portrayed in at least five photographic exhibits in museums in
the Philippines, in Washington, D.C., and in the Netherlands. After Presidential

Decree 1017 (PD-1017 1977) by Ferdinand Marcos established a large reserve for the Tasaday in 1974, "imitation Tasaday" were paraded before Gerald Ford on his state visit to the Philippines.

Somehow connected with the Tasaday have also been threats, counterinsurgency, kidnapping, hostage taking, terrorism, and a lawsuit regarding their identity. In 1988, the Tasaday even became the subject of an investigation by the Philippine Congressional Committee on Cultural Communities.

The 1989 American Anthropological Association (AAA) symposium was the third anthropological conference devoted to the Tasaday, and probably not the last. The issue of political restrictions on academic freedom and scientific inquiry has been raised in resolutions by the department of anthropology of the University of the Philippines in 1987 and the AAA in 1988.

The Tasaday Phenomenon

Clearly the Tasaday are much more than simply another ethnic minority, a newly contacted traditional indigenous group, or even an ethnographic celebrity. Compared to other ethnic minorities, including newly contacted traditional indigenous societies (see Connolly and Anderson 1987; Myers 1988), the Tasaday have received an inordinate amount of attention. For example, in the last two decades at least three dozen indigenous societies, some still using stone tools, have been newly contacted in the Amazon (Schoen 1969a, 1969b, 1971; Yohner 1970); yet none of them has attracted anything even beginning to approach the amount of publicity and controversy surrounding the Tasaday. The Tasaday are more than just a controversy as to whether they are anthropological fact or fiction, reality or image, or some mixture of these. It is more accurate to think of the "Tasaday phenomenon."

Why?

Why are the Tasaday so fascinating? McGrane (1989:95) goes so far as to suggest that "Anthropological discourse isn't concerned with what the tribes are 'in themselves' but with what they represent." At several levels the Tasaday represent a complex symbol with multiple meanings, regardless of whether or not they are in any sense and to whatever degree authentic. This fact has not escaped anthropologists. Most noteworthy is an insightful article by Dumont (1988) who explores the Tasaday as a symbol for the Marcos regime via Panamin and Manuel Elizalde, Jr., for peace concerns in the United States during the Vietnam war, and as the polar extreme to the Yanomami. (Also see Olofson 1989; Rosaldo 1982; and Yengoyan 1977). My purpose here is to develop some of these aspects of the symbolic meaning of the Tasaday, including several points which Dumont did not explore, such as the mutual relevance of the Tasaday and the counterculture movement.

To demystify or decode the extrinsic value of the Tasaday as a complex symbol at multiple levels, there is no better place to begin than with the title of Nance's 1975 book, which is a synthesis of the "Tasaday phenomenon": *The Gentle Tasaday: A Stone Age People in the Philippine Rain Forest.* At the minimum the Tasaday served as (1) an evolutionary symbol from the Stone Age, (2) an ecological symbol from the tropical rain forest, (3) a political symbol from the Philippines, and (4) a peace symbol with political implications from the era of the Vietnam War. (Some of these relationships are illustrated in Figure 1, in which the righthand column represents the United States in the historical context of the Vietnam War and in relation to the "Tasaday phenomenon" and primitivism.)

Anthropological Images

Evolutionary Symbol

As Diamond (1974:203) observed, "The concept of the primitive is as old as civilization because civilized men have always and everywhere been compelled by the conditions of their existence to try to understand their roots and human possibilities." Chronological primitivism refers to the period in time—past, present, future—of the best condition of humankind. Often this is associated with the primeval goodness or happiness of humankind (Lovejoy and Boas 1965:1). Cultural primitivism is the belief that a simpler and less sophisticated life, in some or all aspects, is more desirable than civilization as a whole or in part (Lovejoy and Boas 1965:7). The Tasaday, remote in time as "Stone Age" survivors and in space as supposedly isolated from the urban centers of civilization in a remote wilderness,

FIGURE 1
Symbolic Meaning of the Tasaday

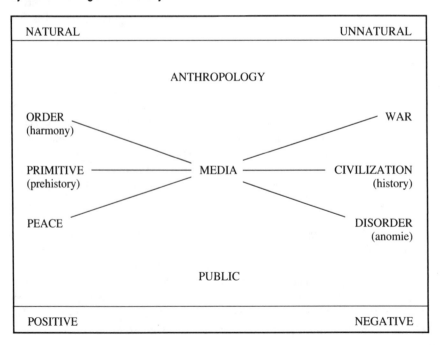

reflect both the chronological and cultural senses of primitivism (see Rosaldo 1982; Torgovnick 1990).

As stone tool–using, nonhunting cave dwellers, surviving in remote, mountainous, tropical rain forest, the Tasaday represented "ultraprimitives," to apply a term from Lindbergh in his foreword to the book by Nance (1975:xi). Similarly, Nance (1981:vii) describes the Tasaday as reflecting "the most elemental levels of human existence." The Tasaday appeared to have many of the attributes of "natural man" or "man in a natural state," following the historical analyses of Barnes (1923) and Lovejoy and Boas (1965:14–15) which remain most useful (see Table 1). Thus in some ways Elizalde's helicopter trips into Tasaday territory were analogous to H. G. Wells's time machine (Nance 1981:vii; cf. McGrane 1989:103).

Although the media, rather than the anthropologists, uncritically applied to the Tasaday characterizations such as "most primitive," "stone age," "cave men," "lost tribe" (Kramer 1975; Life 1972; MacLeish 1972; Nance 1988a:467), as scientists anthropologists have also been keenly interested in the potential insights which research with the Tasaday might provide for understanding the prehistory and evolution of hunter-gatherers (see Headland's three chapters in this volume). Ever since the classical evolutionary ethnologists like Morgan and Tylor, so-called primitive societies have been considered to be—in various ways and to varying degrees—survivals of earlier stages of cultural evolution; and, as such, they can be studied to interpret and amplify the limited material remains in the archaeological record and to reconstruct the stages of cultural evo-

---

TABLE 1
Attributes of "Natural Man" and the Tasaday

Attributes of the "Primitive" present in the Tasaday
    wilderness or forest habitat, "garden of Eden"
    naked (except for leaves)
    nomadic habit (albeit home base in caves), stone tools, fire, foraging (but no hunting of large game)
    egalitarian society based on the family
    cooperation and reciprocity
    simple and contented life
    morals
    language

Attributes of "Civilization" absent in the Tasaday
    sedentary habit with constructed shelter
    agriculture and domesticated animals
    private property
    authority, government, laws and other political institutions
    violence and war
    developed religion

Note: These attributes were originally extracted from historical surveys of theories of "natural man" by Barnes (1923) and by Lovejoy and Boas (1965:14–15).

lution (see Carneiro 1973; Diamond 1974; Kuper 1989; Lovejoy and Boas 1965; Montagu 1968; Pandian 1985; and Stocking 1987).

Unfortunately, there has yet to be an adequate archaeological survey and an ethnoarchaeological study in the Tasaday caves and surrounding region, although the presence or absence of an archaeological record would probably be a decisive factor in assessing the question of a hoax. Another decisive factor would likely be provided by biological anthropology, a subfield of anthropology curiously ignored in both research and debate on the Tasaday. Hair and blood samples, which are usually obtainable, could be used to assess the degree of isolation and distinctiveness of the Tasaday as a biological population in relation to their neighbors (see Cann 1988). Moreover, these archaeological and genetic investigations could still be undertaken and yield significant results, regardless of any cultural and linguistic changes which have occurred among the Tasaday since their "discovery" by Dafal.

Ecological Symbol

As shown by Hudson's *Green Mansions* (1904) and Conrad's *The Heart of Darkness* (1902), among others, Western civilization has long been ambivalent about tropical rain forests, alternately viewing them as either luxurious paradise or green hell (Putz and Holbrook 1988). Indigenous societies in such forests have sometimes been considered as exemplifying Rousseau's (1967) "child of nature" and Chateaubriand's (1952) "noble savage" living in a golden age of harmony within society and with nature—for example the Mbuti (Turnbull 1961)—and other times, via Hobbes (1962), as savages in the jungle living by its cruel natural laws of struggle for survival—for example the Yanomami (Chagnon 1983, 1988).

The Tasaday also neatly fit preconceived stereotypic notions, in this case the positive image of the tropical rain forest and its inhabitants. Lindbergh (1975:ix) described the Tasaday as "living in a Garden of Eden." Fernandez and Lynch (1972) depict the Tasaday as enjoying idyllic conditions: "We saw an apparently healthy, happy people living in close and seemingly contented harmony with their natural environment" (p. 301). "To the Tasaday, the forest is a most congenial environment. Food resources are bountiful in variety and, in certain foods, abundant" (p. 302). The abundance of resources implicit in the "Garden of Eden" image of the tropical rain forest as an earthly paradise (see de Camp 1954) has been challenged on ecological grounds, such as in the case of Headland's application of his "wild yam hypothesis" to the Tasaday in this volume (see also Bailey et al. 1989; Fankhauser this volume; Headland 1987; Headland and Reid 1989; Robson and Yen 1976; Yen 1976b).[1]

Identifying "natural" with "good" (Lovejoy and Boas 1965:12), romantic environmentalists found the Tasaday appealing. They viewed them as noble conservationists living in a small and cooperative community in intimate and harmonious relationship with nature, satisfying only basic needs by gathering and eating natural foods low in the food pyramid and so on (cf. Bennett 1976, Devall and Sessions 1985). According to Kozlovsky (1974:106), the fundamental principle of human ecology is: "Live as simply and as naturally and as close to the earth as possible, inhibiting only two aspects of your unlimited self: your capacity to reproduce and your desire for material things."

Political Symbol

In the Philippines and beyond, the Tasaday emerged as a multivocalic symbol associated with that nation, and especially with Marcos, Panamin, and Elizalde. This is quite clear from Elizalde's own statements in one of the first field reports on the Tasaday in July of 1971 (Elizalde with Fox 1971a):

> In a very real sense the Tasaday are a symbol of PANAMIN's *struggle for a viable program of balanced conservation,* for when the forests disappear, they disappear. The Tasaday provide a *link with our distant past* and through a study of their life-ways, we can achieve a better understanding of man's past and future *relationships with the natural environment* of which he is an integral part. [p. 4, emphasis added]

> The Tasaday are more than just a small group of primitive people who, in the past would simply have been wiped out by civilization; by the agents and forces of change promising them a better life and even a better death. Rather, they are a symbol of Man's variability and *adaptability* and also of his *universality,* for even with the little data we have on hand, we see among the Tasaday the *common denominator* of human life everywhere and at all times—individuals organized into a social system to exploit the environment in which they live with the tools which they know, and with memories of the past and fears of the future. But the future of the Tasaday now rests in our hands, not theirs. It is an awesome *responsibility* which PANAMIN shares with you. [p. 20, emphasis added]

As Chairman of the Panamin Foundation, Elizalde wrote the dedication for the book *Further Studies on the Tasaday* (Yen and Nance 1976:v), which was published as Panamin Foundation Research Series Number 2. There he said:

> Among the achievements of the Marcos Era in Philippine history is a *national reawakening* to the richness of *our indigenous culture,* of our natural and human resources. It is fitting, therefore, that this book be dedicated to President Ferdinand E. Marcos and his First Lady, Mrs. Imelda Romualdez Marcos. Their sustained personal support and *enlightened policies*—particularly for our cultural minorities—have made this series of Panamin publications possible. [emphasis added]

Elizalde clearly recognizes the extrinsic values of the Tasaday as political, evolutionary, and ecological symbols. Since the present author is not an expert on the Philippines, this aspect will not be pursued further, but those interested may read Dumont (1988), Olofson (1989), and Razon and Hensman (1976) for some leads. Nevertheless, the value of the Tasaday as a political symbol for Elizalde and others is probably the single most important reason behind their extraordinary publicity. Yet it should also be pointed out that their political use does not necessarily preclude their authenticity.[2]

Peace Symbol

Models of nonviolent and peaceful societies, whether mythological (Campbell 1972), ethnographic (Collins 1981; Fabbro 1978; Howell and Willis 1989; Montagu 1978:5; cf. Knauft 1987), literary, or otherwise appear to be rare. The non-violent and peaceful image of the Tasaday was embodied in the title of Nance's 1975 book: *The Gentle Tasaday* (see also Nance 1981, 1982). (Nance was the Bureau Chief for the Associated Press in Manila at the time the Tasaday were discovered in 1971.) Perhaps the appealing image of the nonviolent and peaceful Tasaday, even more than the high quality of his writing, explains the popularity of this book (cf. Kramer 1975). Nance wrote:

> Although we could not or would not emulate them and may never extract new principles of behavior from them, we could treasure them as reminders of what was humanly possible; as inspiring emblems of social peace and harmony, of, simply, love. Their love was everywhere—for each other, for their forest, for us—for life. [1975:447]

Similarly, in the *National Geographic Magazine,* Kenneth MacLeish, who visited the Tasaday, wrote:

> perhaps the simplest of living humans, and those closest to nature . . . gentle and affectionate. . . . Our friends have given me a new measure of man. If our ancient ancestors were like the Tasaday, we come from far better stock than I had thought. [1972:248]

One of the early scientific reports on the Tasaday also referred to them as "one of the gentlest people on the face of the earth" (Fernandez and Lynch 1972:293).

The Tasaday offered an island of peace in a sea of violence. In the United States the Tasaday became one of the symbols of peace during the last phase of the Vietnam war, especialy for the media and public who were saturated with reports of killing. For American society groping for some light at the end of the tunnel, the Tasaday provided an ethnographic model of a nonviolent and peaceful egalitarian community living by group consensus in freedom and in harmony with nature. Apparently existing in some mythic age of innocence, the Tasaday had no words for conflict, violence, enemy, war, or murder, and no weapons or enemies. They were one big loving family who just as readily embraced unknown visitors within their community as they did each other. Elkins (1989 and this volume) points out that the Tasaday's public display of affection distinguishes them from other tribal groups in Mindanao and Manobo. Thus, as the "ultraprimitive," the Tasaday led to the hopeful conclusion that, after all, human nature was inherently basically good (Feibleman 1987; Golding 1954; Kohn 1990).

The meaning of the Tasaday as a symbol of peace is reflected in the words of Lovejoy and Boas:

> Merely . . . to point out and to lament the horrors of war was less effective than to picture the felicity of a past and early, or absolutely primeval, condition in which war had been unknown; for this implied that it was not inseparable from human existence and not inherent in the original and universal, and therefore the true, or normal, nature of man; and more vaguely, it could be denounced, from this point of view, in the sacred name of "nature." [1965:16]

As "ultraprimitive" the Tasaday revealed what Diamond (1974:119) has called our "primary human potential," which in their case was very appealing because it seemed so positive (see Cannel and Macklin 1973; Kohn 1990; Stevenson 1987). Dumont (1988:267) even suggests that in the United States the Tasaday represented no less than the Asian antithesis of the Vietcong.

Furthermore, the Tasaday are reminiscent of the hippies in the 1960s—an era which might be called the Old Stoned Age! The Tasaday might even be considered as "paleo-hippies," to borrow a term from Goldschmidt (1977:538), although he didn't apply it to the Tasaday. While the hippies, and more broadly, the counterculture movement, peaked in the late 1960s before the "discovery" of the Tasaday in 1971, that historical fact does not negate the possibility that the Tasaday were of some relevance to later phases of the counterculture movement, nor that the counterculture was of some relevance to the "Tasaday phenomenon." Indeed, Nance (1975:446) mentions that when he read Roszak's (1969) *The Making of a Counter-Culture,* the Tasaday immediately came to mind.

Goldschmidt (1977:532) provides one of the most penetrating anthropological analyses of the counterculture movement. He argues that this movement derived some of its ideology from essentially false notions and romanticizations about the nature of so-called primitive society. If in Goldschmidt's analysis the word *Tasaday* were substituted for *hippie* or *counterculture,* the fit would be remarkably close, although clearly it consists of similarities rather than identities (see Table 2).

According to Roszak (1969:50), the technocratic assumptions about human nature, society, and nature needed to be challenged to restore humane values. Part of the alternative was the intimate personal sociality of communal living without formal structure, hierarchy, and centralized authority (Roszak 1969:54, 60). This involved new patterns of subsistence, shelter, family, sexual mores, arts, and so on, in contrast to the massive technocracy, materialism, alienation, and power politics of the mainstream culture of the United States and Western civilization in general (Roszak 1969:66). While the counterculture movement encompassed radical oppositions to mainstream culture, as an ethnographic reality the Tasaday challenged the moral order simply by sheer contrast, and their challenge was made even more powerful by their "ultraprimitive" status which reflected the elemental condition of humankind.[3]

If the Tasaday had only been discovered earlier, then perhaps they would have provided something of a creation myth for the counterculture. If the Tasaday were invented by Elizalde and/or others, then possibly they were modeled on some of the ideals of the counterculture in order to attract publicity.

In academia the Tasaday are also of special significance as a nonviolent and peaceful society. Yengoyan (1977:136) recognizes this in one of the few reviews of Nance's book by an anthropologist. Montagu, a pioneer in the anthropology of peace studies, considers the Tasaday and their implications in two of his books, *The Nature of Human Aggression* (1976) and *Learning Non-Aggression* (1978). Montagu (1978:4) asserts that, among nearly two dozen societies which are relatively nonviolent and peaceful, the Tasaday are especially important because they appear to lack both intragroup and intergroup aggression. As the most nonviolent society known, the Tasaday, according to Montagu (1978) offer one of

---

TABLE 2

Comparison of the Tasaday and Counterculture

Common to both
    innocence and simplicity
    spontaneity and free expression
    nudity to some degree
    love
    intimacy, communal living, and sharing
    eating natural foods
    living intimately with nature
    isolation and independence from the larger society

Lacking in both
    materialism
    internal structural differentiation (other than age and sex)
    leadership or authority
    organized religion

Lacking in Tasaday but present in the counterculture
    drugs
    free sex
    political action
    anomie and limnality (see Partridge 1973:68–75)

---

the most serious challenges to the ethological argument that human aggression and territoriality are innate drives (proposed by Lorenz, Ardrey, Morris, and others). He suggests (1976:167) that the Tasaday enculturate/socialize children in nonviolence, providing nonviolent role models for children to imitate, rewarding cooperation, and discouraging aggression. However, he laments that he was unable to find anyone who had visited the Tasaday to contribute a chapter on them for the book of case studies he edited on learning nonviolence (Montagu 1978:4).

It is most unfortunate and paradoxical that no systematic scientific research was ever undertaken with a focus on the purportedly nonviolent and peaceful behavior of the Tasaday, even though the media and other visitors to them have repeatedly commented on this as one of their most outstanding characteristics. At least in part, this neglect probably reflects the general bias which appears to be inherent in anthropology and Western culture in favor of attention to violence and war over nonviolence and peace (Sponsel 1989). Yet surely no objective scholar or scientist would deny that nonviolence and peace are legitimate and significant subjects for research (Sponsel 1989, 1990a, 1990b).

Dumont (1988:270–272) follows the central tenet of structuralism, which asserts that there is an inherent tendency in the human mind to create binary oppositions, that is, pairs of antithetical concepts. He identifies the Tasaday and the Yanomami as a binary opposition in anthropology and beyond, and anyone familiar with these two cultures can readily work out the implications (see Table 3).[4]

TABLE 3

Yanomami and Tasaday as Binary Oppositions

Yanomami	Tasaday
negative otherness (e.g., Hobbes)	positive otherness (e.g., Rousseau)
"the fierce people"	"the gentle people"
violence and war (hierarchy of aggression)	nonviolence and peace (no weapons, no enemies, no word for enemy, murder, or war)
swiddening, with foraging also important	foragers (mainly vegetarians) without any farming
growing population	remnant population too small to be viable in the long-term
elaborate shamanistic religion	religion apparently weakly developed
elaborate intra- and inter-village politics albeit no centralized political authority	internally apolitical
scientifically well studied with fairly open access usually allowed by national governments (until recent crisis in Brazil)	scientific studies extremely limited with access greatly restricted by national government
principal American account by anthropologist Chagnon (1983)	principal American account by journalist Nance (1975, 1981)
authenticity unquestioned but controversy over explanation of aggression and conflicting ethnographic representations (Heider 1988, Chagnon 1983, etc.)	authenticity questioned in persistent heated controversy

The Tasaday controversy, like those controversies over the Yanomami (Chagnon versus Lizot), the Samoans (Mead versus Freeman), Tepozlan (Lewis versus Redfield), and the !Kung (Lee versus Wilmsen) points to the increasing recognition of the epistemological problem of the relationship between ethnographic observations and images (see Fabian 1983; Keesing 1987; Kuper 1989; Marcus and Fischer 1986; McGrane 1989; Pandian 1985; Strathern 1987).[5]

Images of Anthropology

Media

The "Tasaday phenomenon" is one of the most remarkable examples of the "Stone Age" meeting the "Media Age" (see Carpenter 1972; Connolly and Anderson 1987; Kottak 1990). To varying degrees many of the symbolic meanings of the Tasaday were conveyed by the media to the public in the Philippines, the United States, and elsewhere in the world. Indeed, in the case of the Tasaday, the media have played a more important role than anthropology. For instance, Nance, a journalist rather than an anthropologist, wrote the only book that approximates an ethnographic monograph on the Tasaday.

Also of special appeal to the public, and therefore to the media, is cult anthropology, and the Tasaday border on this as well. Cult, pseudoscientific, fringe, or fantastic anthropology (Feder 1990; Harrold and Eve 1987) contains unscientific, quasi-religious, and antiestablishment tendencies (Stiebing 1987:7). The four major sources of pseudoscientific ideas are cognitive biases, uncritical media coverage, inadequate or erroneous science education, and sociocultural factors (Eve and Harrold 1987; Singer and Benassi 1981). Because so little regular scientific research with the Tasaday has been permitted by the Philippine government, there has been wide latitude for imaginative, uncritical, and sensationalistic reports by some individuals in the media and public.

Anthropology

In the popular media the Tasaday were often referred to as one of the greatest anthropological discoveries of the century. Yet there is an inverse correlation between the large number of books and articles published on the Tasaday and the very small amount of scientific field research with them, the latter largely because of government restrictions, supposedly to protect them. (The longest period any anthropologist spent with the Tasaday was 38 days in the case of ethnobotanist Yen.) Unlike the media, at least until recently (see Iten's chapter in this volume), most anthropologists have never completely accepted the Tasaday. Moreover, many anthropologists have remained very skeptical from the outset. For instance, in a sample of 20 introductory textbooks on cultural anthropology in the author's library, 85% discuss the Yanomami while only 35% mention the Tasaday, despite the publicity over the latter and their potential significance if authentic. This may reflect the relatively limited scientific documentation on the Tasaday compared to the Yanomami and other societies. Most scientists who have visited them have lamented the paucity and tentative nature of scientific fieldwork, data, and publications on them. Certainly more research with the Tasaday would help us to better know and understand them, even with the profound changes which must have transpired since their "discovery."

Meaning For the 1990s

The Tasaday phenomenon involves more than simply the question of whether they are scientific fact or science fiction. First, in many ways the Tasaday provided, and continue to provide, something like a Rorschach test for our own society. Our fascination with them derives in large measure from their extrinsic value as a complex symbol with multiple meanings at several levels: evolutionary, ecological, political, and peace.

Second, the Tasaday are also relevant as a microcosm of the contemporary rethinking of anthropology in relation to our own traditional binary oppositions of prehistory/history, primitive/civilized, war/peace, image/reality, observer/observed, science/public, anthropology/media, etc.

Third, in all of the Tasaday phenomenon the intrinsic value of the Tasaday as individual human beings has often been overshadowed if not excluded by considerations of their extrinsic value, although Nance (1975) cannot be accused of this. Given our fascination with the scientific and symbolic meaning of the Tasaday, perhaps we have sometimes lost sight of them as people.

Finally, perhaps beyond our concern for the meaning of the Tasaday for us, we should be even more concerned about *our meaning for them*. For instance, Elizalde's 1971 report on their discovery (Elizalde with Fox 1971a) was written for the Smithsonian Institution's Center for Short-Lived Phenomena, a rather sad commentary on the promise which contact with so-called civilization holds for the so-called primitive (see Bodley 1990). Moreover, all of the publicity surrounding the discovery of the Tasaday as a "lost tribe" of "Stone Age" cavedwellers has tended to detract attention away from the serious and urgent concerns for the survival, welfare, and rights of all ethnic minorities in the Philippines (see Razon and Hensman 1976; Rosaldo 1982).

Notes

Acknowledgments. Although I am responsible for any deficiencies in this essay, I am most grateful for the helpful comments on the Tasaday from Irenaus Eibl-Eibesfeldt, Richard Lieban, Judith Moses, John Nance, Harold Olofson, Floro Quibuyan, and Douglas Yen. Thomas Headland, editor of this volume and organizer of the AAA symposium on which it is based, invited me to participate in both forums to explore the reasons for the inordinate fascination with the Tasaday, recognizing my enduring interest in the relationship between anthropology and the so-called primitive. This analysis is based on the available literature, and not on any firsthand field observations on the Tasaday. It is supposed to examine what the Tasaday represent to us, rather than what they are in themselves.

I remain undecided as to whether or not the Tasaday are reality or hoax. However, the 1974 Philippine government prohibition with threat of imprisonment for any social scientist visiting the Tasaday (PD-1017 1977) can only cast serious suspicion on both government motives and the Tasaday situation. At the same time the power of the consensus among several reputable linguists on the AAA panel whose papers were revised for this book cannot be underestimated.

1. Unfortunately, even though diversity is the pivotal characteristic of the tropical rain forest biome, ecological analyses such as that by Headland often tend to advocate monolithic casual explanations without sufficient regard for the complexity and dynamic processes of spatial and temporal variation in such ecosystems. For instance, diversity in tropical rain forest ecosystems is marked in the fact that the forest is composed of a mosaic of plant and associated animal communities at different stages of succession as a result of natural and anthropogenic processes (Colinvaux 1989; Salo 1986; Sanford et al. 1985). There is a whole continuum of ecosystems from poor (oligotrophic) to rich (eutrophic) in terms of biological diversity, productivity, and nutrient availability (Jordan and Herrera 1981). In the case of the Philippines, the ecology of some rain forest areas may be rather distinctive because of their insularity, mountainous terrain, and the

frequency of tropical storms. Also, the "wild yam hypothesis" and similar ones tend to assume a "natural" environment unmodified by humans. There is probably a complex hierarchy of limiting factors, the specific combination of which varies with the particular conditions of a population and with space and time (Sponsel 1986:73–74).

2. Ultimately, to fully understand the Tasaday phenomenon, it would also be necessary to explore the biographies of the major non-Tasaday figures in the situation, especially Dafal as the original "discoverer," Elizalde as head of Panamin, Mai Tuan as the interpreter, and Nance as the principal chronicler and popularizer of the Tasaday (e.g., Rocamora 1979).

3. For additional material on the counterculture see Berke 1969, Brown 1967, Foss 1990, and Partridge 1973. Partridge (1973:9–13) discusses the problem of defining *hippie*.

4. Although the Yanomami are one of the most extensively studied cultures, having been investigated by at least three dozen anthropologists during more than a century, there is significant disagreement concerning ethnographic observations and images about them. There is no doubt that the writings and films of Chagnon (1983, 1988) have depicted the Yanomami as "the fierce people." However, this has been labeled a gross exaggeration by a growing number of other ethnographers who have also spent many years with the Yanomami such as Albert (1985), Good with Chanoff (1991), Lizot (1985, 1989), Ramos (1987), and Early and Peters (1990). (See also Davis 1977; Heider 1988; Sponsel 1983.) Among the Yanomami, nonviolence and peace are far more frequent than violence and war. As pointed out by Campbell (1989) and Heelas (1989), problems arise when an ethnographer labels the essence of a culture as either aggressive or peaceful.

5. Fortunately, several well documented cases of relatively nonviolent and peaceful societies are readily available (Dentan 1968; Howell and Willis 1989; Knauft 1987; Montagu 1978; Robarchek 1977; Robarchek and Dentan 1987).

PART V

Conclusion

● *chapter nineteen*

Conclusion
The Tasaday: A Hoax or Not?

THOMAS N. HEADLAND

M ost people who read this book will be hoping for an answer, preferably a short answer, to one immediate question: Was it a hoax? I have been asked this question countless times since 1986, often by people who acted as though they were allowing me 17 seconds to answer them. For the public, the issue by the end of the 1980s had been reduced to the simple question of whether the Tasaday were a hoax—rain forest phonies who were paid or coaxed to move into the forest and masquerade as Stone Age cave men. The answer to the hoax question, as worded here, is that the Tasaday were not a hoax.

Life is complex, however, and the truth lies somewhere in between the two polar alternatives of deliberate deception versus primitive isolation. The Tasaday did not deliberately deceive the public, but neither were they primitive foragers isolated for hundreds of years from outside contact.

Neither of these polar alternatives is correct. As anthropologists have reanalyzed the issues since Oswald Iten announced the story as a hoax in 1986, the consensus among most anthropologists falls halfway between these two extremes. With new discussion and study since 1986, most no-hoax theorists have moved from their earlier viewpoint that the Tasaday were completely isolated, that they lived alone in a cave for hundreds of years, and that they had a stone-tool technology providing windows for us into the Pleistocene. Most of those anthropologists who claimed that the early reports were a fraud and that these people were paid performers brought in from the outside to fake a primitive life-style before scientists and media cameras have also moved from their position.

While the scholars involved in the controversy in the late 1980s, including the authors in this volume, still differ sharply on many of the details, probably all of them agree that the Tasaday were not following a Paleolithic foraging subsistence. They still disagree as to whether or not the Tasaday were living without iron tools, whether or not they were living independently of cultivated foods, and whether or not they were interacting with farming peoples. But no scholars will argue today that the Tasaday are a Stone Age people, or that the Tasaday never existed. All seem to accept that they are a genuine minority tribal people who, regardless of degree of geographic separation from other peoples, always lived in the general vicinity of where they were found in the early 1970s in South Cotabato. And most of the authors in this volume would agree with the eight facts outlined below and with most (but not necessarily every part) of the proposed hypothesis stated below of Tasaday history before 1971.

Important disagreement continues, however, among the present authors, especially as to whether these 26 people (increased to about 70 in 1986) were a separate ethnic population of foragers, or merely a group of unacculturated Manobo farmers who were asked by Panamin officials to live at the cave site whenever visitors were flown in. Key examples of differences of opinion are whether or not the caves were the Tasaday's main habitation site; to what degree the local area could provide sufficient wild foods for pure foragers; whether or not the Manobo trader Dafal was the only non-Tasaday human they interacted with before 1971; whether or not they did any cultivation; and whether or not they had ever eaten domesticated foods before 1971. While these disagreements remain unresolved, a number of facts that have recently emerged concerning the pre-1971 Tasaday indicate that the journalists, if not the early scientists, exaggerated the "primitiveness" of the Tasaday and led the public to assume that they were more isolated than they actually were. There are eight facts, as I choose to call them, that come to the surface in the chapters of this book which few anthropologists dispute, and which I summarize here.

Eight Little-Known Facts

1. *The Tasaday were not wearing leaves* when discovered in 1971, as the public was led to believe. They were wearing commercially manufactured cloth. They were asked at that time by Manuel Elizalde, Jr., the Panamin director, to discard the cloth and to "wear their traditional" coverings. Thereafter, published films and photographs always showed them either naked or wearing orchid leaves.[1]

2. *The Tasaday had trade goods* before they were discovered in 1971, which indicates that they were not isolated, out of contact with the modern world, or paleolithic. Besides cloth, they had, for example, brass, metal-tipped arrows, bows made from cultivated bamboo (not wild bamboo), iron bush knives, imported baskets, glass beads, and tin cans.[2]

3. *Farming peoples in nearby towns were eating meat from wild game that had been killed and smoke-dried by Tasaday* before 1971 (MacLeish 1972:237). This was probably an important trade item the Tasaday exchanged for the goods mentioned above. Wild meat is a common trade product exchanged for cultivated foods from farmers by tropical forest hunter-gatherers all over the world.

4. *The South Cotabato rain forest lacks sufficient wild plant foods to sustain a pure foraging group.* The evidence strongly supports this. The Tasaday ate a wide variety of wild fruits, roots, palm pith, etc. But these are so widely scattered and difficult to harvest that it is unlikely that foragers could depend on such resources to provide adequate carbohydrate needs unless they also had access to some cultivated starch foods.[3]

5. *No one ever observed the Tasaday subsisting from wild foods.* It was assumed a priori, and reported in the earliest reports (Elizalde with Fox 1971a; Fernandez and Lynch 1972; MacLeish 1972) that their diet was based solely on nondomestic foods; and because of the tight restrictions put on some of the original dozen scientists by the Panamin staff, those scientists never learned otherwise during their fieldwork periods there in 1972. But from June 1971 the Tasaday ate rice, often two and sometimes three times per day, even during the periods when the scientists were there. What is significant is that the rice was often given to them by the Panamin staff without the knowledge of the scientists. The scientists, not knowing this, thought the Tasaday were fulfilling their nutritional needs from wild foods. It was only later that a few of them discovered that rice was secretly being provided for the Tasaday by Panamin employees.[4]

6. *The Tasaday bamboo utensils were of cultivated bamboo, not wild bamboo.* Such utensils include the bamboo tubes in which they cooked their food, their bamboo hunting bows, and their bamboo jew's harps. The question is, where did this bamboo come from? Not from the rain forest. Worldwide, there are some 700 species of bamboo; but the large woody species that stand erect on their own— the types in which the Tasaday cooked their food—are sun-loving, cultivated, and do not grow in shaded primary rain forest. Peralta states in his chapter, "The species of bamboo required did not grow there" (this volume); and Robert Fox (Elizalde with Fox 1971a:8), as well as John Nance (1975:23, 64), also recognized that the bamboo was not wild. The Tasaday, then, either planted the bamboo themselves or got it from Manobo farmers. Thus, since they were making these three tools from a cultivar, they could not have been as ignorant of agriculture as was originally claimed.

7. *The Tasaday stone tools displayed in Manila and shown in photographs were not genuine tools.* The Tasaday were said to have had three simple stone tools in 1971, which were reportedly taken to Manila by Elizalde, where they strangely disappeared. For some unexplained reason, they were never photographed, and no one has seen them since.[5] The stone tools subsequently published in photographs and displayed in the Panamin Museum in Manila were made by Manobo or Tasaday at the request of Panamin personnel for the benefit of newspaper correspondents. The Tasaday may have used some stone in their technology, but they did not use stone tools in the sophisticated way that humans did during the Upper Paleolithic.[6]

8. *The Tasaday do not speak a separate language or unintelligible dialect.* They speak a *dialect* of the nearby Cotabato Manobo language, one of more than 20 languages making up the Manobo subgroup of the Southern Philippine Austronesian language family. About 85% of Tasaday words are identical to Cotabato Manobo. If shared cognates are taken into consideration, the percentage would, of course, be higher. In 1989, Tasaday conversations tape-recorded by Molony in 1972 were played by Johnston in several Manobo villages. As Johnston reports in his chapter, the Manobo had no trouble understanding these although they did notice that the "tune" (i.e., the accent) was different. It is important to note, however, that all the linguists who reviewed the Tasaday language data agree that

the Tasaday speak a separate dialect of Manobo. Their speech is not identical with Cotabato Manobo speech, or with any Manobo dialect yet studied. A full Manobo dialect survey has yet to occur. Reid states in his chapter, and Molony and Elkins now concur in theirs, that this shows that the Tasaday have lived apart from Manobo people for at least 100–150 years. Thus the linguistic data we have to date, admittedly incomplete, support the no-hoax theory. Molony's observation that the Tasaday speech lacks borrowed words and agricultural terms makes it difficult to accept the view that these people were nothing more than farmers who had just moved into a cave to pose as something prehistoric.

These eight points, although they do not prove that the early Tasaday reports were a hoax do, however, indicate that the people were not as isolated and "primitive" as first reported. It was more the fault of the journalists and Panamin officials—not the original dozen scientists who were more conservative in their analyses—that the story turned into a media circus.[7]

A Hypothesis of Tasaday History before 1971

While we still know little about how the Tasaday lived in the recent past, from the data available it may be inferred that the Tasaday were a group of foragers who, during the first half of the 20th century, lived much like other hunter-gatherer groups in Southeast Asia such as the Agta, Batak, Batek, Negrito, and Semang. Linguistic analyses of the Tasaday language data by Elkins, Molony, Johnston, and Reid provide strong evidence that the Tasaday separated from a Cotabato Manobo agricultural group recently—sometime in the 19th century—and moved deeper into the rain forest of South Cotabato near the site where they live today. Their economy then shifted from farming to a seminomadic forager subsistence. They probably lived in simple huts, sleeping in rock shelters only occasionally when on overnight foraging trips. They ate wild foods, but also domestic foods. Some of the domestic foods they may have planted themselves in tiny plots, but they secured most of it by trading minor forest products with Manobo farmers. In this hypothetical scenario they lived separate—but neither alone nor isolated—from other Manobo groups. They had at least periodic interaction based on trade with other peoples living in South Cotabato, especially with the people of Blit, the name of the agricultural village located in the late 1960s just 4 kilometers (2.5 miles) southwest of the Tasaday cave, but which in earlier decades may have been as distant as 30 kilometers from the caves.

Critical Research Needed

The original claims in 1972 were that the Tasaday had been living for hundreds of years in a cave (actually, three adjacent caves, but they dwelt mainly in Cave III). While many outsiders visited the Tasaday at this cave site in 1972–73, the Panamin director did not allow any archaeological investigation to be done there. The research most needed at present, then, is archaeological. As Longacre stated in 1989 and in his chapter in this volume, it would take a "blue-ribbon" team of archaeologists only three or four days of digging at the cave site to collect the data needed to find out if humans had ever lived in the cave and, if they had, when, and what their subsistence was like. Even cave people leave garbage. A search by a qualified archaeologist should be made for a cave midden. If no midden is found, that would be convincing proof that humans had never lived in the caves. If one is found, a small sample bore into it would furnish valuable data that would probably settle the whole controversy once and for all. It is uncertain, however, whether the political leaders in South Cotabato, and the former Panamin leaders (some of whom are now leaders of the new Tasaday Community Care Foundation, Inc.), would allow such an archaeological investigation—even a simple three-day one—to be carried out. These political heads, and sometimes armed guerrilla forces roaming the area, as well, have kept the Tasaday area closed to independent outside researchers almost continually since 1972.[8] Nance (1991:57) was not exaggerating when he recently said, "At least eight expeditions intending Tasaday research [most since 1986] have been interrupted or halted by gunmen or threats of violence."

We already have available some important ethnographic and linguistic data from the 1970s, and these have been reanalyzed by several of the authors of this volume. But all of the data collected in the 1970s are seriously limited because of the extreme restrictions that Panamin put upon the scientists then and because some of the important data collected by them have reportedly been lost. Examples of data unavailable for examination are the three stone tools described by Peralta in his chapter, three of Molony's four audio tapes, and the tapes of the Tasaday conversation secretly recorded by Elizalde at the cave in 1972, English translations of which appear in 29 pages of text in Nance's (1975) book.[9] One important piece of linguistic data still lacking is a word list of the language of the Manobo farmers at Blit village. We need that to answer the important question, is the Blit speech identical to the Cotabato Manobo language studied by Johnston? If not, how similar is it to Tasaday speech?

Another potentially productive line of investigation involves studies of the genetic distance between the Tasaday and their neighboring Tboli and Manobo tribal groups. Through genetic studies it might be possible to calculate the degree of admixture between the Tasaday and other populations. For example, if the Tasaday have lived genetically separate from other groups for long enough (and 100 years would not be long enough), it might be possible using mitochondrial DNA (mtDNA) analysis to estimate the number of generations since they and a neighboring group had a common female ancestor (Cann 1988; Vigilant et al. 1991). The exciting new technique of isolating mtDNA from hair (Vigilant et al. 1989) makes this line of investigation relatively simple and noninvasive. Again, a team of qualified scientists would find it difficult to collect Tasaday hair samples without first securing the permission of the local political bodies mentioned above, including the former Panamin director.

The Hoax Question

Before we can attempt to answer the question stated in the opening sentence of this chapter, we must clarify the antecedent to the pronoun in the question. Does *it* refer to the Tasaday people themselves, to others who wrote about them in the 1970s, or to the critics who in 1986 attacked the original story? We must also figure out what the asker means by the word *hoax,* a very overloaded term in the present controversy. If the asker conceptualizes *hoax* in the extreme sense as referring to nontribal people who were paid or coaxed to move into the forest and disguise themselves as Stone Age cave dwellers, then the early reports were, in my opinion, not a hoax.

We can better address this question if we remove the loaded word *hoax* from the argument, and instead ask the more sensible and less sensational question: Were any of the reports of the Tasaday exaggerated or false? To this we can answer *yes* with little hesitation. Few of the authors in this book would disagree with Lee's point in his chapter that the Tasaday could not be what they were originally claimed to be. It should be evident to anyone who reads through this book that the early reports of the 1970s overemphasized the primitiveness of the Tasaday; and some people involved, whether unwittingly or purposely, hid certain facts and details from both the original scientists and the public.[10] But it was not just defenders of the early reports that may have done this. Rogel-Rara and Nabayra's chapter suggests that there was false information presented to the public in 1986 by some of Panamin's opponents, as well.

It is evident, then, to anyone who has studied the controversy in detail that there was some withholding or distortion of information, both in the early 1970s and in 1986. It must be emphasized that this was done by people on *both* sides of this controversy. Let me give some examples.

First, the public was not told that when the Panamin discovery team first met the Tasaday in June 1971 the Tasaday were wearing commercial cloth and had a wide variety of trade goods including tin cans. Instead, the eight million subscribers (in 1972) of *National Geographic* were told that the Tasaday had "no woven cloth; leaves serve as clothing" (MacLeish 1972:242). While two of the scientists (Fernandez and Lynch 1972), and journalist Nance (1975), noted that the Tasaday wore cloth, this detail was ignored by the media. The public was not told that the stone tools displayed in Manila were counterfeits, nor that the Tasaday's primitive cooking vessels were of *cultivated* bamboo, nor that the Tasaday's cave home was a mere 4 kilometers (2.5 miles) away from a Manobo farming village. Neither was it made clear to the public that the Tasaday's speech was fully understandable—indeed, almost identical—to the speech spoken by thousands of Manobo farmers living in southern Mindanao. We now know that Panamin employees were purposely deceiving the scientists, as these employees covertly took rice up to the caves almost every night for the Tasaday. Indeed, it seems evident that many such facts that should have caused people to question the isolationist vision of the Tasaday were hidden from various visitors and from the public. Even the Tasaday themselves were apparently not averse to playing the "professional primitive" role that Richard Fox (1969) describes for other hunter-gatherer groups in Asia. I myself have observed Agta foragers hide their shorts or T-shirts and put on G-strings when they knew a government official from Manila was coming.[11] As Peralta observed when he made his second visit to the Tasaday in 1986, and as he states in his chapter,

> The Tasaday were putting on the leaves for the benefit of outsiders who had come to see and photograph them, having been conditioned to this in the past. The less reticent among them even knew what was wanted of them in terms of action and poses. It appeared that they were conscious of the image that was wanted of them and, in fact, they were putting on a visual and even an auditive performance. There was no indication from any of the dialogue that they had been asked to attempt this seeming deception. It appeared rather to be a spontaneous attempt to maintain an appearance because of the economic benefits that it brought. [this volume]

Another example of one who may have overstated his claims about the Tasaday is Dafal, the Manobo trader who reportedly said he was the first to discover the Tasaday around 1966. In 1971 he allegedly told the Panamin party that it was a six-day walk to the Tasaday homes; and *National Geographic* journalists joined him in giving the same report (MacLeish 1972:222). Still another example occurred when Panamin allegedly had a Tboli named George Tanedo dress up and pose as a Tasaday in a cultural parade for former President Gerald Ford's state visit to the Philippines.

The credibility of Mai Tuan, the Tboli mayor who made so many grand statements about the primitive Tasaday, must be brought into question because of two illogical claims he made on Central Independent Television in 1987. One was that the Tasaday were still living in their caves in 1987 "just as when we first saw them." Ambiguity also surrounds Mai Tuan's degree of fluency in the Tasaday dialect, for when the television interviewer asked him, "How can you understand [the Tasaday speech]?", he answered in English, "We do not understand the [Tasaday] dialect. . . . Even now I do not speak fluently yet their dialect." If this second claim is true, how was Mai Tuan able in 1972 to translate into English the 29 pages published in Nance's 1975 book of Tasaday conversation that Elizalde had tape-recorded?[12]

These foregoing examples of how certain pieces of information were exaggerated or kept hidden from scientists and the public help explain why the early media reports perpetuated an overstated false view of the primitiveness of the Tasaday. So whether or not one should call the story a hoax, there was certainly some exaggeration. If Panamin employees such as Dafal, Mai Tuan, and George Tanedo were being less than forthright in the instances described here, how much credibility can we give to the rest of the Panamin stories?

Now, all this is different than saying that the Tasaday people themselves were a hoax, or that they intended to trick or dupe the public. Blame the press, perhaps, or the Panamin agency, but let's not accuse the Tasaday people of causing the confusion. Probably most of the authors of this volume agree with the 1988 conclusion of the Philippine Congressional Committee on the Tasaday, when they stated in their Resolution 405 that the Tasaday "exist and are an authentic cultural minority group." The people themselves were not a hoax because they were, and are, real people who lived in the forest. While they were probably not completely isolated, certain evidence suggests that they did indeed live geographically separate from farmers in South Cotabato.[13]

It should be remembered that if some defenders of Elizalde's discovery may have been less than aboveboard in their statements, they were not the only ones: On the other side, some of the attackers of the original story may have also fabricated some false information. It now appears evident from Rogel-Rara and Nabayra's genealogical data that one particular individual, George Tanedo, may have pulled off the biggest hoax of all. Salazar, in his chapter, presents a set of genealogies which he elicited primarily from Tanedo in 1986. These data not only disagree with the genealogical data collected by the early ethnographers in 1972–73, but also show that several Tasaday are related by blood to local farmers. If Salazar's genealogies collected from Tanedo are correct, then the Tasaday story was indeed a complete and outrageous fabrication. When Rogel-Rara and Nabayra went to the field in 1987 to check Tanedo's genealogies, they not only found his information to be completely different from the data they elicited, but they report that they were able to locate 14 non-Tasaday people who had in 1986 impersonated, or were claimed by Tanedo to be, actual Tasaday individuals. Photographs of 12 of these "Tasaday poseurs," as Rogel-Rara and Nabayra call them, appear in their chapter in this book, along with adjacent photos of the actual Tasaday that each poseur was reportedly impersonating.

From this example, it appears obvious that someone here is trying to pull the wool over the eyes of the entire anthropology world. It is not Salazar who, like any anthropologist, accepted his informant Tanedo's information in good faith. Some hoax theorists may suggest that it is Rogel-Rara and Nabayra who have collected incorrect material. Any reader, however, who studies their chapter carefully will find it difficult to doubt the authenticity of their data and analysis. Therefore, if we cannot reject Rogel-Rara and Nabayra's thesis, we must then conclude that Tanedo (along with a group of local non-Tasaday people) is attempting to deceive us here. At this point, it is left up to the reader to decide, by reading the chapters herein, who is presenting the incorrect data.

Conclusion

Once the "discovery" story exploded into the international headlines in late 1971, most of the outsiders that Panamin permitted to visit the Tasaday seemed eager themselves, without outside prompting from anyone, to highlight the primitiveness of these 26 people.[14] Whether people on both sides of the controversy were purposefully exaggerating, or just being carried away by their own self-fulfilling hypotheses, it is clear that the public was not being given the whole story. While the original dozen scientists allowed to the visit the Tasaday were more conservative in their reports, they were so restricted by Panamin, both in the amount of time allowed them and what they could study, that they could only report what they saw.

In conclusion, then, there can be little doubt that the Tasaday exist and that they have lived for a very long time in South Cotabato. In spite of whatever questions we may have concerning their "primitiveness" or original degree of isolation until 1971, they are an indigenous minority people whose rights and lands should be protected, and, as Duhaylungsod and Hyndman make clear in their chapter, this concern is perhaps as important as are the scientific issues which have been the primary focus of this volume.

Notes

1. The chapters by Berreman, Iten, and Headland question the leaf clothing; but see also Molony's chapter, which gives a more personal account of their leaf clothing.
2. See Berreman's and Headland's chapters on this point.
3. Fankhauser's chapter analyzes quantitatively the nutritional account of these wild-food data, which are also discussed by Headland in his chapter.
4. Salazar especially discusses this point in his chapter.
5. See Peralta's chapter, and Nance (1975:67).
6. See Carneiro's and Salazar's chapters on this.
7. Iten makes this point clear in his chapter. Sponsel also looks at the role of the media, going on to explore the engaging question of why the Western world and anthropologists are so fascinated with, and anxious to find, primitive peoples in the first place.
8. The Introduction chapter of this book describes the powerfully intimidating Presidential Decree No. 1017 (PD-1017 1977) which threatens imprisonment for any scientists attempting to enter the Tasaday area without the permission of Panamin.
9. One valuable data bank which has not been lost are the records of John Nance. Nance (personal correspondence) reported that between 1971 to 1974 and 1986 to 1989 he acquired 20,000 photographs, many hours of audio/video recordings, and several drawers of field notes, all in the Tasaday area. In two letters to me (dated 8/14/89 and 3/16/91) Nance stated that he was willing to make some or all of these materials available to any of the panelists of the 1989 Washington symposium. He said in his letters that he put no conditions on the potential use of these materials, or that the use include him. He stated that the 1971 photos and negatives have been archived with the Associated Press in New York since 1971; most of the photos and other materials from 1972 are with Nance where he presently lives in Portland, Oregon. He pointed out that all black and white photos are numbered by the roll in chronological sequence, meaning that, as he noted, "Any alterations or tampering with individual photos or the roll in printing or by retouching would be evident." This may be an extremely valuable archival resource for future researchers, and I state the source here for the record.
10. This point is emphasized in the chapters by Berreman, Iten, Salazar, and Duhaylungsod and Hyndman.
11. I know of three specific instances of this among the Agta: (1) On May 7, 1964, when the then-Secretary of Education for the Philippines, Alehandro Roces, visited the Agta and had lunch in our home. (2) On July 4, 1977, when the then-Minister of Defence, Juan Ponce Enrile, visited Casiguran, and about 40 Agta men greeted him when his helicopter landed, all dressed in the same-colored G-strings, and no shirts. (3) In 1976, when three farmer women, all one-fourth Agta by blood (but who do not speak Agta), went to Manila, dressed in wrap-around Agta-style skirts and Agta necklaces and arm bands, and reportedly made a call upon the Panamin directors to request help. I personally observed the first two cases. The third case was later described to me by two of the three women. The majority of Agta men normally wear cotton G-strings (usually with shirts); but in the above cases they purposely undressed themselves or, in case 2, were ordered to do so by the local military commander, in order to look exotic in front of outsiders they wanted to impress.

12. The quotes in this paragraph are statements made by Mai Tuan in the documentary film, "Scandal: The Lost Tribe" (Central Independent Television 1987). The ellipsis in the second quote is as follows: "because they speak different from my tribe. So we have to be there with them and speak by signs until we get [a] few words from each other." See also Mai Tuan's statement in Nance 1988a:469.
13. This evidence is their minor differences in speech style described by Johnston and their separate genealogical linkages described by Rogel-Rara and Nabayra.
14. Sponsel discusses this point in his chapter.

References Cited

ABC-TV
 1986   The Tribe That Never Was. An August 14 documentary film for ABC-TV's 20/
        20 show. Judith Moses, prod. New York: American Broadcasting Company. [A type-
        script of the narration was produced by Herman S. Jaffe Reporting and Transcribing
        Services, Inc., New York. Page numbers cited are from that typescript.]
Adler, Christian
 1986   The Tasaday Hoax, The Never-Ending Scandal. Paper presented at the Interna-
        tional Conference on the Tasaday Controversy and Other Urgent Anthropological Is-
        sues, August 15–17. University of the Philippines.
Albert, Bruce
 1985   Temps du Sang, Temps des Cendres: Representations de la Maladie, Systeme
        Ritual et Espace Politique chez les Yanomami du Sud-est (Amazonie Bresilienne).
        Ph.D. dissertation, University of Paris.
Allen, Melinda S.
 1985   The Rain Forest of Northeast Luzon and Agta Foragers. *In* The Agta of North-
        eastern Luzon: Recent Studies. P. B. Griffin and A. Estioko-Griffin, eds. Pp. 45–68.
        Cebu City, Philippines: San Carlos Publications.
Artajo, Juan
 1977   Integrated Civilian Home Defense Force (ICHDF) Organized by Philipine Con-
        stabulary (PC) within Panamin Areas. Unpublished document prepared for Panamin,
        February 22.
Asiaweek
 1986   Controversies: Return to the Tasaday. Asiaweek 12(24):26–38. June 15.
Azurin, Arnold Molina
 1988   The Tasaday: Media Circus and Sci-Fi. Diliman Review 36(1):1, 19–24.
Bailen, Jerome, compiler
 1986   A Tasaday Folio. Quezon City: UGAT [Philippine Social Science Center, Room
        208, Commonwealth Ave., Diliman, Quezon City].
Bailen, Jerome, ed.
 n.d.   The Tasaday Controversy: Proceedings of the International Conference on the
        Tasaday Controversy and Other Urgent Anthropological Issues. Quezon City, Phil-
        ippines, August 15–17, 1986. Vol. 1. Quezon City: University of the Philippines. (In
        press.)
Bailey, Robert C.
 1988   The Significance of Hypergyny for Understanding Subsistence Behaviour among
        Contemporary Hunters and Gatherers. *In* Diet and Subsistence. Brenda V. Kennedy
        and Genevieve M. LeMoine, eds. Pp. 57–65. Calgary: Chacmool (The Archaeolog-
        ical Association of the University of Calgary).
 1990   Exciting Opportunities in Tropical Rain Forests: A Reply to Townsend. Ameri-
        can Anthropologist 92:747–748.

Bailey, Robert C., Mark Jenike, and Robert Rechtman
    1991   Reply to Colinvaux and Bush. American Anthropologist 93:160–162.
Bailey, Robert C., G. Head, M. Jenike, B. Owen, R. Rechtman, and E. Zechenter
    1989   Hunting and Gathering in Tropical Rain Forest: Is It Possible? American An-
           thropologist 91:59–82.
Bailey, Robert C., and Nadine R. Peacock
    1988   Efe Pygmies of Northeast Zaire: Subsistence Strategies in the Ituri Forest. In
           Coping with Uncertainty in Food Supply. I. de Garine and G. A. Harrison, eds. Pp.
           88–117. Oxford: Clarendon Press.
Baradas, David B.
    1972   Preface. Philippine Sociological Review 20:277–278. Co-published as Panamin
           Foundation Series No. 1.
Barnard, Myra Lou, Alice Lindquist, and Vivian Forsberg
    1955   Cotabato Manobo Survey. Philippine Social Sciences and Humanities Review
           20(2):121–136.
Barnes, Harry E.
    1923   The Natural State of Man. The Monist 33(1):33–80.
Begley, Sharon, and Debbie Howard
    1986   Back from the Stone Age? Newsweek (April 28):55.
Benedicto, Rey
    1987   Reply to 20/20. Documentary video film, 30 min. Previewed at the December
           10, 1987, Congressional Committee Hearing on the Tasaday Controversy, House of
           Representatives, Philippines.
Bennett, John W.
    1976   The Ecological Transition: From Equilibrium to Disequilibrium. In The Ecolog-
           ical Transition: Cultural Anthropology and Human Adaptation. John W. Bennett, ed.
           Pp. 123–155. New York: Pergamon Press.
Benterrak, Krim, Stephen Muecke, and Paddy Roe
    1984   Reading the Country. Freemantle, Western Australia: Freemantle Arts Press.
Berke, Joseph, ed.
    1969   Counter Culture. London: Peter Owen.
Berreman, Gerald D.
    1960   Cultural Variability and Drift in the Himalayan Hills. American Anthropologist
           62:774–794.
    1989   The Incredible "Tasaday": Deconstructing the Myth of a "Stone-Age" People.
           Paper presented at the 88th Annual Meeting of the American Anthropological Asso-
           ciation, Washington, DC, Nov. 15–19.
    1991   The Incredible "Tasaday": Deconstructing the Myth of a "Stone-Age" People.
           Cultural Survival Quarterly 15(1):2–45.
Bird-David, Nurit
    1983   Conjugal Families and Single Persons: An Analysis of the Naiken [South India]
           Social System. Ph.D. dissertation, Cambridge University.
Blust, Robert
    1983   Variation in Retention Rate in Austronesian Languages. Paper presented at the
           Third International Conference on Austronesian Linguistics, Bali.
Bodley, John H.
    1975   Victims of Progress. Menlo Park, CA: Benjamin Cummings.

1986 The Tasaday Controversy: An Assessment. Unpublished report to the Tasaday Commission, International Conference on the Tasaday Controversy and Other Urgent Anthropological Issues. Department of Anthropology, University of the Philippines, Diliman, Quezon City.

1990 Victims of Progress. 3rd edition. Palo Alto: Mayfield.

Bolinger, Dwight
1968 Aspects of Language. New York: Harcourt, Brace, and World.

Bower, Bruce
1989a A World That Never Existed: Reassessing Hunter-Gatherers. Science News 135(17):264–266. April 29.
1989b The Strange Case of the Tasaday: Were They Primitive Hunter-Gatherers or Rain-Forest Phonies? Science News 135(18):280–281, 283 (May 6). [Reprinted in Anthropology Newsletter 30(7):25–26. October 1989.]

Brosius, J. Peter
1990 Penan Hunter-Gatherers of Sarawak, East Malaysia. Anthroquest 42:1–7.

Brown, J. D.
1967 The Hippies. New York: Time.

Brownlee, Shannon
1990 If Only Life Were So Simple. U.S. News & World Report. February 19, pp. 54–56.

Campbell, Alan
1989 Peace. In Societies at Peace: Anthropological Perspectives. S. Howell and R. Willis, eds. Pp. 213–224. New York: Routledge.

Campbell, Joseph
1972 Mythologies of War and Peace. In Myths to Live By. Pp. 174–206. New York: Bantam.

Cann, Rebecca L.
1988 DNA and Human Origins. Annual Review of Anthropology 17:127–143.

Cannel, Ward, and June Macklin
1973 The Human Nature Industry. Garden City, NY: Anchor/Doubleday.

Carneiro, Robert L.
1973 The Four Faces of Evolution: Unilinear, Universal, Multilinear, and Differential. In Handbook of Social and Cultural Anthropology. J. J. Honigmann, ed. Pp. 89–110. Chicago: Rand McNally.
1974 On the Use of the Stone Axe by the Amahuaca Indians of Eastern Peru. Ethnologische Zeitschrift Zurich 1:107–122.
1979a Tree Felling with the Stone Ax: An Experiment Carried Out among the Yanomamö Indians of Southern Venezuela. In Ethnoarchaeology, Implications of Ethnography for Archaeology. Carol Kramer, ed. Pp. 21–58. New York: Columbia University Press.
1979b Forest Clearance among the Yanomamö, Observations and Implications. Antropológica (Caracas) 52:39–76.
1988 Public letter to Judith Moses, regarding "Tasaday Stone Axes." [Quoted with permission of the author.]
1989 Comments on the Tasaday Debate. Comments read at the 88th Annual Meeting of the American Anthropological Association, Washington, DC, November 16.

Carpenter, Edmund
1972 Oh, What a Blow That Phantom Gave Me! New York: Bantam Books.

Central Independent Television
    1987   Scandal: The Lost Tribe. John Edwards, prod, Ian Taylor, dir. Central Indepen-
    dent Television: Birmingham, England.
Chagnon, Napoleon A.
    1983[1968]   Yanomamö: The Fierce People. 3rd edition. New York: Holt, Rinehart
    and Winston.
    1988   Life Histories, Blood Revenge, and Warfare in a Tribal Population. Science
    239:985–991.
Chateaubriand, Francois-Rene de
    1952   Atala. Berkeley: University of California Press.
Chikwendu, V. E., and C. E. A. Okezie
    1989   Factors Responsible for the Ennoblement of African Yams: Inferences from Ex-
    periments in Yam Domestication. In Foraging and Farming: The Evolution of Plant
    Exploitation. David R. Harris and Gordon C. Hillman, eds. Pp. 344–357. London:
    Unwin Hyman.
Clark, C., and J. B. Turner
    1973   World Population Growth and Future Food Trends. In Man, Food and Nutrition.
    M. Recheigl, Jr., ed. Pp. 55–77. Cleveland: CRC Press.
Clark, J. Desmond
    1989   Public letter dated April 4, to G. Berreman, regarding plausibility of the Tasaday
    claims, read at the 88th Annual Meeting of the American Anthropological Associa-
    tion, Washington, DC, November 15–19.
Colchester, Marcus
    1984   Rethinking Stone Age Economics: Some Speculations Concerning the Pre-Co-
    lumbia Yanomama Economy. Human Ecology 12:291–314.
Colinvaux, Paul A.
    1989   The Past and Future Amazon. Scientific American 260(5):102–108.
Colinvaux, Paul A., and Mark B. Bush
    1991   The Rain-Forest Ecosystem as a Resource for Hunting and Gathering. American
    Anthropologist 93:153–160.
Collins, James X.
    1981   An Anthropological Understanding of Non-Aggressive Social Systems. In Ap-
    plied Systems and Cybernetics. G. E. Lasker, ed. Pp. 553–557. New York: Perga-
    mon.
Collins, Mark
    1990   The Last Rain Forests: A World Conservation Atlas. New York: Oxford Uni-
    versity Press.
Committee on National Cultural Communities
    1988   Report on the Congressional Investigation Conducted on the Tasaday Per House
    Resolution No. 405. House of Representatives, Congress of the Philippines, Quezon
    City.
Conklin, Harold C.
    1957   Hanunoo Agriculture. Rome: Food and Agriculture Organization of the United
    Nations (FAO).
Connolly, Bob, and Robin Anderson
    1987   First Contact: New Guinea's Highlanders Encounter the Outside World. New
    York: Viking Penguin.
Conrad, Joseph
    1902   The Heart of Darkness. Baltimore: Penguin.

Dandan, Virginia B., ed.
1989 Readings on the Tasaday. Tasaday Community Care Foundation, Publication No. 1. Manila: Tasaday Community Care Foundation.

Davis, Shelton H.
1977 The Yanomamö: Ethnographic Images and Anthropological Responsibilities. *In* The Geological Imperative: Anthropology and Development in the Amazon Basin of South America. S. H. Davis and R. O. Matthews, eds. Pp. 6–21. Boston: Anthropology Resource Center.

de Camp, Lyon S.
1954 Lost Continents: The Atlantis Theme in History, Science, and Literature. New York: Dover Press.

De Mille, Richard
1980 The Don Juan Papers. Santa Barbara, CA: Ross-Erikson Publishers.

Dentan, Robert K.
1968 The Semai: A Nonviolent People of Malaya. New York: Holt, Rinehart and Winston.

Devall, Bill, and George Sessions
1985 Deep Ecology: Living As If Nature Mattered. Salt Lake City: Gibbs M. Smith.

Diamond, Stanley
1974 In Search of the Primitive: A Critique of Civilization. New Brunswick: Transaction Books.

DuBois, Carl
n.d. Sarangani Manobo Dictionary. Unpublished computer printout. Manila: Summer Institute of Linguistics.
1988 Tagabawa Dictionary. Unpublished computer printout. Manila: Summer Institute of Linguistics, Philippines. (Pacific and Asian Language Archives, University of Hawaii.)

Dufour, Darna L.
1989 Factors Determining Wild Plant Food Use in Northwest Amazonia. Paper presented at the 88th Annual Meeting of the American Anthropological Association, Washington, DC, November 15–19.

Duhaylungsod, Fabian
1989 Interview. Maitum, South Cotabato, February 4–16. From field notes of L. Duhaylungsod and D. Hyndman.

Duhaylungsod, Levita, and David C. Hyndman
1989 Behind and Beyond the "Tasaday": The Untold Struggle Over Resources of Indigenous People. Paper presented at the 88th Annual Meeting of the American Anthropological Association, Washington, DC, November 15–19.

Duhaylungsod, Samuel
1989 Interview. Maitum, South Cotabato, February 4–16. From field notes of L. Duhaylungsod and D. Hyndman.

Duhaylungsod, Tim
1989 Interview. Maitum, South Cotabato, February 4–16. From field notes of L. Duhaylungsod and D. Hyndman.

Dumont, Jean-Paul
1988 The Tasaday, Which and Whose? Toward the Political Economy of an Ethnographic Sign. Cultural Anthropology 3:261–275.

Dyen, Isidore
1970 Qualitative Confirmation of a Subgrouping Hypothesis. Philippine Journal of Linguistics 1(1):1–11.

Early, John D., and John F. Peters
  1990   The Population Dynamics of the Mucajai Yanomama. San Diego: Academic
         Press.
Eder, James F.
  1987   On the Road to Tribal Extinction: Depopulation, Deculturation, and Adaptive
         Well-Being among the Batak of the Philippines. Berkeley: University of California
         Press.
Edralin, Napoleon
  1989   Interview. Maitum, South Cotabato, February 4–16. From field notes of L. Du-
         haylungsod and D. Hyndman.
Elizalde, Manuel, Jr.
  1971a The Tao Tasaday. Typescript, 10 pp., with word list supplied by Robert B. Fox
         for research on the Tao Tasaday. Unpublished ms. in the files of the Tasaday Com-
         munity Care Foundation, Manila.
  1971b Radiogram sent to Robert B. Fox regarding information on new tribe [Tasaday
         Manobo]; 6:45 A.M., June 9. In the files of Panamin Foundation, Inc. Copies available
         upon request from the Tasaday Community Care Foundation, Manila.
Elizalde, Manuel, Jr., with Robert B. Fox
  1971a The Tasaday Forest People. A Data Paper on a Newly Discovered Food Gath-
         ering and Stone Tool Using Manubo Group in the Mountains of South Cotabato, Min-
         danao, Philippines. Typescript, viii, 20 pp., + 5 unnumbered pages of 10 photo-
         graphs. Dated July 1971. Washington, DC: Smithsonian Institution, Center for Short-
         lived Phenomena.
  1971b The Tasaday Project: A Research Design. 55 pp. August 15, 1971. Unpub-
         lished Panamin document in the files of the Tasaday Community Care Foundation,
         Manila.
Elkins, Richard E.
  1968   Manobo-English Dictionary. Oceanic Linguistics Special Publication No. 3.
         Honolulu: University of Hawaii Press.
  1971   Comments [on The Tasaday Language So Far, by Llamzon]. Philippine Journal
         of Linguistics 2(2):31–33. [Reprinted in Philippine Sociological Review 20:325–327;
         copublished as Panamin Foundation Series No. 1.]
  1972   A Tasaday Word List. Unpublished typescript on file in the Manila office of the
         Summer Institute of Linguistics.
  1973–74 A Preliminary Proto-Manobo Word List. Philippine Journal of Linguistics
         4–5(1–2):23–40.
  1974   A Proto-Manobo Word List. Oceanic Linguistics 13:601–641.
  1977   Root of a Language: How One Manobo Word Led to Another. Filipino Heritage
         2:523–527. [Singapore: Lahing Pilipino.]
  1983   An Extended Proto-Manobo Word List. Philippine Journal of Linguistics (spe-
         cial issue) 14(2), 15(1):218–229.
  1984   An Extended Proto-Manobo Word List. In Panagani, Language Planning, Im-
         plementation, and Evaluation: Essays in Honor of Bonifacio P. Sibayan on His Sixty-
         Seventh Birthday. Andrew Gonzales, ed. Pp. 218–229. Manila: Linguistic Society of
         the Philippines.
  1989   The Tasaday: Some Observations. Paper presented at the 88th Annual Meeting
         of the American Anthropological Association, Washington, DC, November 15–19.

Elkins, Richard E., and Betty Elkins
    1954   Vocabulary of Central Mindanao Manobo. Typescript. Manila: Summer Institute of Linguistics and Ministry of Education and Culture.
Endicott, Kirk
    1979   Batek Negrito Religion: The World-View and Rituals of a Hunting and Gathering People of Peninsular Malaysia. Oxford: Clarendon Press.
Errington, Ross
    1979a   Discourse Types and Tense Patterns in Cotabato Manobo. Studies in Philippine Linguistics 3(2):218–222.
    1979b   A Transition Network Grammar of Cotabato Manobo. Studies in Philippine Linguistics 3(2):105–163.
    1984   Hortatory Mitigation: The Case of the Camouflaged Backbone. Studies in Philippine Linguistics 3(2):218–222.
    1988   The Magic of the Cotabato Manobos. Studies in Philippine Linguistics 7(1):153–164.
Errington, Ross, and Ellen Errington
    1981   Cotabato Manobo Dictionary. Unpublished computer printout. Manila: Summer Institute of Linguistics.
Eve, Raymond A., and Frank B. Harrold
    1987   Pseudoscientific Beliefs: The End of the Beginning or the Beginning of the End? *In* Cult Archaeology and Creationism: Understanding Pseudoscientific Beliefs about the Past. F. B. Harrold and R. A. Eve, eds. Pp. 134–151. Iowa City: University of Iowa Press.
Fabbro, David
    1978   Peaceful Societies: An Introduction. Journal of Peace Research 15:67–83.
Fabian, Johannes
    1983   Time and the Other: How Anthropology Makes Its Object. New York: Columbia University Press.
Fankhauser, Barry
    1989   A Nutritional Analysis of the Philippine Tasaday Diet. Unpublished paper.
Feder, Kenneth L.
    1990   Frauds, Myths, and Mysteries: Science and Pseudo Science in Archaeology. Mountain View, CA: Mayfield.
Feibleman, James K.
    1987   The Underside of Human Nature. New York: Peter Lang.
Fernandez, Carlos A.
    1977   The Tasaday: The Inside Story on One of the Century's Most Dramatic Discoveries in Terms of a Surviving Stone Age Group. Filipino Heritage, vol. 2. Pp. 100–112. Manila: Lahing Pilipino.
Fernandez, Carlos A., and Frank Lynch
    1972   The Tasaday: Cave-Dwelling Food Gatherers of South Cotabato, Mindanao. Philippine Sociological Review 20(3):279–313, 328–330. [Co-published as Panamin Foundation Series No. 1.]
Food and Agriculture Organization (FAO)
    1954   Food Composition Tables. Nutritional Studies 11. Rome: Food and Agriculture Organization.
    1972   Food Composition Tables for Use in East Asia. Rome and Washington, DC: U.S. Dept. of Health, Education and Welfare, Food and Agriculture Organization.

Forsberg, Vivian, and Alice Lindquist
    1955   Tagabili [Tboli] Vocabulary. Manila: Summer Institute of Linguistics and Institute of National Language, Department of Education.
Forrest, Thomas (Captain)
    1780   A Voyage to New Guinea and the Moluccas. London: G. Scott.
Foss, Daniel
    1990   Freak Culture: Life Style and Politics. New York: Library of Art and Social Science.
Fox, Richard G.
    1969   "Professional Primitives": Hunters and Gatherers of Nuclear South Asia. Man In India 49:139–160.
Fox, Robert B.
    1970   The Tabon Caves: Archaeological Exploration and Excavations on Palawan Island, Philippines. Manila: National Museum of the Philippines.
    1971a   Radiogram sent to Sec. Manuel Elizalde, Jr. [in reply to radiogram sent by MEJ, June 9]. Dated June 9. In the files of Panamin Foundation, Inc. [Copies available upon request from the Tasaday Community Care Foundation, Manila.]
    1971b   Time Catches Up with the Tasaday. The Asian, October 24–30, p. 7.
    1976   Notes on the Stone Tools of the Tasaday, Gathering Economies in the Philippines, and the Archaeological Record. In Further Studies on the Tasaday. Panamin Foundation Research Series No. 2. D. E. Yen and John Nance, eds. Pp. 3–12. Makati, Rizal, Philippines: Panamin Foundation.
Francisco, Juan R.
    1964   Indian Influences in the Philippines. Philippine Social Sciences and Humanities Review 28(1,2,3).
Garvan, John M.
    1931   The Manobos of Mindanao. Memoirs of the National Academy of Sciences 23:1. Washington, D.C.: U.S. Government Printing Office.
Golding, William
    1954   Lord of the Flies. New York: Capricorn Books.
Goldschmidt, Walter
    1977   An Anthropological View of the Counter-Culture Movement. In Exploring the Ways of Mankind: A Text-Casebook. W. Goldschmidt, ed. Pp. 531–540. New York: Holt, Rinehart and Winston.
Good, Kenneth, with David Chanoff
    1991   Into the Heart: One Man's Pursuit of Love and Knowledge among the Yanomama. New York: Simon and Schuster.
Gordon, Robert
    1991   People of the Great White Lie? Cultural Survival Quarterly 15(1):49–51.
Griffin, P. Bion
    1988   National Policy on Minority Cultural Communities: The Philippine Case. Southeast Asian Journal of Social Science 16(2):5–16.
Griffin, P. Bion, and Agnes Estioko-Griffin, eds.
    1985   The Agta of Northeastern Luzon: Recent Studies. Cebu City, Philippines: San Carlos Publications.
Grumet, Robert S.
    1990   Anthropology. In 1990 Britannica Book of the Year: Events of 1989. Pp. 141–143. Chicago: Encyclopaedia Britannica, Inc.

Gutierrez, Dinualdo
1989 On Tasaday Reservation. (Open Letters.) Lunay S'bung: Newsletter of the South Cotabato Tribes. Koronadal, South Cotabato: Santa Cruz Mission.

Harmon, Carol W.
1979 Reconstructions of Proto-Manobo Pronouns and Case Marking Particles. Papers in Philippine Linguistics 10. Pacific Linguistics, Series A, 55.

Harris, David R., and Gordon C. Hillman, eds.
1989 Foraging and Farming: The Evolution of Plant Exploitation. London: Unwin Hyman.

Harrold, Francis B., and Raymond A. Eve, eds.
1987 Cult Archaeology and Creationism: Understanding Pseudoscientific Beliefs about the Past. Iowa City: University of Iowa Press.

Hart, Terese B., and John A. Hart
1986 The Ecological Basis of Hunter-Gatherer Subsistence in African Rain Forests: The Mbuti of Eastern Zaire. Human Ecology 14:29–55.

Headland, Thomas N.
1981 Taxonomic Disagreement in a Culturally Salient Domain: Botany Versus Utility in a Philippine Negrito Taxonomic System. Ann Arbor: University Microfilms International.
1985 Comment on "Mode of Subsistence and Folk Biological Taxonomy." Current Anthropology 26:57–58.
1986 Why Foragers Do Not Become Farmers: A Historical Study of a Changing Ecosystem and Its Effect on a Negrito Hunter-Gatherer Group in the Philippines. Ann Arbor: University Microfilms International.
1987 The Wild Yam Question: How Well Could Independent Hunter-Gatherers Live in a Tropical Rain Forest Ecosystem? Human Ecology 15:463–491.
1988 Ecosystemic Change in a Philippine Tropical Rainforest and its Effect on a Negrito Foraging Society. Tropical Ecology 29:121–135.
1989a What Did the Tasaday Eat? Paper presented at the 88th Annual Meeting of the American Anthropological Association, Washington, DC, November 15–19.
1989b Quotations about Rice Being Given to or Eaten by Tasaday. Typescript, 2 pages. Compiled by Thomas Headland and distributed at 88th Annual Meeting of the American Anthropological Association, Washington, DC, November 15–19.
1989c Primitives or Poseurs? The Sciences 29(2):8 (March-April).
1989d Introduction to "The Tasaday Controversy: An Assessment of the Evidence." Paper presented at the 88th Annual Meeting of the American Anthropological Association, Washington, DC, November 15–19.
1990a What Are Plant Specifics? A Critique of Olofson's Search for the Tasaday. Philippine Quarterly of Culture and Society 18:22–32.
1990b Paradise Revised. The Sciences 30(5):45–50.
1992 Tasaday: A Cultural Summary. In Encyclopedia of World Cultures: Southeast Asia Volume. Paul Hockings, volume ed., and David Levinson, ed.-in-chief. Sponsored by the Human Relations Area Files. Boston: G. K. Hall. (In press.)

Headland, Thomas N., and Janet D. Headland
1974 A Dumagat [Agta] (Casiguran)-English Dictionary. Canberra: Australian National University.

Headland, Thomas N., and Lawrence A. Reid
1989 Hunter-Gatherers and Their Neighbors from Prehistory to the Present. Current Anthropology 30:43–66.

Heelas, P.
   1989   Identifying Peaceful Societies. *In* Societies at Peace: Anthropological Perspectives. S. Howell and R. Willis, eds. Pp. 225–243. New York: Routledge.
Heider, Karl G.
   1988   The Rashomon Effect: When Ethnographers Disagree. American Anthropologist 90:73–81.
Henson, Florante G.
   1986   The Unmasking of a Hoax—The Tau't Bato. Paper presented at the International Conference on the Tasaday Controversy and Other Urgent Anthropological Issues, Quezon City, August 16. [Forthcoming in The Tasaday Controversy: Proceedings of the International Anthropological Conference on the Tasaday Controversy and Other Urgent Anthropological Issues, Quezon City, August 15–17, 1986. Vol. 1.]
Hidalgo, Araceli, and Cesar A. Hidalgo
   1989   The Tasadays, Distinct and Isolated: The Linguistic Evidence. Typescript, 66 pp. (limited circulation).
Hobbes, Thomas
   1962   Leviathan. New York: Collier Books.
Hoffer, Eric
   1951   The True Believer: Thoughts on the Nature of Mass Movements. New York: Harper and Brothers.
Hoffman, Carl
   1984   Punan Foragers in the Trading Networks of Southeast Asia. *In* Past and Present in Hunter Gatherer Societies. Carmel Schrire, ed. Pp. 123–149. Orlando: Academic Press.
   1986   The Punan: Hunters and Gatherers of Borneo. Ann Arbor: UMI Research Press.
Howell, Signe, and Roy Willis, eds.
   1989   Societies At Peace: Anthropological Perspectives. New York: Routledge.
Hudson, William H.
   1904   Green Mansions. New York: Bantam.
Hurtado, A. Magdalena, and Kim Hill
   1989   Experimental Studies of Tool Efficiency among Machiguenga Women and Implications for Root-Digging Foragers. Journal of Anthropological Research 45:207–217.
Hyman, Ray
   1989   The Psychology of Deception. Annual Review of Psychology 40:133–154.
Hyndman, David C., and Levita Duhaylungsod
   1990   The Development Saga of the Tasaday: Gentle Yesterday, Hoax Today, Exploited Forever? Bulletin of Concerned Asian Scholars 22(4):38–54.
Illustrated Encyclopedia
   1990   Tasaday: Philippines. *In* The Illustrated Encyclopedia of Mankind, Vol. 14. Pp. 1752–1755. London: M. Cavendish.
Iten, Oswald
   1986a   Die Tasaday—Ein Philippinisher Stinzeitschwindel. Neue Zürcher Zeitung, April 12–13 (Wochenende section), pp. 77–79. Zürich.
   1986b   The Tasaday—A Stone Age Swindle. Swiss Review of World Affairs (June), pp. 14–19.
   1988   The Tasaday: First a Hoax and then a Cover-Up. Paper presented at the 12th International Congress of Anthropological and Ethnological Sciences. Zagreb, July 28.

1989 The "Tasaday" and the Press. Paper presented at the 88th Annual Meeting of the American Anthropological Association, Washington, DC, November 15–19.
1990 The Tasaday. Anthropology Today 6(5):24.

Iten, Oswald, and Joey Lozano
1986 A Swiss Journalist Says the Tasaday Could Be the Great Stone Age Hoax. Sunday Magazine, Malaya 2(47):3–7.

Johnston, E. Clay
1968 Cotabato Manobo Dictionary. Unpublished typescript. Manila: Summer Institute of Linguistics.
1975 The Verb Affixation of Cotabato Manobo. Philippine Journal of Linguistics 6(1):26–50.
1979 Cotabato Manobo First Person Narrative: Major Features of Discourse and Paragraph. Papers in Philippine Linguistics 9. Pacific Linguistics Series A, 50, pp. 1–17. Canberra: Australian National University.
1988 Letter to Carol Molony, dated November 28. [Quoted with permission of the author.]
1989 The Tasaday Language: Is It Cotabato Manobo? Paper presented at the 88th Annual Meeting of the American Anthropological Association, Washington, DC, November 15–19.

Jones, Clayton
1989 Tales from the Philippine Woods. World Monitor. January: 66–71.

Jordan, Carl F., and Rafael Herrera
1981 Tropical Rainforests: Are Nutrients Really Critical? American Naturalist 117:167–180.

Keesing, Roger M.
1981 Cultural Anthropology: A Contemporary Perspective. 2nd edition. New York: Holt, Rinehart and Winston.
1987 Anthropology as Interpretive Quest. Current Anthropology 28:161–176.

Kerr, Harland B.
1965 The Case-marking and Classifying Function of Cotabato Manobo Voice Affixes. Oceanic Linguistics 4:15–47.
1988a Cotabato Manobo Grammar. Studies in Philippine Linguistics 7(1):1–123.
1988b Cotabato Manobo Ethnography. Studies in Philippine Linguistics 7(1):125–151.

Knauft, Bruce
1987 Reconsidering Violence in Simple Human Societies. Current Anthropology 28:457–500.

Kohn, Alfie
1990 The Brighter Side of Human Nature: Altruism and Empathy in Everyday Life. New York: Basic Books.

Kottak, Conrad P.
1990 Prime-Time Society: An Anthropological Analysis of Television and Culture. Belmont, CA: Wadsworth.

Kozák, Vladimír
1972 Stone Age Revisited. Natural History 81(8):14, 16, 18–22, 24.

Kozák, Vladimír, David Baxter, Laila Williamson, and Robert L. Carneiro
1979 The Héta Indians: Fish in a Dry Pond. Anthropological Papers of the American Museum of Natural History 5 (Part 6):349–434.

Kozlovsky, Daniel G.
   1974   An Ecological and Evolutionary Ethic. Englewood Cliffs, NJ: Prentice-Hall.
Kramer, Jane
   1975   The Gentle Tasaday. The New York Times Book Review 7:1–5 (June 1).
Kronholz, June
   1986   Tangled Tale: Saga of a Lost Tribe in the Philippines Is Illustrative of the Dark
          Side of Marcos Era. Wall Street Journal, September 15:1, 14.
Kuper, Adam
   1989   The Invention of Primitive Society. London: Routledge.
La Nación
   1986a   Ministerio Publico Actuará en Caso Elizalde. September 3. (San José, Costa
           Rica.)
   1986b   Piden a Arias Decidir Contratacion de Mujeres. September 18. (San José, Costa
           Rica.)
Leacock, Eleanor, and Richard Lee, eds.
   1982   Politics and History in Band Societies. Cambridge: Cambridge University Press.
Lee, Richard B.
   1981   Is There a Foraging Mode of Production? Canadian Journal of Anthropology
          2:13–19.
   1988   Reflections on Primitive Communism. In Hunters and Gatherers, vol. 1. T. In-
          gold, D. Riches, and J. Woodburn, eds. Pp. 252–268. Oxford: Berg.
Lerner, Bettina, prod.
   1989   Trial in the Jungle. Documentary film produced by Broadcasting Support Ser-
          vices for the BBC Horizon Series. London: BBC Television. [A written transcription
          of the narration was published in a 26-page booklet by Broadcasting Support Services,
          P.O. Box 7, London W3 6XJ, for BBC Horizon. Page numbers cited are from that
          booklet.]
Lewin, Roger
   1988   New Views Emerge on Hunters and Gatherers. Science 240:1146–1148.
Life
   1972   The Beat of Life. Life Magazine 73(5):6–9.
Lindbergh, Charles A.
   1975   Foreword. In The Gentle Tasaday: A Stone Age People in the Philippine Rain
          Forest. J. Nance. Pp. ix–xi. New York: Harcourt Brace Jovanovich.
Lizot, Jacques
   1985   Tales of the Yanomami: Daily Life in the Venezuelan Forest. New York: Cam-
          bridge University Press.
   1989   Sobre la Guerra: Una Respuesta a N. A. Chagnon (Science, 1988). La Iglesia en
          Amazonas 44:23–34.
Llamzon, Teodoro A.
   1971a   A Tasaday Manobo Word List. Unpublished typescript.
   1971b   The Tasaday Language So Far. Philippine Journal of Linguistics 2(2):1–30 [Re-
           printed in Philippine Sociological Review 20(3):314–324 [1972]. Co-published as
           Panamin Foundation Series No. 1.]
Lopez, José
   1989   OSCC and Its Role. Prepared by the Undersecretary of the Office of Southern
          Cultural Communities. [Photocopy in the files of Duhaylungsod and Hyndman.]
Lopez, Maria Elena
   1986   Rethinking the Tasaday Controversy. PSSC Social Science Information 14(3):8–
          9, 24.

Lovejoy, Arthur O., and George Boas
1965 Primitivism and Related Ideas in Antiquity. New York: Octagon Books.
Lunay S'bung
1989 On Tasaday Reservation. Lunay S'bung: Newsletter of the South Cotabato Tribes. Koronadal, South Cotabato: Santa Cruz Mission.
Lyman, Thomas J.
1971 Hierarchical Phonological Features of Cotabato Manobo. The Archive 2 (New Series) 1:39–56. Quezon City: The Archives of Philippine Languages and Dialects, and Philippine Linguistic Circle, University of the Philippines.
Lynch, Frank, Robert B. Fox, Teodoro Llamzon, and Carlos Fernandez
1973 The Tasaday: Stone Age Tribe of Mindanao. Yearbook of Science and the Future. Chicago: Encyclopaedia Britannica. Pp. 50–65.
Lynch, Frank, and Teodoro A. Llamzon
1971 The Blit Manobo and the Tasaday. Philippine Sociological Review 19(1–2):91–92.
Mabandos, Helen
1989 On Blit Proximity to the Tasaday. Typescript. [Copies available upon request from the Tasaday Community Care Foundation, Manila.]
MacLeish, Kenneth
1972 Stone Age Cavemen of Mindanao. National Geographic 142(2):219–249.
Malayang, Jerry P.
1986 Elizalde's Tasadays: The Fame Syndrome. An Insider's Notes on an Alleged Anthropological Hoax. Malaya [Manila] Series of four articles on consecutive days, May 6–9.
Manuel, E. Arsenio
1948 Chinese Elements in the Tagalog Language. Manila: Filipiniana Publications.
Marcus, George E., and Michael M. J. Fisher
1986 Anthropology as Cultural Critique: An Experimental Moment in the Human Sciences. Chicago: University of Chicago Press.
McCarry, Charles
1988 Three Men Who Made the Magazine. National Geographic 174(3):287–316.
McDonagh, Fr. Sean
1984 To Care for the Earth. Quezon City: Claretian Publications.
1987 What about the Tasadays Themselves? Philippine Daily Globe December 9:5.
McFarland, Curtis D.
1980 A Linguistic Atlas of the Philippines. Study of Languages and Cultures of Asia and Africa, Monograph Series No. 15. Tokyo: Tokyo University of Foreign Studies.
McGrane, Bernard
1989 Beyond Anthropology: Society and the Other. New York: Columbia University Press.
McKaughan, Howard P., and Batua A. Macaraya
1967 A Maranao Dictionary. Honolulu: University of Hawaii Press.
Merrill, A. L., and B. K. Watt
1955 Energy Value of Foods—Basis and Derivation. U.S. Department of Agriculture Handbook 74. Washington, DC: U.S. Department of Agriculture.
Mills, C. Wright
1959 The Sociological Imagination. New York: Grove Press.
Molony, Carol H.
1988 The Truth About the Tasaday: Are They a Primitive Tribe—or a Modern Hoax? The Sciences, September/October: 12–20.

1989a   The Tasaday Language: Evidence for Authenticity? Paper presented at the 88th Annual Meeting of the American Anthropological Association, Washington, DC, November 15–19.

1989b   Who are the Tasaday? Stanford Magazine 17(4):50–55.

Molony, Carol H., with Dad Tuan

1976   Further Studies on the Tasaday Language: Texts and Vocabulary. *In* Further Studies on the Tasaday. Panamin Foundation Research Studies No. 2. D. E. Yen and John Nance, eds. Pp. 13–96. Makati, Rizal, Philippines: Panamin Foundation.

Montagu, Ashley

1976   The Nature of Human Aggression. New York: Oxford.

1978   Learning Non-Aggression: The Experience of Non-Literate Societies. New York: Oxford University Press.

Montagu, Ashley, ed.

1968   The Concept of the Primitive. New York: Free Press.

Morris, Brian

1982   Forest Traders: A Socio-Economic Study of the Hill Pandaram [India]. London: Athlone Press.

Moses, Judith

1988   The Tribe That Never Was. Paper read at the 12th International Congress of Anthropological and Ethnological Sciences, Zagreb, July 28.

Musin, Philip

1989   Interview. Koronadal, South Cotabato, February 4–16. Field notes of L. Duhay-lungsod and D. Hyndman.

Mydans, Seth

1986a   The Tasaday Revisited: A Hoax or Social Change at Work? New York Times, May 13.

1986b   In Mindanao, Ancient Tribe or 70s Hoax? New York Times, December 7.

1986c   From Forest to Manila, Stranger in a Strange Land. New York Times, December 27.

1987   In Mindanao: Ancient Tribe or a Hoax from the 1970s? New York Times, December 7:6.

1988   20th Century Lawsuit Asserts Stone Age Identity. New York Times, October 29:4.

Myers, Fred R.

1988   Locating Ethnographic Practice: Romance, Reality, and Politics in the Outback. American Ethnologist 15:609–624.

Nance, John

1975   The Gentle Tasaday: A Stone Age People in the Philippine Rain Forest. New York: Harcourt Brace Jovanovich.

1981   Discovery of the Tasaday, A Photo Novel: The Stone Age Meets the Space Age in the Philippine Rain Forest. Manila: Vera-Reyes. Hongkong: Toppan Printing Co.

1982   Lobo of Tasaday: A Photographic Account For Young Readers. New York: Pantheon.

1988a[1975]   The Gentle Tasaday: A Stone Age People in the Philippine Rain Forest. Boston: David R. Godine.

1988b   What's Behind the Strange Tasaday Hoax Charges. New York Times, Letters to the Editor, January 30.

1991   Letter to the editor. Cultural Survival Quarterly 15(2):56–57.

National Geographic Society
1971 First Glimpse of a Stone Age Tribe. National Geographic 140(6):880–882b.
1972 The Last Tribes of Mindanao. Dennis Azarella, prod.-dir. Documentary film.
NBC-TV
1971 Tasaday Contacted. Jack Reynolds, Correspondent. Series of reports for NBC Nightly News, July 1971.
1972 The Cave People of the Philippines. A documentary film for NBC Reports. Gerald Green, Prod. New York: National Broadcasting Company.
1986 Tasaday Revisited and Authentic. Jack Reynolds, correspondent. Reports on NBC Nightly News and Today Show. June 1986. [Copies available upon request from the Tasaday Community Care Foundation, Manila.]
NDR-TV
1972 Ein Mann Mit Vielen Namen [A Man With Many Names]. 16 mm., 90 minutes, color. Hamburg: Norddeutscher Rundfunk-TV.
Neel, James V.
1979 Health and Disease in Unacculturated Amerindian Populations. In Health and Diseases in Tribal Societies. Ciba Foundation Symposium 49. Amsterdam, Oxford, New York: Excerpta Medica.
Non, Domingo
1989 Interview. General Santos City, South Cotabato, February 4–16. Field notes of L. Duhaylungsod and D. Hyndman.
Okamura, Jonathan
1987 The Politics of Neglect. Tribal Forum 8:5–30.
Olofson, Harold
1989 Looking for the Tasaday: A Representation. Philippine Quarterly of Culture and Society 17:3–39.
Panamin
1972 Protecting Man's Right to Choice. O. V. Trinidad, ed. (Brochure.) Manila: Panamin Foundation. [Copies available upon request from the Tasaday Community Care Foundation, Manila.]
Pandian, Jacob
1985 Anthropology and the Western Tradition: Toward an Authentic Anthropology. Prospect Heights, IL: Waveland Press.
Partridge, William L.
1973 The Hippie Ghetto: The Natural History of a Subculture. New York: Holt, Rinehart and Winston.
PD-1017
1977 Presidential Decree No. 1017, "Prohibiting persons from entering into unexplored tribal grounds and providing penalty therefore." Official Gazette 73(14):2589–110 to 2589–111. April 4.
Peralta, Jesus T.
1971a Field Notes on the Tasaday. Unpublished photocopy of handwritten notes. (In the files of L. Reid.)
1971b Tasaday Family Units. Unpublished field notes. (June 1971). National Museum. [Copies available upon request from the Tasaday Community Care Foundation, Manila.]
1987 Tasaday Revisited. Man and Culture in Oceania (Special Issue) 3:61–70.
1988 Manila Standard [title of newspaper]. November 21.

Philippine Atlas
    1975   The Philippine Atlas. Vol. 1. Manila: Fund for Assistance to Private Education.
Philippine Yearbook
    1977   Philippine Yearbook 1977. Manila: National Census and Statistics Office.
Piperno, Dolores R.
    1989   Non-affluent Foragers: Resource Availability, Seasonal Shortages, and the
            Emergence of Agriculture in Panamanian Tropical Forests. *In* Foraging and Farming:
            The Evolution of Plant Exploitation. David R. Harris and Gordon C. Hillman, eds.
            Pp. 538–554. London: Unwin Hyman.
Police of Kiamba, South Cotabato
    1987   Report to the Provincial Commander/Police Superintendent, General Santos
            City, Regarding Police Record of Eliezer [*sic*] Boone Y Dalendan, dated October 14,
            1987. Typescript, 3 pp. [Copies available upon request from the Tasaday Community
            Care Foundation, Manila.]
Police of Maitum, South Cotabato
    1987   Report to the Provincial Commander/Police Superintendent, General Santos
            City, Regarding Killing of Eliezer [*sic*] Boone, dated October 14, 1987. Typescript,
            2 pp. [Copies available upon request from the Tasaday Community Care Foundation,
            Manila.]
Provincial Inspectorate, South Cotabato Constabulary, Integrated National Police
    1987   Report to the Provincial Commander/Police Superintendent, General Santos
            City, Regarding Feedback on IR's Mysterious Death of Eliezer [*sic*] Boone dated Oc-
            tober 20, 1987. Typescript, 2 pp. [Copies available upon request from the Tasaday
            Community Care Foundation, Manila.]
PPDO
    1988a   South Cotabato: The Bread Basket of the South. Koronadal, South Cotabato:
            PPDO, Office of the Provincial Government. Provincial Planning and Development
            Office.
    1988b   Socio-Economic Profile of South Cotabato. Koronadal, South Cotabato:
            PPDO, Office of the Provincial Government. Provincial Planning and Development
            Office.
Putz, Francis E., and N. Michele Holbrook
    1988   Tropical Rain-Forest Images. *In* People of the Tropical Rain Forest. J. S. Den-
            slow and C. Padoch, eds. Pp. 37–52. Berkeley: University of California Press.
Ramos, Aicida R.
    1987   Reflecting on the Yanomami: Ethnographic Images and the Pursuit of the Exotic.
            Cultural Anthropology 2:284–304.
Razon, Felix, and Richard Hensman
    1976   The Oppression of the Indigenous Peoples of the Philippines. Document 25. Co-
            penhagen: International Work Group for Indigenous Affairs.
Reid, Lawrence A., ed.
    1971   Philippine Minor Languages: Word Lists and Phonologies. Oceanic Linguistics
            Special Publications 8. Honolulu: University of Hawaii Press.
Robarchek, Clayton A.
    1977   Frustration, Aggression and the Nonviolent Semai. American Ethnologist
            4:762–770.
Robarchek, Clayton A., and Robert K. Dentan
    1987   Blood Drunkenness and the Bloodthirsty Semai: Unmaking Another Anthropo-
            logical Myth. American Anthropologist 89:356–365.

Robson, John R., and Douglas E. Yen
1976   Some Nutritional Aspects of the Philippine Tasaday Diet. Ecology of Food and
        Nutrition 5:83–89. [Reprinted in Dandan 1989:256–262.]
Rocamora, Joel
1979   The Political Uses of Panamin. Southeast Asia Chronicle 67:11–21.
Rocamora, Joel, et al., eds.
1979   Tribal People and the Marcos Regime: Cultural Genocide in the Philippines.
        Southeast Asia Chronicle, No. 67 (October).
Rogel, Amelia
1972   Tasaday Genealogy. Unpublished field data chart. (April 1972.) Panamin Foun-
        dation. [Copies available upon request from the Tasaday Community Care Founda-
        tion, Manila.]
Rogel-Rara, Amelia, and Emmanuel S. Nabayra
1988a   A Critique to Salazar's Third and Final Footnote's Genealogical Evidence on
        the Tasaday. Unpublished working paper No. 1. 165 pp. Manila: Tasaday Commu-
        nity Care Foundation. [Copies available upon request from the Tasaday Community
        Care Foundation, Manila.]
1988b   A Composite Genealogical Chart of the Tasaday as Reconstructed from the
        Field Data of Elizalde and Fox (June 1971); Peralta (June 1971); Lynch and Fernandez
        (March 1972); Rogel (April 1972); Molony (1972); Nance (1972–74); Yen and Nance
        (December 1972); Trinidad and Nance (1979); and Peralta and Fernandez (April
        1986). [Copies available upon request from the Tasaday Community Care Founda-
        tion, Manila.]
1988c   A Composite Genealogy of the So-called Tasaday and Their Relatives (Tasaday
        Poseurs) Based on Zeus Salazar's eight genealogical charts presented at the Interna-
        tional Conference on the Tasaday Controversy and Other Urgent Anthropological Is-
        sues, University of the Philippines (August 15–17, 1986) and at the 12th ICAES,
        Zagreb (July 17, 1988). [Copies available upon request from the Tasaday Community
        Care Foundation, Manila.]
1988–89 Population Census of the Tasaday-B'lit Reservation and its Neighbouring
        Communities, Gathered between the Period August 1988 to May 1989. (Compiled
        with the help of the Office of Southern Cultural Communities, General Santos City).
        [Copies available upon request from the Tasaday Community Care Foundation, Ma-
        nila.]
1989   Survival Strategy of the Tasaday: Genealogical Evidence. Paper presented at the
        88th Annual Meeting of the American Anthropological Association, Washington,
        DC, November 15–19.
Rosaldo, Renato
1982   Utter Savages of Scientific Value. In Politics and History in Band Societies.
        Eleanor Leacock and Richard Lee, eds. Pp. 309–325. New York: Cambridge Uni-
        versity Press.
Roszak, Theodore
1969   The Making of a Counter Culture. Garden City, NY: Doubleday.
Rousseau, Jean-Jacques
1967   The Social Contract and Discourse on the Origin of Inequality. New York:
        Pocket Books.
Sahlins, Marshall D.
1972   Stone Age Economics. New York: Aldine.

Salazar, Zeus A.
   1971   Footnote on the Tasaday. Philippine Journal of Linguistics 2(2):34–38.
   1973   Second Footnote on the Tasaday. Asian Studies 11(2):97–113.
   1986   Genealogical Charts of the "Tasaday Relatives." Charts presented at the International Conference on the Tasaday Controversy and Other Urgent Anthropological Issues, University of the Philippines, Diliman, August.
   1988   Third and Final Footnote on the Tasaday. Paper presented at the 12th International Congress on Anthropological and Ethnological Sciences (ICAES), Zagreb, July 28.
   1989   Another Footnote to a Never-Ending Story. Paper presented at the 88th Annual Meeting of the American Anthropological Association, Washington, DC, November 15–19.
   n.d.   Critical Views on Claims on the Authenticity of the Tasaday IV. In The Tasaday Controversy: Proceedings of the International Conference on the Tasaday Controversy and Other Urgent Anthropological Issues. Quezon City, Philippines, August 15–17, 1986. Vol. 1. Quezon City: University of the Philippines. (In press.)
Salo, Jukka, et al.
   1986   River Dynamics and the Diversity of Amazon Lowland Forest. Nature 322:254–258.
Sanford, Robert L., Jr., et al.
   1985   Amazon Rain-Forest Fires. Science 227:53–55.
Scherz, H., G. Kloos, and F. Senser
   1986   Food Composition and Nutrition Tables 1986/87. Wissenschaftliche Verlagsgesellschaft mbH: Stuttgart.
Schlegel, Stuart A.
   1971   Tiruray-English Lexicon. Berkeley: University of California Press.
Schoen, Ivan L.
   1969a   Contact with the Stone Age. Natural History 68(1):10–18, 66.
   1969b   Report on the Second Contact with the Akurio (Wama) Stone Age Tribe, Surinam, September 1968. Washington, DC: Smithsonian Institution, Center for Short-Lived Phenomena.
   1971   Report of the Emergency Trip Made by the West Indies Mission to the Akoerio Indians, June 1971. Washington, DC: Smithsonian Institution, Center for Short-Lived Phenomena.
Schrire, Carmel, ed.
   1984   Past and Present in Hunter-Gatherer Societies. Orlando: Academic Press.
Scrimgeour, David J.
   1979   Health Care of Australian Aborigines with No Previous European Contacts. Mimeo. Pintupi Homelands Service, PMB 13, Alice Springs, N.T. 5751.
Singer, Barry, and Victor A. Benassi
   1981   Occult Beliefs. American Scientist 69:49–55.
Solway, Jacqueline S., and Richard B. Lee
   1990   Foragers, Genuine or Spurious? Situating the Kalahari San in History. Current Anthropology 31:109–146.
Sponsel, Leslie E.
   1983   Yanomama Warfare, Protein Capture, and Cultural Ecology: A Critical Analysis of the Arguments of the Opponents. Interciencia 8:204–210.
   1986   Amazon Ecology and Adaptation. Annual Review of Anthropology 15:67–97.

1989   An Anthropologist's Perspective on Peace and Quality of Life. *In* Peace and Development: An Interdisciplinary Perspective. D. S. Sanders and J. K. Matsuoka, eds. Pp. 29–48. Honolulu: University of Hawaii School of Social Work.
1990a   The Mutual Relevance of Anthropology and Peace Studies. Human Peace Quarterly 7(3–4):3–9.
1990b   Ultraprimitive Pacifists: The Tasaday as a Symbol of Peace. Anthropology Today 6(1):3–5.
Stevenson, Leslie
1987   Seven Theories of Human Nature. New York: Oxford University Press.
Stiebing, William H., Jr.
1987   The Nature and Dangers of Cult Archaeology. *In* Cult Archaeology and Creationism: Understanding Pseudoscientific Beliefs about the Past. F. B. Harold and R. A. Eve, eds. Pp. 1–10. Iowa City, University of Iowa Press.
Stocking, George W.
1987   Victorian Anthropology. New York: Free Press.
Strathern, Marilyn
1987   Out of Context: The Persuasive Fictions of Anthropology. Current Anthropology 2:251–282.
Sudaria, Olivia
1989   Interview. General Santos City, South Cotabato, February 4–16. Field notes of L. Duhaylungsod and D. Hyndman.
Sueno, Ismael
1989   Interview. Koronadal, South Cotabato, February 4–16. Field notes of L. Duhaylungsod and D. Hyndman.
Sukhatme, P. V.
1975   Human Protein Needs and the Relative Role of Energy and Protein in Meeting Them. *In* The Man/Food Equation. F. Steele and A. Bourne, eds. Pp. 53–75. London: Academic Press.
Tan, Michael
1986   The Tasaday and Other Urgent Issues in Anthropology. Philippine Social Science Information 14:2 (July-September). Pp. 11, 26.
Tanedo, George
1989   Interview. Maitum, South Cotabato, February 4–16. Field notes of L. Duhaylungsod and D. Hyndman.
Terry, Edith
1971   Field notes on the Tasaday: Observations and Interviews During First Contacts with the Tasaday at the Forest Edge and the Manobo People at Blit from June 13–17, 1971. Unpublished field notes. [Copies available upon request from the Tasaday Community Care Foundation, Manila.]
1989   Letter to Eugene L. Sterud and the American Anthropological Association, dated June 12. [Terry visited the Tasaday, in company with Panamin people, from July 13 to 17, 1971.]
Tico Times (San José, Costa Rica)
1986   Elizalde Wants to Come Back; Calderon Sues [San Jose, Costa Rica]. September 19.
Torgovnick, Marianna
1990   Gone Primitive: Savage Intellects, Modern Lives. Chicago: University of Illinois Press.

Townsend, Patricia K.
  1990   On the Possibility/Impossibility of Tropical Forest Hunting and Gathering.
         American Anthropologist 92:745–747.
Townsend, William H.
  1969   Stone and Steel Tool Use in a New Guinea Society. Ethnology 8:199–205.
Tribal Forum
  1985   Land Our Lost Heritage: How Do We Regain It? Tribal Forum 7:1–52.
Turnbull, Colin
  1961   The Forest People. Garden City, NY: Doubleday.
Tyrrell, D. A. J.
  1979   Aspects of Infection in Isolated Communities. In Health and Diseases in Tribal
         Societies. Ciba Foundation Symposium 49. Amsterdam, Oxford, New York: Ex-
         cerpta Medica.
Unger, Walter, and Jay Ullal
  1986   Der Grosse Schwindel im Regenwald [The Great Bluff in the Rain Forest]. Stern
         39(17):20–33, 179 (April 17).
University of the Philippines
  1987   Statement of the UP Anthropology Department. Philippine Daily Inquirer, De-
         cember 10. Reprinted in Diliman Review 39(1):36; and in Anthropology Newsletter
         29(2):4.
USAID
  1984   Grant Application No. AID 492.0367-G-SS 4070-00, dated February 27.
Vigilant, Linda, R. Pennington, H. Harpending, T. Kocher, and A. Wilson
  1989   Mitochondrial DNA Sequences in Single Hairs from a Southern African Popu-
         lation. Proceedings of the National Academy of Sciences 86:9350–9354.
Vigilant, Linda, M. Stoneking, H. Harpending, K. Hawkes, A. Wilson
  1991   African Populations and the Evolution of Human Mitochondrial DNA. Science
         September 27:1503–1507.
Villanueva, Virgilio
  1989   Interview. Maitum, South Cotabato, February 4–16. Field notes of L. Duhay-
         lungsod and D. Hyndman.
Walton, Charles
  1979   A Philippine Language Tree. Anthropological Linguistics 21:70–98.
White, Joyce C.
  1989   Ethnoecological Observations on Wild and Cultivated Rice and Yams in North-
         eastern Thailand. In Foraging and Farming: The Evolution of Plant Exploitation.
         David R. Harris and Gordon C. Hillman, eds. Pp. 152–158. London: Unwin Hyman.
World Health Organization (WHO)
  1985   Energy and Protein Requirements. World Health Organization, Food and Agri-
         culture Organization of the United Nations and the United Nations University Joint
         Report. World Health Organization Technical Report Series 724. Geneva: World
         Health Organization.
Wilmsen, Edwin N.
  1989   Land Filled with Flies: A Political Economy of the Kalahari. Chicago: University
         of Chicago Press.
Wilmsen, Edwin N., and James R. Denbow
  1990   Paradigmatic History of San-Speaking Peoples and Current Attempts at Revi-
         sion. Current Anthropology 31:489–524.

Wilson, Peter J.
 1988 The Domestication of the Human Species. New Haven and London: Yale University Press.
Wolf, Eric
 1982 Europe and the People without History. Berkeley: University of California Press.
Yap, Fe Aldave
 1977 A Comparative Study of Philippine lexicons. Manila: Institute of National Language.
Yen, Douglas E.
 1976a The Ethnobotany of the Tasaday, II: Plant Names of the Tasaday, Manobo Blit and Kemato Tboli. *In* Further Studies on the Tasaday. Panamin Foundation Research Series No. 2. D. E. Yen and John Nance, eds. Pp. 137–158. Makati, Rizal, Philippines: Panamin Foundation.
 1976b The Ethnobotany of the Tasaday, III: Notes on the Subsistence System. *In* Further Studies on the Tasaday. Panamin Foundation Research Series No. 2. D. E. Yen and John Nance, eds. Pp. 159–183. Makati, Rizal, Philippines: Panamin Foundation.
 1989 Reconsidering the Tasaday Environment—17 Years On. Paper presented at the 88th Annual Meeting of the American Anthropological Association, Washington, DC, November 15–19.
Yen, D. E., and Hermes G. Gutierrez
 1974 The Ethnobotany of the Tasaday: The Useful Plants. The Philippine Journal of Science 103:97–139. [Reprinted in Yen and Nance, eds., 1976, pp. 97–136.]
Yen, D. E., and John Nance, eds.
 1976 Further Studies on the Tasaday: Panamin Foundation Research Series No. 2. Makati, Rizal, Philippines: Panamin Foundation.
Yengoyan, Aram A.
 1977 Paradise Lost? The American Scholar 46:134–138.
 1991 Shaping and Reshaping the Tasaday: A Question of Cultural Identity. A Review Article. The Journal of Asian Studies 50:565–573.
Yohner, Arthur, Jr.
 1970 Contact with a New Group of Akurijo Indians of Surinam. Washington, DC: Sithsonian Institution, Center for Short-Lived Phenomena.

Index

246

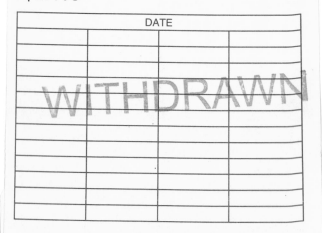